ENVIRONMENT, SCARCITY, AND VIOLENCE

ENVIRONMENT, SCARCITY, AND VIOLENCE

Thomas F. Homer-Dixon

PRINCETON UNIVERSITY PRESS   PRINCETON AND OXFORD

The Library of Congress has cataloged the cloth edition of this book as follows
Homer-Dixon, Thomas F.
Environment, scarcity, and violence / Thomas F. Homer-Dixon.
p.   cm.
Includes bibliographical references (p.) and index.
ISBN 0-691-02794-3 (CL : alk. paper)
1. Violence—Environmental aspects—Developing countries.
2. Social conflict—Developing countries.   3. Environmental
degradation—Social aspects—Developing countries.
4. Renewable natural resources—Developing countries.
5. Scarcity—Social aspects.   6. Developing countries—
Environmental conditions.   I. Title.
HN981.V5H65   1999
303.6—dc21   98-34878

British Library Cataloging-in-Publication Data is available

This book has been composed in Times Roman

Material in chapters 1, 4, 5, and 7 is similar to that in Thomas F.
Homer-Dixon, "On the Threshold: Environmental Changes as Causes of
Acute Conflict," *International Security* 16, no. 2 (fall 1991): 76–116.
Material in chapter 2 is similar to that in Thomas F. Homer-Dixon,
"Environmental Scarcity, Mass Violence, and the Limits to Ingenuity,"
Current History 95, no. 604 (November 1996): 359–65. The material
in the text and appendixes of chapters 5 and 7 is similar to that in
Thomas F. Homer-Dixon, "Strategies for Studying Causation in
Complex Ecological-Political Systems," *Journal of Environment &
Development* 5, no. 2 (June 1996): 132–48; and idem, "Environmental
Scarcities and Violent Conflict: Evidence from Cases," *International
Security* 19, no. 1 (summer 1994): 5–40. Chapter 6 is similar to material
in Thomas F. Homer-Dixon, "The Ingenuity Gap: Can Poor Countries
Adapt to Resource Scarcity?" *Population and Development Review* 21,
no. 3 (1995): 587–612.

Printed on acid-free paper. ∞

www.pup.princeton.edu

Printed in the United States of America

10   9   8   7   6   5   4

For Doug ————————————————————————————

"The magnitude of the land problem can be summed up here," the Communist Party official said, gesturing around us toward the bare, rocky mountains where *kaingeros* (slash-and-burn farmers) were losing their fight to scrape a living from the tired soil. "Look at these people, trying to cultivate this rocky hillside. They have no other place to go."

We were sitting in an NPA [New People's Army] camp in the Cordillera Mountains of Nueva Vizcaya province in 1988 with a bird's-eye view of the desperate plight of Filipino peasants in this rugged corner of the northern Philippines. In all directions, the mountains had been almost entirely stripped of trees by logging companies owned by powerful politicians. Erosion was cutting deep grooves into the severe slopes and carrying away the thin remaining layer of precious topsoil. By night, the mountainsides twinkled with the orange glow of fires set by *kaingeros* as they prepared plots wrested from the hardscrabble for June planting. By day, an acrid pall of smoke and haze hung above the treeless hills, which shimmered like a desert mirage in the baking tropical sun.

(*Gregg Jones*, Red Revolution: Inside the Philippine Guerrilla Movement)

Contents

Figures

Tables

Acknowledgments ─────────────────────────────────

THIS BOOK would not have been possible without the extraordinary help of countless people over the last ten years. I have synthesized and built upon material that I have published, sometimes with coauthors, in journals, books, and monographs since 1990 (for a partial list, see the items under Homer-Dixon in "General Readings on Environmental Security"). The previously published material and this book present the results of several large international research projects on the links between environmental stress and violence in developing countries. In total, these projects involved about one hundred researchers and advisors from fifteen countries on four continents.

I am particularly grateful to Jeffrey Boutwell of the American Academy of Arts and Sciences, who worked with me as codirector of two of these research projects. George Rathjens, of the Massachusetts Institute of Technology also played a key role in the early stages of this work. Both Jeffrey and George have been the finest colleagues I could have wished for in these endeavors. At the University of Toronto, Peter Gizewski, Philip Howard, Kimberley Kelly, and Valerie Percival made up a team of tremendously dedicated researchers. (Material that I coauthored with these researchers has been incorporated into the book at various points, as indicated in those chapters' endnotes.) Valerie Percival and Philip Howard, in particular, helped keep multiple projects moving at the same time, sometimes under very difficult circumstances. Jane Willms gathered key materials and set up our extremely useful computerized database (which is accessible via the World Wide Web). Jessica Blitt worked closely with me to complete the book manuscript; she was responsible for all fact checking, figures, and diagrams. Michele Rizoli provided vital administrative support in Toronto as did Annette Mann Bourne (who also edited and prepared many of our occasional papers) in Cambridge, Massachusetts. To Jane, Jessica, Michele, and Annette: thank you so much for your superb work.

Key researchers and advisors outside the University of Toronto included Charles Barber, Edward Barbier, Janet Welsh Brown, Elizabeth Economy, Sergio Diaz-Briquets, Peter Gleick, Jack Goldstone, Fen Hampson, John Harris, Shaukat Hassan, Sanjoy Hazarika, Emmy Hafild, John Holdren, Michael Horowitz, Jad Issac, Calestous Juma, Zhao Junlin, Atul Kohli, Ashok Khosla, Diana Liverman, Miriam Lowi, William Moomaw, Tom Naff, Bernard Nietschmann, Charles Okidi, Nancy Peluso, Celso Roque, Lester Ross, David Runnalls, Thayer Scudder, Jonathan Schwartz, Blair Seaborn, Vaclav Smil, Astri Suhrke, Shibley Telhami, and Myron Weiner.

Others who contributed valuable help and ideas were Hayward Alker, Tahir Amin, Jesse Ausubel, John Bongaarts, James Boyce, Wallace Broecker, David Brooks, Tony Campbell, Peter Cebon, Robert Chen, Nazli Choucri, Richard

Cincotta, William Clark, Joel Cohen, Robert Couchman, Paul Craig, Geoffrey Dabelko, Ning Datong, Paul Diehl, Paul Demeny, David Dessler, Daniel Deudney, David Dewitt, Paul Diesing, Tanja Ellingsen, Robert Engleman, John Evans, Darya Farha, Anne Florini, Claire Fortier, Joshua Foster, Madhav Gadgil, Shen Ganqing, Susan Gibbs, Michael Glantz, Nils Petter Gleditsch, Gary Goertz, Leela Gulati, Ernst Haas, Allen Hammond, Arthur Hanson, Wenche Hauge, George Haynal, Ramaswamy Iyer, Robert Jervis, Colin Kahl, Daniel Kammen, Robert Kaplan, Stephen Kellert, Michael Klare, Shmitu Kothari, Mary Kritz, John Last, Jill Lazenby, Ned Lebow, Shin-Wha Lee, Marc Levy, Stephan Libiszewski, Eugene Linden, Ronnie Lipschutz, Steve Lonergan, Thomas Lovejoy, Sean Lynn-Jones, James MacNeill, Jessica Tuchman Mathews, Richard Matthew, Geoffrey McNicoll, Steven Miller, Ted Moran, Fraser Mustard, Ashis Nandy, James Nickum, Vicki Norberg-Bohm, William Overholt, Ted Parson, Per Pinstrup-Andersen, Dennis Pirages, Peter Poole, Zhang Qishun, Laura Reed, David Rejeski, Judith Reppy, James Risbey, Richard Rockwell, Paul Romer, Michael Ross, Kartikeya Sarabhai, Thomas Schelling, Susan Sechler, Sara Seims, Deng Shoupeng, Seth Shulman, Steven Sinding, Alan Simmons, P. J. Simmons, Eugene Skolnikoff, Brian Smith, Dan Smith, Martha Snodgrass, Marvin Soroos, Kurt Spillman, Janice Stein, William Stevens, Ashok Swain, Urs Thomas, Monica Toft, Barbara Boyle Torrey, Winxie Tse, Hugh Vernon-Jackson, David Victor, Peter Wallensteen, Tom Wander, Arthur Westing, Jennifer Seymour Whitaker, Anne Whyte, Mark Zacher, and Lyuba Zarsky.

Financial support for the research reviewed in this book was provided by the Canadian Institute for International Peace and Security, the Donner Canadian Foundation, the W. Alton Jones Foundation, the MacArthur Foundation, the Global Stewardship Initiative of the Pew Charitable Trusts, the Rockefeller Foundation, the Rotary Club of Toronto, the Royal Society of Canada, and the Social Sciences and Humanities Research Council of Canada. During the writing of the manuscript, I received support as an Associate Fellow of the Canadian Institute for Advanced Research. I am exceedingly grateful for the confidence of these funders over the years.

Lastly, I wish to thank my students and my critics. I often feel that I learn more from my students than they do from me. There is no better test of an idea's clarity and usefulness than trying to explain it to students and then facing their questions about it. As for my critics, almost all of their comments over the years have been constructive and thoughtful. My work has been greatly improved by their attention. They have encouraged me to make my arguments sharper, my logic clearer, and my evidence deeper and better marshaled. They are not responsible for the failures of this volume, but they can take great credit for its successes.

Toronto, Canada
January 1998

Abbreviations

ARIJ	Applied Research Institute in Jerusalem
CFC	chlorofluorocarbon
FAO	UN Food and Agriculture Organization
GDP	gross domestic product
GLASOD	Global Assessment of Soil Degradation
IIASA	International Institute for Applied Systems Analysis
NDF	National Democratic Front
NGO	nongovernmental organization
NPA	New People's Army
PKK	Kurdish Workers Party
PRI	Partido Revolucionario Institucional
UN	United Nations
UV	ultraviolet
UV-B	ultraviolet-B
WEC	World Energy Council
WMO	World Meteorological Organization
WRI	World Resources Institute

ENVIRONMENT, SCARCITY, AND VIOLENCE

1

Introduction

IN RECENT YEARS, a number of analysts have argued that human-induced environmental pressures might seriously affect national and international security.[1] These experts offer interesting and important arguments. But the topic of "environmental security" encompasses an almost unmanageable array of sub-issues, especially if we define "security" broadly to include general physical, social, and economic well-being.[2] For example, is the potential inundation of coastal cities caused by climate change and rising seas a threat to security? Does loss of biodiversity from deforestation risk the security of future generations by limiting their opportunities to create new crops and medicines?

We can narrow the scope of the problem by focusing on how environmental stress affects *conflict* rather than security. Still the topic is too vast. Environmental stress might contribute to conflicts as diverse as war, terrorism, or diplomatic and trade disputes. Moreover, it might have a great range of causal roles: in some cases, it might be a proximate and powerful cause of conflict, whereas in others, it might be only a minor and distant player in a tangled story that involves many political, economic, and physical factors.

We can narrow the scope further by focusing on how environmental stress affects *violent* national and international conflict. Intuitively, this topic seems more tractable. In the 1970s and 1980s, experts suggested various ways such violence might arise. Some proposed, for example, that environmental stress might shift the balance of power among states either regionally or globally, producing power instabilities that cause war.[3] Others suggested that, as global environmental damage increases the gap between the industrialized and developing worlds, poor nations might militarily confront the rich for a fairer share of the planet's wealth.[4] Warmer temperatures could lead to contention over new ice-free sea-lanes in the Arctic or more accessible resources in the Antarctic.[5] Bulging populations and land stress might produce waves of environmental refugees that spill across borders and that undermine the domestic stability of receiving countries.[6] Countries could fight among themselves over dwindling supplies of river water and the effects of upstream pollution.[7] In poor countries that depend on agriculture, a sharp drop in food-crop production could lead to strife between urban and rural dwellers or between nomads and sedentary farmers.[8] If environmental degradation tightens food supplies, exporters might use food as a weapon.[9] More generally, some of these experts argued, environmental stress could cause the gradual impoverishment of societies, both rich and poor, which would aggravate class and ethnic cleavages, undermine liberal regimes, and spawn insurgencies.[10]

In sum, these experts suggested that environmental pressures could "ratchet up" the level of stress within national and international society, increasing the likelihood of many different kinds of conflict and impeding cooperative solutions.[11] Unfortunately, the early writings on the links between environment and violence were often speculative, anecdotal, and imprecise. Some of the more recent work of the subject—work that has received considerable attention—is little better.[12]

With this book, I hope to make the discussion less speculative and more precise. Since 1989, I have been privileged to study the issue as a leader of several large research projects that involved over one hundred experts from fifteen countries. Organized principally by the Peace and Conflict Studies Program at the University of Toronto and the American Academy of Arts and Sciences in Cambridge, Massachusetts, these projects examined in detail sixteen regional and country cases.[13] Taken in conjunction with research by other groups, especially in Switzerland and Norway, a clearer picture of the links between environmental stress and violence has emerged.[14] This picture is still, in some ways, only a preliminary sketch; much research remains to be done. Nevertheless, we can now say a good deal about how and where environmental stress—or what I have come to call "environmental scarcity"—contributes to social breakdown and violence.

In the following chapters, I survey and synthesize these recent findings. As far as possible, I have written for a general audience, although the material here should also be useful to scholars and students. The main body of the text, especially the first chapters, will be accessible to a wide readership because all technical elaborations are in the endnotes and appendices, where readers who want to pursue matters further should find all the information they need.

Although careful analysis of past and current cases reveals the most likely connections between environmental scarcity and violence, some of these connections may not be widely observable until well into the next century. On the basis of the preliminary research reported in this book, however, I believe that in coming decades the world will probably see a steady increase in the incidence of violent conflict that is caused, at least in part, by environmental scarcity. Developing countries are likely to be affected sooner and more severely than developed countries. They tend to be much more dependent on environmental goods and services for their economic well-being; they often do not have the financial, material, and human capital resources to buffer themselves from the effects of environmental scarcities; and their economic and political institutions tend to be fragile and riven with discord. It is probable, therefore, that poor countries will be less able to apprehend, prevent, or adapt to environmental problems.

During coming decades, environmental scarcity could plausibly produce five general types of violent conflict affecting these countries. Moving from the most local to the most global type, these are:

1. Disputes arising directly from local environmental degradation caused, for instance, by factory emissions, logging, or dam construction

2. Ethnic clashes arising from population migration and deepened social cleavages due to environmental scarcity

3. Civil strife (including insurgency, banditry, and coups d'état) caused by environmental scarcity that affects economic productivity and, in turn, people's livelihoods, the behavior of elite groups, and the ability of states to meet these changing demands

4. Scarcity-induced interstate war over, for example, water

5. North-South conflicts (i.e., conflicts between the developed and developing worlds) over mitigation of, adaptation to, and compensation for global environmental problems like global warming, ozone depletion, threats to biodiversity, and decreases in fishstocks[15]

Of these five types, the first is unlikely to cause more than sporadic, localized violence. And, although some scholars emphasize the plausibility of the fifth type of conflict, I believe that major, organized violence between the North and the South will not occur. Of the remaining three types, I will show that the fourth—interstate scarcity wars—is the least probable. Much of this book, therefore, focuses on the remaining two types: ethnic clashes and civil strife.

Social conflict—even violent conflict—is not always a bad thing. Mass mobilization and civil strife can produce useful change in the distribution of land and wealth and in institutions and processes of governance. Similarly, environmental scarcity is not always a bad thing: it can stimulate technological entrepreneurship and institutional change, and it can produce international cooperation by confronting states and transnational groups with tasks that require collaboration.[16] Moreover, because in repressive societies the environment is often one of the few subjects of public discussion around which people can organize relatively unhindered political activity, opposition groups often use environmental issues as vehicles to rally dissent.

But I will argue here that many developing countries face increasingly complex, fast-moving, and interacting environmental scarcities. These scarcities can overwhelm efforts to produce constructive change and can actually reduce a country's ability to deliver reform. Consequently, environmental scarcity sometimes helps to drive societies into a self-reinforcing spiral of violence, institutional dysfunction, and social fragmentation. The negative effects of severe environmental scarcity will often outweigh the positive.

Aim and Structure of the Book

Our research program did not aim to identify all the factors that cause violent conflict around the world; rather, it sought to determine whether a specific factor—environmental scarcity—can be an important cause of violent conflict.

This is not the type of goal generally thought to guide social-scientific inquiry. Usually, researchers are interested in the whole range of factors that influences the value of a specific "dependent variable," such as the incidence of violent conflict. They therefore ask, What factors—what "independent variables"—cause or explain changes in the value of dependent variable? But researchers studying the links between environmental scarcity and conflict have a different goal. They want to know whether, and how, a *particular* independent variable (in this case, environmental scarcity) can cause changes in the value of the dependent variable (the incidence of conflict). Their emphasis therefore shifts from explaining the value of the dependent variable to understanding the current and potential causal roles of a specific independent variable and to understanding the specific nature of the causal relationship between the two variables.[17]

This shift in focus is not uncommon. It is reasonable, for example, when two conditions hold: first, when the value of a variable in a complex system is changing significantly, or is thought likely to change significantly in the future; and, second, when researchers want to know if this change will affect other variables that interest them.[18]

These two conditions apply in environment-conflict research: evidence suggests that environmental scarcity is getting worse rapidly in many parts of the world; and the incidence of violent conflict around the world is of concern to many researchers, analysts, and policymakers. Therefore, these people might reasonably ask the following questions:

1. Can environmental scarcity contribute to violent conflict?
2. If yes, how can it contribute to conflict?
3. Is this contribution important?

This book addresses the above three questions. Identifying how environmental scarcity can contribute to conflict—that is, answering question 2— means identifying scarcity's possible *causal roles*. To do this, I divide the question into two further questions that correspond to the two arrows, or causal steps, shown in figure 1.1: What are the important social effects (such as impoverishment and migrations) of environmental scarcity? And what types of violent conflict, if any, are most likely to result from these social effects? I also address some of the key factors that causally precede environmental scarcity on the left of the figure, and I discuss important feedback loops (what social scientists sometimes call *reciprocal causation)* from violent conflict to environmental scarcity.

Environmental Scarcity ⟶ Social Effects ⟶ Violent Conflict

Figure 1.1. Two Causal Steps

Arrow diagrams like figure 1.1 play a prominent role in the following chapters (for an explanation of how to read such diagrams, see the appendix to chapter 3). They bring order into the profusion of predictions about the links between environmental scarcity and violent conflict. They help us identify key interactions among simultaneous environmental problems, specify intervening and interacting variables, and identify causal links across levels of analysis (for example, from the urban level to the national and international levels). These diagrams also help us answer the third question above, Is environmental scarcity's contribution to violence important?

Some skeptics argue that environmental scarcity is rarely an important cause of violent conflict.[19] Clearly, as I will stress in the following chapters, environmental scarcity by itself is neither a necessary nor sufficient cause: there are many conflicts around the world in which environmental scarcity plays little role; and, when it does play a role, it always interacts with other contextual factors—be they physical or social—to generate violence. But this fact should not lead analysts to the conclusion that environmental scarcity is always unimportant. After all, it is hard to identify any cause of violence that is, by itself, either necessary or sufficient; the causes of specific instances of violence are always interacting sets of factors, and the particular combination of factors can vary greatly from case to case. If we want to gauge the causal power of environmental scarcity's contribution to a specific instance of violence, therefore, we must gauge its power relative to the other factors contributing to that violence.

This task, it turns out, is especially intractable; in fact, for many specific cases it may well be impossible (I address the problem briefly in the appendix to chapter 5). In this book, I therefore try to avoid entangling myself in the metaphysical debate about the relative importance of causes. Instead, given the preliminary nature of our research, I adopt a purely pragmatic criterion for judging environmental scarcity's importance in specific cases of violent conflict: Can the sources and nature of the conflict, I ask, be adequately understood without including environmental scarcity as part of its causal story? For many conflicts around the world—conflicts that preoccupy researchers, policymakers, and others—the answer is clearly "no." For example, much of the recent civil violence in Chiapas, South Africa, Pakistan, the Philippines, and Haiti cannot be properly understood or explained without taking into account the causal role of environmental scarcity. We must integrate ecological and environmental factors into our explanations of these conflicts; and it seems reasonable to conclude, therefore, that environmental scarcity is an important cause of these conflicts.

In the following seven chapters, I present my arguments in support of this and other key conclusions. Chapter 2 is a nontechnical overview of the findings of our research. In chapters 3 through 7, I present a theory of environment-conflict linkages. Chapter 3 reviews—in greatly simplified form—the two-century debate between optimists and pessimists over the effects of population growth and resource scarcity on prosperity, and it identifies the particular contribution of this book to that debate. Chapter 4 defines environmental scarcity, specifies its main causes, and briefly describes the severity and likely trajectory of the key environmental scarcities that currently affect our planet. Chapter 5 then discusses ways in which the causes of environmental scarcity interact. The chapter's principal concern, however, is the nature of the causal relationships represented by the left-hand arrow in figure 1.1; it identifies environmental scarcity's main negative social effects, including constrained agricultural and economic productivity, migration, social segmentation, and disrupted institutions.

Chapter 6 addresses the central issue of why some societies are able to adapt well to environmental scarcity and do not, as a result, exhibit turmoil and violence, whereas others experience major social stress. I argue that the latter societies exhibit an "ingenuity gap" between the amount of social and technical ingenuity they need and the amount they actually supply. I also identify several factors that can facilitate or hinder ingenuity supply.

In chapter 7, I bring all these ideas and arguments together into one core model. I also specifically address the right-hand arrow in figure 1.1 by discussing in detail the main types of violent conflict likely to arise from environmental scarcity and its negative social effects. In addition, I review the relationship between rapid urban growth and urban violence, the implications of chronic strife within developing countries for international security, and (in the chapter's appendix) the logic of case selection to test and illustrate hypotheses.

In chapter 8, the book's conclusion, I briefly recapitulate our research program's key findings, reply to some common skeptical arguments, and offer suggestions for further research.

Key Research Concepts, Methods, and Goals

The concepts of "resource," "resource scarcity," and "environmental scarcity" are key to my argument. *Environmental scarcity*, as I use the term, is scarcity of renewable resources, such as cropland, forests, river water, and fish stocks. This scarcity can arise, as we will see in chapter 4, from depletion or degradation of the resource, from increased demand for it, and from unequal distribution. Unlike many analysts, I interpret all types of environmental depletion or damage as various forms of scarcity of renewable resources. Deforestation increases the scarcity of forest resources, water pollution increases the scarcity of clean water, and climate change increases the scarcity of the regular patterns of rainfall and temperature on which farmers rely.

As noted above, the effects of these environmental scarcities on society are hard to analyze: causal processes are exceedingly complex, involving multiple physical and social variables, feedback loops, interactive effects, and nonlinear responses. Analysts often must trace out long and tangled chains of causation, and data on key variables and processes are rarely abundant or of high quality. Although the underlying influence of environmental factors on conflict may sometimes be great, the complex and indirect causation in these systems means that the scanty evidence available is always open to many interpretations. To complicate matters further, understanding environmental-social systems involves specifying links across levels of analysis usually regarded as quite independent.

To cope with these difficulties, therefore, our researchers used an exacting, step-by-step analysis of the causal processes operating in each of our regional and country cases. Although we invariably encountered serious problems of data quantity and quality, this "process tracing" nonetheless allowed us to identify general patterns of environment-conflict linkages across multiple cases. Each case, in other words, served as a data point in our general analysis; as we produced more of these data points, we were able to induce from them a general answer to the "how" question discussed above.

Our researchers had to adopt a pragmatic, but not cavalier, disregard for disciplinary boundaries. Study of the relationship between environmental stress and violence inevitably involves a daunting range of highly technical fields, from soil science to developmental economics, from atmospheric chemistry to social psychology, and from demography to political science. Members of our research team were drawn from at least a dozen fields in the natural and social sciences. We developed tolerance for the idiosyncrasies and jargons of fields other than our own, we practiced making the ideas within our specialties accessible to nonspecialists, and we worked together to combine the most useful of these ideas into tools that helped us understand if and how environmental scarcity contributes to violence. In the process, we have produced new syntheses and concepts that cross disciplinary boundaries and that sometimes violate conventions within specific disciplines. I hope that the specialists among the readers of this book will be tolerant of our trespasses, appropriations, and new constructions.

In the following chapters, I do not predict specific events in our future world or specific characteristics of that world, although I do try to cast our view forward several decades. Some readers might question whether it is possible to offer any useful forecasts that far into the future about the environmental and social problems that human societies will face. But there are two reasons why we should try. First, as we will see in chapter 4, we actually know enough about the trends in human population growth and in the depletion and degradation of the planet's environmental resources to say a good deal about what our physical world will look like several decades from now, although the political and social consequences of these trends are highly uncertain. Second, we are passing through a moment in history when political and economic events are fluid and social structures are more malleable than they have been for decades. This situation provides opportunities for reform of our economic, political, and social systems, but it also presents dangers. Many of the choices we make during the next years—even small ones—will have large consequences far into the future. If we are to do better than blindly stumble into the next century, we must project these consequences as far into the future as we can.

The middle years of the next century are not as distant as they seem. Well over one-third of the people currently alive will still be alive in 2050.[20] The children around us today will live with the consequences of the decisions we make today.

Although I hope this book will be useful to policymakers, it does not offer detailed policy recommendations. The book is diagnostic, not prescriptive. The current policy environment is changing so rapidly—with changing aid budgets, government restructuring, and economic globalization—that any specific recommendations will either be quickly outdated or entirely hortatory. Moreover, each case of environmentally induced conflict is complex and unique: each has a specific ecosystem, history, culture, economy, set of actors, and set of power relations among these actors. Policy tools available in one case will not be available in another, for wholly idiosyncratic reasons. Successful policy intervention thus requires customization based on a careful analysis of the character of the specific case and of the policy tools available in that case. In this book, therefore, I can do no more than give policymakers a rough understanding of key causal processes and of useful intervention points in these processes.

Nonetheless, I can offer four general comments about interventions. First, there is no single solution or magic bullet that will always break the links between environmental scarcity and violence. The causal systems in question encompass huge numbers of interacting variables; interventions must therefore operate at many points to capitalize on these systems' natural synergies. Policymakers need to implement a broad and integrated set of responses at the international, regional, national, and community levels. Second, early intervention is generally better than late intervention. If policymakers wait till widespread violence has broken out, it will probably be too intractable, too complex, and too charged with emotion to resolve. Moreover, environmental scarcity tends to produce diffuse and subnational violence of a kind that our conventional military institutions do not, in general, handle well. Policymakers should therefore emphasize proactive interventions that break the early links in the causal chains described in this book.

Third, policy responses do not have to be capital-intensive: they can be simultaneously effective and relatively inexpensive. Examples include greater support for nongovernmental organizations that are rehabilitating local environmental resources and for research on crops that can grow with eroded soil and polluted water. Fourth and finally, effective policy interventions will not necessarily be unique or special. The analysis in this book simply presents another set of reasons for a range of interventions—from selective debt relief to enhancement of indigenous technical capacity—that many experts have long believed necessary to produce humane and rapid economic development in poor countries around the world.

2

Overview

PRELIMINARY RESEARCH indicates that scarcities of critical environmental resources—especially of cropland, freshwater, and forests—contribute to violence in many parts of the world. These environmental scarcities usually do not cause wars among countries, but they can generate severe social stresses within countries, helping to stimulate subnational insurgencies, ethnic clashes, and urban unrest. Such civil violence particularly affects developing societies, because they are, in general, highly dependent on environmental resources and less able to buffer themselves from the social crises that environmental scarcities cause.

Although this violence affects developing societies most, policymakers and citizens in the industrialized world ignore it at their peril. It can harm rich countries' national interests by threatening their trade and economic relations, entangling them in complex humanitarian emergencies, provoking distress migrations, and destabilizing pivotal countries in the developing world.

In South Africa, for example, severe land, water, and fuelwood scarcities in the former black homelands have helped drive millions of poor blacks into squatter settlements around the major cities. The settlements are often constructed on the worst urban land, in depressions prone to flooding, on hillsides vulnerable to slides, or near heavily polluting industries. Scarcities of land, water, and fuelwood in these settlements help provoke interethnic rivalries and violent feuds among settlement warlords and their followers. This strife jeopardizes the country's transition to democratic stability and prosperity.

In Pakistan, shortages and maldistribution of good land, water, and forests in the countryside have encouraged millions of the rural poor to migrate into major cities, such as Karachi and Hyderabad. The conjunction of this in-migration with high fertility rates is causing city populations to grow at an astonishing 4 to 5 percent a year, producing fierce competition—and often violence—among ethnic groups over land, basic services, and political and economic power. This turmoil exacts a great toll on the national economy.

In Chiapas, Mexico, Zapatista insurgents rose against land scarcity and insecure land tenure caused by ancient inequalities in land distribution, by rapid population growth among groups with the least land, and by changes in laws governing land access. The insurgency rocked Mexico to the core, helped trigger a peso crisis, and reminded the world that Mexico remains—despite the pretenses of the country's economic elites—a poor and profoundly unstable developing country.

The Critical Role of Environmental Resources

It is easy for the billion-odd people living in rich countries to forget that the well-being of about half of the world's population of 6.0 billion remains directly tied to local natural resources. Sixty to seventy percent of the world's poor people live in rural areas, and most depend on agriculture for their main income; a large majority of these people are smallholder farmers, including many who are semisubsistence (which means they survive mainly by eating what they grow). Over 40 percent of people on the planet—some 2.4 billion— use fuelwood, charcoal, straw, or cow dung as their main source of energy; 50 to 60 percent rely on these biomass fuels for at least some of their primary energy needs. Over 1.2 billion people lack access to clean drinking water; many are forced to walk far to get what water they can find.

The cropland, forests, and water supplies that underpin the livelihoods of these billions are renewable. Unlike nonrenewable resources such as oil and iron ore, renewables are replenished over time by natural processes. In most cases, if used prudently, they should sustain an adequate standard of living indefinitely. Unfortunately, in many regions where people rely on renewables, they are being depleted or degraded faster than they are being renewed. From Gaza to the Philippines to Honduras, the evidence is stark: aquifers are being overdrawn and salinized, coastal fisheries are disappearing, and steep uplands have been stripped of their forests leaving their thin soils to erode into the sea.

This environmental scarcity helps generate chronic, diffuse, subnational violence—exactly the kind of violence that bedevils conventional military institutions. Around the world, we see conventional armies pinned down and often utterly impotent in the face of interethnic violence or attacks by ragtag bands of lightly armed guerrillas and insurgents. As yet, environmental scarcity is not a major factor behind most of these conflicts, but we can expect it to become a more important influence in coming decades because of larger populations and higher per capita resource consumption rates.

In 1900, when the world's human population was about 1.65 billion, its annual growth was around 10 million; today, with a base of about 6.0 billion, the annual growth is about 80 million. The fourfold increase in total world population since 1900 has combined with much higher per capita consumption of materials and energy to produce huge jumps in global energy consumption, carbon emissions, water use, fish consumption, land degradation, and deforestation.

Currently, the human population is growing by 1.3 percent a year. This figure peaked at about 2.1 percent between 1965 and 1970 and has fallen since then. In recent years, fertility rates have dropped surprisingly sharply in most poor countries; women are having, on average, significantly fewer children. But it is wildly premature to declare, as some commentators have, that the problem of human population growth is behind us. The largest cohorts of girls ever born have yet to reach their reproductive years, which ensures tremendous momentum behind global population growth. Consequently, even under the most optimistic projections, the planet's population will expand by almost a third, or by about 2 billion people, by 2025.

Real economic product per capita is also currently rising by about 1.0 percent a year. Combined with global population growth, Earth's total economic product is therefore increasing by about 2.3 percent annually. With a doubling time of around thirty years, today's global product of about $30 trillion should exceed $50 trillion in today's dollars by 2025.

A large component of this two-thirds growth will be achieved through yet higher consumption of the planet's natural resources. Already, as the geographers R. Kates, B. L. Turner, and W. C. Clark write, "transformed, managed, and utilized ecosystems constitute about half of the ice-free earth; human-mobilized material and energy flows rival those of nature."[1] Such changes are certain to increase, because of the ever-greater scale and intensity of human economic activity. We will see a decline in the total area of high-quality cropland, along with the widespread loss of remaining virgin forests. We will also see continued degradation and depletion of rivers, aquifers, and other water resources, and the further decline of wild fisheries.

Regional scarcities of these renewables are already affecting large populations in poor countries. But during the last decade, global environmental problems, especially climate change and stratospheric ozone depletion, have generally received more attention in the popular media in the industrialized world. The social impacts of these problems, in particular of climate change, may eventually be very large, but these impacts will probably not be decisively clear until well into the next century. Moreover, climate change is most likely to have a major effect on societies, not by acting as an isolated environmental pressure, but by interacting with other long-present resource pressures, such as degraded cropland and stressed water supplies.[2] Although global atmospheric problems are important, policymakers, the media, and the public in rich countries should focus more of their attention on regional environmental scarcities of cropland, water, and forests in the developing world.

Sources of Environmental Scarcity

Environmental scarcities usually have complex causes. The depletion and degradation of a resource are a function of the physical vulnerability of the resource, the size of the resource-consuming population, and the technologies and practices this population uses in its consumption behavior. The size of the population and its technologies and practices are, in turn, a result of a wide array of other variables, from women's status to the availability of human and financial capital.

In addition, resource depletion and degradation are together only one of three sources of environmental scarcity. Depletion and degradation produce a decrease in total resource *supply* or, in other words, a decrease in the size of the total resource "pie." But population growth and changes in consumption behavior can also cause greater scarcity by boosting the *demand* for a resource. Thus, if a rapidly growing population depends on a fixed amount of cropland, the amount of cropland per person—the size of each person's slice of the resource pie—falls inexorably. In many countries, resource availability is being squeezed by both these supply and demand pressures.

Finally, scarcity is often caused by a severe imbalance in the distribution of wealth and power that results in some groups in a society getting disproportionately large slices of the resource pie, whereas, others get slices that are too small to sustain their livelihoods. Such unequal distribution—or what I call *structural* scarcity—is a key factor in virtually every case of scarcity contributing to conflict. Often the imbalance is deeply rooted in institutions and class and ethnic relations inherited from the colonial period. It is frequently sustained and reinforced by international economic relations that trap developing countries into dependence on a few raw material exports. It can also be reinforced by heavy external debts that encourage countries to use their most productive environmental resources—such as their best croplands and forests—to generate hard currency rather than to support the most impoverished segments of their populations.

In the past, analysts and policymakers have usually addressed these three sources of scarcity independently. But research shows that supply, demand, and structural scarcities interact and reinforce each other in extraordinarily pernicious ways.

One type of interaction is *resource capture*. It occurs when powerful groups within a society recognize that a key resource is becoming more scarce (due to both supply and demand pressures) and use their power to shift in their favor the laws and institutions governing resource access. This shift imposes severe structural scarcities on weaker groups. Thus, in Chiapas, worsening land scarcities, partly caused by rapid population growth, encouraged powerful landowners and ranchers to exploit weaknesses in the state's land laws in order to seize lands from campesinos and indigenous farmers. Gradually these peasants were forced deeper into the state's lowland rain forest, farther away from the state's economic heartland, and deeper into poverty.

In the Jordan River basin, Israel's critical dependence on groundwater flowing out of the West Bank—a dependence made acute by an increasing Israeli population and salinization of aquifers along the Mediterranean coast—has encouraged Israel to restrict groundwater withdrawals on the West Bank during the occupation. These restrictions have been far more severe for Palestinians than for Israeli settlers. They have contributed to the rapid decline in Palestinian agriculture in the region, to the dependence of Palestinians on day labor within Israel and, ultimately, to rising frustrations in the Palestinian community.

Another kind of interaction, *ecological marginalization*, occurs when a structural imbalance in resource distribution joins with rapid population growth to drive resource-poor people into ecologically marginal areas, such as upland hillsides, areas at risk of desertification, and tropical rain forests. Higher population densities in these vulnerable areas, along with a lack of the capital and knowledge needed to protect local resources, causes local resource depletion, poverty, and eventually further migration, often to cities.

Ecological marginalization affects hundreds of millions of people around the world, across a wide range of geographies and economic and political systems. We see the same process in the Himalayas, Indonesia, Central America, Brazil, Rajasthan, and the Sahel. For example, in the Philippines, an extreme imbalance in cropland distribution between landowners and peasants has interacted with high population growth rates to force large numbers of the landless poor into interior upland regions of the archipelago. There, the migrants use slash-and-burn agriculture to clear land for crops. As more millions arrive from the lowlands, new land becomes hard to find; and as population densities on the steep slopes increase, erosion, landslides, and flash floods become critical. During the 1970s and 1980s, the resulting poverty helped drive many peasants into the arms of the communist New People's Army insurgency that had a stranglehold on upland regions. Poverty also drove countless others into wretched squatter settlements in cities like Manila.

The Importance of Context

Of course, numerous contextual factors have combined with environmental and demographic stress to produce these outcomes. Environmental scarcity is never a sole or sufficient cause of large migrations, poverty, or violence; it always joins with other economic, political, and social factors to produce its effects. In the Filipino case, for example, the lack of clear property rights in upland areas encouraged migration into these regions and discouraged migrants from conserving the land once they arrived. And President Marcos's corrupt and authoritarian leadership reduced regime legitimacy and closed off options for democratic action by aggrieved groups.

Analysts often overlook the importance of such contextual factors and, as a result, jump from evidence of simple correlation to unwarranted conclusions about causation. Some commentators, for instance, have asserted that rapid population growth, severe land scarcity, and the resulting food shortfalls caused the 1994 Rwandan genocide. In an editorial in August 1994, the Washington Post argued that, while the Rwandan civil war was "military, political, and personal in its execution," a key underlying cause was "a merciless struggle for land in a peasant society whose birthrates have put an unsustainable pressure on it."[3] Yet close analysis shows that the genocide arose mainly from a conventional struggle among elites for control of the Rwandan state. Land scarcity played at most a peripheral role by reducing regime legitimacy in the countryside and restricting alternatives for elite enrichment outside of government.[4]

Although context is important, analysts should avoid swinging to the opposite extreme, in which the causal role of environmental scarcity is entirely subordinated to that of contextual factors. For example, some skeptics claim that environmental scarcity's contribution to conflict merits little independent attention, because scarcity is wholly a result of political, economic, and social factors, such as failed institutions and policies.[5] Since these factors are the ultimate causes of the conflict, policymakers trying to prevent conflict should focus on them and not on the scarcity. But our research has identified three reasons why such arguments are incomplete at best.

First, environmental scarcity is not only influenced by social factors like institutions and policies, it can itself affect these institutions and policies in harmful ways. In other words, we should not assume that institutions and policies, taken together, are a completely independent and external starting point in the causal chain; it turns out that they can be shaped by environmental scarcity, sometimes negatively. For instance, during the 1970s and 1980s the prospect of chronic food shortages and a serious drought encouraged governments along the Senegal River to build a series of irrigation and flood-control dams. Because of critical land scarcities elsewhere in the region, land values in the basin shot up. In order to profit from this change, the Mauritanian government, controlled by Moors of Arab origin, captured the resource by rewriting the laws governing land ownership and abrogating the traditional rights of black Mauritanians to farm, herd, and fish along the Mauritanian side of the river. Thus, regional land and water scarcity influenced Mauritania's institutions and laws of land ownership in a way that harmed the interests of a substantial fraction of the country's population.

Second, the degree of environmental scarcity a society experiences is not, as it turns out, wholly a result of economic, political, and social factors, such as failed institutions and policies; it is also partly a function of the particular physical characteristics of the society's surrounding environment. These characteristics are, in some respects, independent of human activities. For instance, the depth of soils in the Filipino uplands prior to land-clearing and the features that make Israel's aquifers vulnerable to salt intrusion are physical "givens" of these environmental resources. Third, once environmental scarcity becomes irreversible (as, for example, when Haiti's vital topsoil washes into the sea), then the scarcity is, almost by definition, an external influence on society. Even if enlightened reform of institutions and policies removes the underlying political and economic causes of the scarcity, because the scarcity itself is irreversible, it will remain a continuing burden on society.

Policymakers will neither adequately understand nor respond to many important cases of civil violence around the world—cases such as the Filipino insurgency or the chronic instability in Haiti—if they do not take into account the independent causal role of environmental scarcity.

Pivotal Countries

Scarcity-induced resource capture by Moors in Mauritania helped ignite violence over water and cropland in the Senegal River basin, producing tens of thousands of refugees. Expanding populations, land degradation, and drought spurred the rise of the Sendero Luminoso guerrillas in the southern highlands of Peru. In Haiti, forest and soil loss has worsened a persistent economic crisis that generates strife and periodic waves of boat people. And land shortages in Bangladesh, exacerbated by fast population growth, have prompted millions of people to migrate to India—an influx that has, in turn, caused ethnic strife in the state of Assam.

Close study of such cases shows that severe environmental scarcity can constrain local food production, aggravate poverty of marginal groups, spur large migrations, enrich elites that capture resources, deepen divisions among social groups, and undermine a state's moral authority and capacity to govern. Marginal groups that are highly dependent on increasingly scarce resources find themselves trapped in a vise between rising scarcity on one side and institutional and policy failures on the other. These long-term, tectonic stresses can slowly tear apart a poor society's social fabric, causing chronic popular unrest and violence by boosting grievances and changing the balance of power among contending social groups and the state. (Support for this claim comes not only from close qualitative study of multiple cases: statistical analysis of data from over one hundred countries on land degradation, water pollution, and forest loss shows a significant correlation between environmental degradation and civil strife.[6])

Thus, environmental scarcity is mainly an *indirect* cause of violence, and this violence is mainly *internal* to countries. It is not the type of violence that analysts commonly assume will occur when critical resources are scarce—that is, "resource wars" among countries, in which scarcity directly stimulates one country to try to seize the resources of another.

Although this internal violence may not be as conspicuous or dramatic as wars among countries, it may nonetheless have broad implications. Some of the countries worst affected by internal environmental scarcity are *pivotal*; in other words, their stability and well-being profoundly affect broader regional and world security.[7] These countries include South Africa, Mexico, Pakistan, India, and China. India and China deserve particular attention because of their size and importance; together they make up nearly 40 percent of the world's population. Although neither currently exhibits widespread violence in which environmental factors play a role, in both cases, there are clear reasons to believe that environmentally induced violence may be widespread in the future.

India

Since independence, India has often seemed on the brink of disintegration. But it has endured, despite enormous difficulties, and by many measures the country has made real progress in bettering its citizens' lives. Recent economic liberalization has produced a surge of growth and a booming middle class (often estimated at 150 million strong). However, the country's prospects remain uncertain at best.

Although India has reduced its fertility rates significantly, the rate of population growth in 1998 is still high, at about 1.5 percent a year. India's population in 1998 is 975 million, and it expands by some 15 million people annually, which means it adds the equivalent of Indonesia to its population every 14 years. About 700 million of these people live in the countryside, and one-third still lack the income to buy a nutritionally adequate number of calories.[8] The UN's latest low and medium projections for India's population in 2025 are 1.22 and 1.33 billion, respectively.[9]

Already, water scarcities and cropland fragmentation, erosion, and salinization are widespread. Fuelwood shortages, deforestation, and desertification also affect broad tracts of countryside. Robert Repetto writes:

In most respects, India's environment has deteriorated markedly since [1970]. In canal-irrigated areas, dams are rapidly silting up because of deforestation upstream, and millions of hectares of farmland have become waterlogged or salinized because water has been applied improperly. In large areas where tubewell development has been intensive, water tables are falling; in coastal areas, salt water is invading and ruining the aquifers, depriving tens of millions of people of drinking and irrigation water. In areas of intensive farming, deficiencies in organic matter and micronutrients have emerged and limit crop yields.

In the uncultivated parts of rural India, two thirds of the total area, overharvesting of fuelwood and overgrazing of livestock—combined with unsustainable rates of commercial exploitation—have devegetated the landscape. . . . Large-scale soil erosion and disruption of hydrological flows have resulted. Increasing shortages of fuelwood, fodder, and other useful products of India's commons have added to the deprivations of the rural poor, especially women, who are most dependent on those resources.[10]

Rural resource scarcities and population growth have combined with an inadequate supply of rural jobs and economic liberalization in cities to widen wealth differentials between countryside and urban areas. These differentials propel waves of rural-urban migration. The growth rates of many of India's cities are nearly twice that of the country's population, which means that cities like Delhi, Mumbai, and Bangalore double in size every twenty years. Their infrastructures are overtaxed: Delhi has among the worst urban air pollution in the world, power and water are regularly unavailable, garbage is left in the streets, and the sewage system can handle only a fraction of the city's wastewater.

India's growing population has sometimes impeded the loosening of the state's grip on the economy: as the country's workforce expands by 6.5 million a year, and as resentment among the poor rises against those castes and classes that have benefited most from economic liberalization, left-wing politicians have been able to exert strong pressure to maintain subsidies of fertilizers, irrigation, and inefficient industries and to retain statutory restrictions on corporate layoffs. Rapid population growth has also led to fierce competition for limited status and job opportunities in government and education.[11] Attempts to hold a certain percentage of such positions for lower castes have caused bitter intercaste conflict. The right-wing Bharatiya Janata Party has often capitalized on upper- and middle-caste resentment of encroachment on their privileges, mobilizing this resentment against minorities like Muslims.

These pressures are largely beyond the control of India's increasingly corrupt and debilitated political institutions. At the district and state levels, politicians routinely hire local gang leaders or thugs to act as political enforcers. At the national level, kickbacks and bribes have become common in an economic system still constrained by bureaucracy and quotas. The central government in Delhi and many state governments are widely seen as unable to manage India's rapidly changing needs and, as a result, have lost much of their legitimacy. Furthermore, the mid-1990s have seen a sharp weakening of the Congress Party, which has traditionally pulled together the interests of multiple sectors of Indian society. The parties that have gained at Congress's expense represent a profusion of narrow caste, class, religious, and regional interests.

Although in recent decades the exploding megacities of the developing world have been remarkably quiet, India shows the record may be changing: the country's widespread urban violence in early 1993, following the demolition of Babri Masid mosque, was concentrated in the poorest slums of cities like Ahmadabad and Mumbai. Gang rapes, murders, and acts of arson continued for months after the demolition. Although Western commentators usually described the unrest as strictly communal between Hindus and Muslims, in actual fact Hindus directed many of their attacks against recent Hindu migrants from rural areas.[12] B. K. Chandrashekar, a sociology professor at the Indian Institute of Management, says that "the communal violence was quite clearly a class phenomenon. Indian cities became the main battlegrounds because of massive migrations of the rural poor in the past decades."[13]

Indian social institutions and democracy are now under extraordinary strain. The strain arises from a rapid yet incomplete economic transition, from widening gaps between the wealthy and the poor, from chronically weak political institutions, and, not least, from continued population growth and worsening environmental scarcities. Should these converging pressures cause major internal violence—or, in the worst case, should they cause the country to fragment into contending regions—the economic, migration, and security consequences for the rest of the world would be staggering.

China

Population growth and environmental scarcities are also putting extreme pressure on China's populace and government. Most experts and commentators on China have been distracted by the phenomenal economic boom in the country's coastal areas. They have tended to project these trends onto the rest of the country and to neglect the dangers posed by demographic and environmental stresses.[14] But, as with India, the costs of misreading the Chinese situation could be very high. The country has over a fifth of the world's population, a huge military with growing power-projection capability, and unsettled relations with some of its neighbors. The effects of Chinese civil unrest and internal disruption could spread far beyond its borders.

In recent years, China has embarked on an economic and social transition that is almost unimaginably complicated. Countless urgent problems, some small and some very large, must be addressed immediately as the country develops at breakneck speed. Given China's vast population, this transition will be far harder than that of South Korea or Taiwan, two countries that optimistic commentators often consider exemplars. The management demands on the central, provincial, and local Chinese governments are without precedent in human history.

Chinese leaders recognize that unchecked expansion of the country's already huge population—now around 1.25 billion—will make economic development far more difficult. Fertility rates peaked during the Cultural Revolution between 1969 and 1972. Population growth peaked at about 13 million per year in the mid-1990s, as the babies born during the Cultural Revolution reached their reproductive years.

In the late 1980s and early 1990s, specialists tempered their optimism about Chinese ability to bring population growth down to replacement rate.[15] Market liberalization in the countryside had undermined the one-child policy. In rural areas, state coercion seemed less effective, and peasants enriched by market reforms could more easily pay fines levied for having too many children. In some provinces, therefore, it became common for mothers to bear two or more children. More recent evidence, however, suggests that Chinese authorities have renewed their commitment to limiting population growth. In response to often extremely coercive measures by low-level officials, fertility rates have fallen below two children per woman for the first time.[16] But experts are not sure that this accomplishment can be sustained for long, and even if it is, China's population will continue to grow well into the next century. The UN's current low and medium projections for China's population in 2025 are 1.37 and 1.48 billion, respectively.

Larger populations and higher per capita resource consumption (resulting from economic growth) aggravate regional scarcities of water and land. Water shortages in much of northern and western China are now critical and constrain development.[17] In 1995, the great Yellow River, still referred to as the "sorrow of China" because of its catastrophic floods in years passed, was dry at its mouth for over one hundred days because of upstream withdrawals. The aquifers under Beijing supply 50 percent of the city's water, but their water levels are falling by a meter a year, causing the ground to sink throughout the region as groundwater is extracted. The central government has responded by announcing plans to build a giant canal to move 15 billion metric tons of water annually from a tributary of the Yangtze River in the south to northern regions, including Beijing, a distance of almost fourteen hundred kilometers. If built, this canal will be one of the great engineering feats of human history, cutting across hundreds of geological formations, streams, and rivers; the current plan is to construct an eight-kilometer siphon to suck the water under and past the Yellow River.[18]

The industrial city of Taiyuan, the capital of the central province of Shanxi, is a microcosm of the challenges faced by China's resource managers.[19] Situated in a valley surrounded by mountains that are rich with coal, Taiyuan is an important and rapidly growing producer of steel and chemicals. Long ago the city's demand for water for its industries, homes, and agriculture outstripped the supply of the local Fen River, requiring ever-higher extractions of groundwater from wells. As in Beijing, the water table is dropping rapidly. A large spring in the valley used for irrigation, a site marked by one of China's best-known Buddhist temples, has almost gone dry. To make matters worse, the city and its industries produce hundreds of thousands of tons of heavily polluted waste water each day, much of which is dumped into the Fen untreated or only minimally treated.

Because agricultural land is so scarce in the region, as throughout China, Taiyuan cannot afford to stop irrigating the rice, wheat, and vegetable fields in the valley. But Fen River water is increasingly laden with dangerous chemicals and salts, most seriously cancer-causing benzene. Local water managers acknowledge that the use of Fen water is slowly ruining the valley's soil, poisoning its crops, and lowering agricultural yields. The only solution is to dilute the river water with groundwater, but this resource is already overtaxed. The managers must therefore make a dreadful trade-off between further damaging the valley's soils and food production and maintaining water supplies to the city's industries and homes.

Senior officials in Taiyuan readily admit that the water problems, if not solved, will eventually cap economic growth in the region; already they must sometimes shut down factories in summer because of shortages. But all the potential solutions—more conservation and recycling, or pumping water 150 kilometers from the already depleted Yellow River—demand new technologies and large amounts of capital. The officials say that they do not have the know-how or funds to solve their water crisis adequately.

Water scarcity is only one of a host of evermore tangled resource problems in China.[20] At about a tenth of a hectare per capita, cropland availability is among the lowest in the developing world. Several hundred thousand hectares of farmland are lost every year to erosion, salinization, and urban expansion. Tracts of villas and suburban-style homes are gobbling up rich rice fields around major cities. Near many towns and cities, new Special Economic Zones—industrial parks that offer tax and service advantages to foreign investors—sprawl across good farmland. Each new auto-assembly plant, poultry-processing site, or paint factory takes a further chunk of valuable farmland. When these losses are combined with population growth, the amount of cropland per person is falling steadily by 1.5 percent a year.

Continued population growth and worsening environmental scarcities make China's rapid economic and social transition harder in many ways. First of all, they increase wealth gaps between the cosmopolitan coast, which is linked to the Pacific economy, and the more conservative interior and northern regions where water and fuelwood are desperately scarce and the land often badly damaged. Although economic growth in many interior regions has been fast, it has tended to lag far behind growth in regions closer to the coast. This widening gap has spurred a circular migration of people in search of economic opportunity—a huge flow, often estimated at 100 million people, moving back and forth between rural areas and coastal cities.

One of human history's great migrations, this movement has gone largely unremarked in the West, yet a visitor sees its evidence everywhere. The halls, corridors, and stairwells of major train stations teem with weathered and disheveled peasants from the countryside on their way to the city. In big cities, construction sites are lined with the tents and shacks of workers from rural areas; in Shanghai alone, over a million newcomers live on construction sites, moving from one to another as work demands. This flood of rural migrants has produced a jump in crime and a widely remarked drop in cleanliness and hygiene in the big cities.

Resource shortages increase wealth gaps not only between regions, but also between rich and poor people within regions. Shortages of land and water increase opportunities for powerful members of China's elite—often well-connected members of the Communist Party or their family members—to gain windfall profits through speculation.

In addition, environmental problems and population growth boost the already huge capital demands faced by the state and the economy. New dams and canals have to be built to store scarce water and move it around, cheap housing is needed for rural-urban migrants, and agricultural stations and research laboratories need funding to increase food output. Yet between 1978 and 1994, central and local government revenues as a percentage of gross domestic product (GDP) fell by almost two-thirds; the figure for central government revenue alone (at a mere 3.9 percent in 1994) was among the lowest in the world.[21] As a result, one sees rooms full of advanced equipment sitting idle in leading research labs—including labs dedicated to solving China's critical water and agricultural problems—while scientists read novels for lack of research funds. Meanwhile, in the private sector, too much capital is being channeled into high-margin luxury shopping centers, villas, and office buildings in cities like Shanghai.

Finally, resource and environmental stresses increase the susceptibility of the Chinese economy and society to sudden shocks like droughts, floods, and sharp changes in the international economy. A visitor gets the overriding impression that the country has a razor-thin margin for error when it comes to basics such as energy, food, and water. The leadership, media, and general public are acutely aware, for instance, of national food production. A slight shortfall in grain production in 1994 pushed up inflation sharply; in each June, the whole country seems to breath a sigh of relief if a good wheat harvest is announced. Serious environmental scarcities and population pressures mean there is little slack in the system to keep the effects of sudden, unanticipated shocks from propagating through the economy and society.

These three problems—rising wealth differentials, capital shortfalls, and susceptibility to shocks—are not unmanageable, but they demand consistently strong, competent, and resilient government at all levels of society. Unfortunately, the Chinese national government today lacks robust moral authority among the Chinese public. A high degree of moral authority—or *legitimacy* as political scientists like to call it—is key to the country's long-term stability.

It is true that the Communist Party has a deep reservoir of support among the Chinese, because it unified China, made the country respected around the world, and guaranteed the basics of life to its people. Yet communist ideology no longer serves as a moral glue; in the wake of the Cultural Revolution, it attracts virtually no support. Moreover, the crackdown following the 1989 Tiananmen Square massacre halted the evolution of alternative political ideas and institutions that might have formed the foundation for a newly legitimized Chinese state. Debate over central political questions—the rate of democratization, the nature of political representation, and the like—has been largely suspended. In this vacuum, the legitimacy of China's national government now mainly rests on two pillars: continued economic growth and nationalism. The nationalism, in turn, centers on a cluster of issues, including Chinese dominion over Taiwan, Tibet, and several groups of tiny islands in the South China Sea.

Even a brief slackening of economic growth would accentuate the underlying stresses posed by increasing wealth differentials and capital shortfalls. During this delicate period of economic transition, marginal groups—such as poor farmers, rural-urban migrants, and workers in state industries that are being streamlined—are especially vulnerable. The Chinese state no longer guarantees an "iron rice bowl," or bottom-line social security, for the weakest members of its population. Yet the labor force grows relentlessly by 6 million people a year. If the economy falters, the potential for urban and rural unrest could encourage a regime struggling for legitimacy to retreat to evermore aggressive nationalism.

We all have a stake in the success of the grand Chinese experiment with economic liberalization. In a land of scarce environmental resources and a still-expanding population, rapid economic growth is essential to provide capital, jobs, and know-how. But this rapid growth itself often worsens the country's underlying resource scarcities and environmental problems, and these problems, in turn, threaten growth. Whether and how China breaks out of this vicious cycle will shape much of human history for decades, if not centuries, to come.

Ingenuity and Adaptation

Some people reading the preceding accounts of India and China will say "non-sense!" They will argue that market reforms and adequate economic growth will enable these countries to manage their problems of population growth, environmental stress, and poverty relatively easily.

These optimists, who are often economists, generally claim that few if any societies face strict limits to population or consumption. Many intervening factors—physical, technological, economic, and social—permit great resilience, variability, and adaptability in human-environmental systems. In particular, they claim, properly functioning economic institutions, especially markets, can provide incentives to encourage conservation, resource substitution, the development of new sources of scarce resources, and technological innovation. Increased global trade allows resource-rich areas to specialize in production of goods (like grain) that are derived from environmental resources, while other areas specialize in nonresource-intensive production, such as services and high technology. These economic optimists are commonly opposed by neo-Malthusians—often biologists and ecologists—who claim that finite natural resources place strict limits on the growth of human population and consumption both regionally and globally; if these limits are exceeded, poverty and social breakdown result.

The debate between these two camps is now largely sterile. Nevertheless, although neither camp tells the whole story, each grasps a portion of the truth. The economic optimists are right to stress the extraordinary ability of human beings to surmount scarcity and improve their lot. The dominant trend over the past two centuries, they point out, has not been rising scarcity but increasing aggregate wealth. In other words, most important resources have become *less* scarce, at least in economic terms.

The optimists also provide a key insight that we should focus on the supply of human ingenuity in response to increasing resource scarcity rather than on strict resource limits. Many societies adapt well to scarcity without undue hardship to their populations; in fact, they often end up better off than they were before. In these societies, necessity is the mother of invention; they supply enough ingenuity in the form of new technologies and new and reformed social institutions—like efficient markets, clear and enforced property rights, and effective government—to alleviate the effects of scarcity.

The critical question then is, What determines a society's ability to supply this ingenuity? The answer is complex: different countries—depending on their social, economic, political, and cultural characteristics—will respond to scarcity in different ways and, as a result, they will supply varying amounts and kinds of ingenuity.

In the next decades, growing populations, rising per capita resource consumption, and persistent inequalities in resource access guarantee that scarcities of renewables will affect many poor countries with unprecedented severity, speed, and scale. As a result, resource substitution and conservation tasks will be more urgent, complex, and unpredictable, boosting the need for many kinds of ingenuity. In other words, these societies will have to be smarter—technically and socially—in order to maintain or increase their well-being in the face of rising scarcities.

Optimists often make the mistake of assuming that an adequate supply of the right kinds of ingenuity is always assured. But supply will be constrained by a number of factors, including the brain drain out of many poor societies, limited access to capital, and often incompetent bureaucracies, corrupt judicial systems, and weak states. Moreover, markets in developing countries frequently do not work well: property rights are unclear; prices for water, forests, and other common resources do not adjust accurately to reflect rising scarcity; and thus incentives for entrepreneurs to respond to scarcity are inadequate. Most importantly, however, the supply of ingenuity can be restricted by stresses generated by the very resource crises the ingenuity is needed to solve. Scarcity can engender intense rivalries among interest groups and elite factions that impede the development and delivery of solutions to resource problems.

It changes the behavior of subgroups within societies by changing their profit and loss calculations in ways that can exacerbate political conflict.

It turns out that we cannot leave to economists the task of predicting the social consequences of severe environmental scarcity. Politics—the sometimes nasty struggle for relative advantage and power among narrow groups—is a key factor affecting whether or not societies adapt successfully to environmental scarcity.

In Haiti, for example, shortages of forests and soil have inflamed competition among social groups; this competition, in turn, obstructs technical and institutional reform. In some cases, powerful groups that profit from high fuelwood prices have ripped up the seedlings of reforestation projects to keep the supply of fuelwood limited. In the Indian state of Bihar, which has some of the highest population growth rates and rural densities in the country, land scarcity has deepened divisions between landholding and peasant castes, promoting intransigence on both sides that has helped bring land reform to a halt. In South Africa, scarcity-driven migrations into urban areas, and the resulting conflicts over urban environmental resources (such as land and water), have encouraged communities to segment along lines of ethnicity or residential status. This segmentation has shredded networks of trust and eviscerated local institutions. Powerful warlords, linked to Inkatha or the African National Congress, have taken advantage of these dislocations to manipulate group divisions within communities, often producing horrific violence and further institutional breakdown.

Societies like these face a widening "ingenuity gap" as their requirement for ingenuity to deal with environmental scarcity rises while their supply of ingenuity stagnates or drops. A persistent and serious ingenuity gap raises grievances and erodes the moral and coercive authority of government, which boosts the probability of serious civil turmoil and violence. This violence further undermines the society's ability to supply ingenuity. If these processes continue unchecked, the country may fragment as the government becomes enfeebled and peripheral regions come under the control of renegade authorities. Countries with a critical ingenuity gap therefore risk becoming trapped in a vicious cycle, in which severe scarcity further undermines their capacity to mitigate or adapt to scarcity.

In coming decades, we can expect an increasing division of the world into those societies that can keep the ingenuity gap closed—thus adapting to environmental scarcity and avoiding turmoil—and those that cannot. If several pivotal countries fall on the wrong side of this divide, humanity's overall prospects will dramatically worsen. Such a world will be neither environmentally sustainable nor politically stable. The rich will be unable to fully isolate themselves from the crises of the poor, and there will be little prospect of building the sense of global community needed to address the array of grave problems—economic, political, as well as ecological—that humanity faces.

3

Two Centuries of Debate

DISCUSSION of the relationship between population growth, natural resource scarcity, and prosperity dates back to Confucius and Plato. But vigorous debate began only with the writings of the British clergyman and economist Thomas Malthus in the late eighteenth century.

At some risk of oversimplification, I identify three main positions in today's version of this debate, two of which I have already highlighted in the previous chapter.[1] As noted there, neo-Malthusians, who are often biologists or ecologists, claim that finite natural resources place strict limits on the growth of human population and consumption; if these limits are exceeded, poverty and social breakdown result.[2] Economic optimists, in contrast, say that there need be few, if any, strict limits to population and prosperity. These optimists are a diverse group including neoclassical economists, economic historians, and agricultural economists.[3] They say that properly functioning economic institutions, especially markets, provide incentives to encourage conservation, resource substitution, development of new sources of scarce resources, and technological innovation.[4] Finally, analysts whom I call *distributionists* (and whom I did not mention in the previous chapter, because they currently receive much less attention in the popular debate) say that the real problem is the maldistribution of resources and wealth. Poverty and inequality, in their view, are causes, not consequences, of high population growth rates and practices that deplete resources.[5]

This debate has become sterile. In most popular accounts, it is two-sided: the protagonists are arch-optimists like Julian Simon, who believe there are no limits to human population growth and wealth, and arch-pessimists like Paul Ehrlich, who argue that the human population is already far too large for the earth's resource base.[6] Although these bitter exchanges accomplish little, the underlying dispute is not frivolous. The paradigms underpinning the three positions have tremendous influence in the world. In particular, economic optimism guides the responses of the World Bank and other multilateral development agencies to resource problems in poor countries; and it informs commentary in influential business-oriented newspapers, magazines, and books.[7] The neo-Malthusian view prevails in the mass media and in the green movement. Distributionist sentiment saw its widest influence in the 1970s and 1980s, especially in developing countries.

Often, it seems, such perspectives reflect deep personal orientations to the world more than empirical evidence. The political scientist Kal Holsti notes that people face "multiple realities" when considering these issues; it is possible to build a thoroughly supported case for a great range of points of view. "My impression is that many of the theoretical arguments . . . are really debates about optimism and pessimism, our very general outlooks toward the world in which we live."[8] Looking back over the countless exchanges since Malthus' time, one might therefore think that we have progressed little in our understanding of key underlying questions. Despite the sterility of much of the current debate, however, I believe we have learned much.

In the following pages, I summarize my interpretation of the debate's main stages. I start with the three positions mentioned above; I then turn to important new contributions by geochemists, ecologists, and other scientists who have enriched our understanding of complex environmental systems; and finally I identify the particular contribution of this book, which is an attempt to unify and move beyond the current debate.

Some specialists will object to my simplification—even caricature—of this debate. Nonetheless, nonspecialists often become lost amid the welter of attacks and counterattacks by specialists, and they will benefit from a schematic outline of the debate's main structure. Interested readers can find more nuanced accounts elsewhere.[9]

Neo-Malthusians versus Economic Optimists

Malthus argued that brutal hardship was unavoidable, because human population grows exponentially when unconstrained, while food production only grows linearly.[10] He said that population tends to grow to the limit of subsistence, where it will be held in check by famine, disease, and war. Figure 3.1 represents a core Malthusian idea that scarcity and, in turn, poverty are a consequence of two factors: the physical availability of resources and total resource demand (which is the product of population size and per capita resource demand).

Later economists interpreted Malthus's core idea to mean that population growth causes a drop in per capita food production (and an increase in poverty) because of diminishing returns to labor. If the supply of cropland is static while the population grows, at some point the extra increment of food produced by an additional person—that is, the marginal product of labor—starts to fall; eventually, it falls below the amount of food the additional person eats.[11]

More recently, some economists have suggested that a rapidly growing population causes poverty by diverting capital from savings and investment to

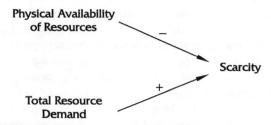

Figure 3.1. Basic Malthusianism. See the appendix of this chapter for information on how to read a systems diagram.

consumption, which lowers the long-term productivity of the economy.[12] Moreover, population growth might induce changes in agrarian structure, such as smaller and more inefficient farms, that constrain food output.[13] Finally, some analysts have claimed that a larger population increases environmental degradation, such as soil erosion, and in turn poverty.

Empirical studies do not wholly support any of these neo-Malthusian arguments. Technological change and greater inputs of capital have dramatically increased labor productivity in agriculture; the link between population growth and low savings is unclear; changes in agrarian structure induced by such growth can sometimes increase food output; and larger populations can lower environmental degradation, if, for example, they use certain labor-intensive technologies (like slope terracing).

More generally, the neo-Malthusian view has suffered because, during the last two centuries, humankind has breached many resource barriers that seemed unchallengeable. Even in Malthus's time, the French utopian Marquis de Condorcet proclaimed that

> new instruments, machines, and looms can add to man's strength and improve at once the quality and accuracy of man's productions, and can diminish the time and labor that has to be expended on them. . . . A very small amount of ground will be able to produce a great quantity of supplies . . . , more goods will be obtained for a small outlay, the manufacture of articles will be achieved with less wastage of raw materials and will make better use of them.[14]

History seems to have justified Condorcet's optimism. A century later, the population of Malthus's England had quadrupled and per capita income was much higher. Time and again, modern societies have avoided the scarcity crises predicted by Cassandras, including the feared timber shortage in America in the late nineteenth century and the "energy crisis" of the 1970s and 1980s.[15] (Many energy-supply predictions made in the 1970s are now truly embarrassing. For example, in 1973 the Cornell ecologist David Pimentel and his colleagues asserted that "if current use patterns continue, fuel costs are expected to double or triple in a decade and to increase nearly fivefold by the turn of the century."[16] In 1998, real petroleum costs were little higher than in 1973.)

Economic optimists seem better able to explain and predict this adaptability. Loosely extrapolating from past experience, they generally assume that standard economic responses will maintain or increase the stream of utility provided by scarce resources. The agricultural economist Ester Boserup shows, for example, that cropland scarcity often stimulates harder work by agricultural laborers, greater labor specialization, and land-saving changes in cropping practices.[17] Societies also compensate through growth in invested capital like agricultural machinery and fertilizer plants and through higher capital productivity. Capital growth arises from increased savings, and higher productivity from technological innovation. A key vehicle for many of these adaptations, especially technological innovation, is the market, which provides price signals and incentives for firms and entrepreneurs. Extensive research by Jacob Schmookler shows that profit opportunities are the usual stimulus for technological innovation;[18] these opportunities are often sharpest in imperfectly competitive markets, where entrepreneurs can make profits from (usually transitory) monopoly control of new technologies.[19]

A particularly interesting argument is *induced innovation* theory, which was pioneered in the 1930s by J. R. Hicks.[20] Lately, Yujiro Hayami and Vernon Ruttan, in particular, have elaborated this theory and applied it specifically to the development of agriculture in the United States, Japan, and other countries.[21] In successful economies, they propose, changes in factor endowments of, for example, land, labor, and energy are reflected in market price signals. These signals stimulate technological innovation that loosens constraints on growth, very much as Schmookler argued. Hayami and Ruttan acknowledge the critical intervening role—between price and technological innovation—of social institutions like property rights, financial agencies, and land and labor markets. However, they argue that demand for new institutions is largely determined, once again, by changes in factor endowments.[22]

Figure 3.2 summarizes these economists' main response to the grim Malthusian forecast. The key additional variable is the "quality of institutions, policies, and technologies." For simplicity, I have left out of the figure the effects of increased availability of labor and capital arising from population and economic growth (labor and capital can both substitute for resources). Most economists, in their debates with Malthusians, stress that government policies, technologies, and institutions—especially markets—are the factors of ultimate importance in the human response to resource scarcity. I have also left out of the figure the cultural, historical, and ecological forces that fundamentally shape institutions, because few economists explicitly acknowledge the role of these forces.

According to the schema in figure 3.2, better institutions, policies, and technologies can directly boost the physical availability of resources and reduce

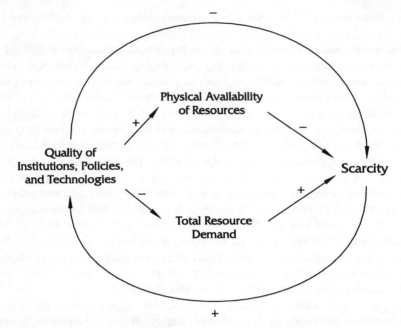

Figure 3.2. The Economists' Response

total resource demand. Price changes in efficient markets encourage people to tap new sources of scarce resources, for instance, by opening up new lands for agriculture; they promote resource substitution, such as the use of fertilizer to compensate for depleted soils; and they stimulate resource conservation, which decreases resource demand, for example, by encouraging people to use contour plowing to reduce soil erosion. New technologies, such as drip-irrigation techniques or hybrid grains that grow in high-salinity soil, curb demand and increase resource availability.

   The arrow across the top of figure 3.2 shows that scarcity and poverty are fundamentally influenced by many factors other than physical availability of resources and resource demand, in particular by the quality of government and its policies. The arrow across the bottom represents the induced-innovation argument that scarcity can stimulate beneficial institutional and technological change. Taken together, the changes from Figure 3.1 to figure 3.2 make the variables of resource supply and demand *fully determined* by other variables in the causal system—that is, they become entirely *internal* (or endogenous) to the causal system.[23] Social and technological factors explain resource supply with little (if any) reference to the physical availability of resources. The revised conceptual model thus dramatically downplays the importance of physical availability.

The economic optimists' view has three important implications. The first is that natural resources are more homogenous than commonly thought, since the right institutions and technologies allow substitution among resources.[24] As a result, Harold Barnett and Chandler Morse note, the "reservation of particular resources for later use may contribute little to the welfare of future generations."[25] Much more valuable to posterity will be a heritage of capital, knowledge, and institutions. Some optimists even argue that eventually all material scarcities will be reduced to energy scarcities, because, given sufficient energy, we can extract all basic resources from common rock and transmute one element into another. Moreover, human ingenuity will eventually find a boundless source of energy. Thus, Barnett and Morse continue: "Advances in fundamental science have made it possible to take advantage of the uniformity of energy/matter—a uniformity that makes it feasible, without preassignable limit, to escape the quantitative constraints imposed by the character of the earth's crust."[26]

Second, the optimists' view implies that the human species is biologically exceptional and that our modern economies are historically exceptional. Economic optimists celebrate the creativity and adaptability that they believe make us different from other forms of life. (Neo-Malthusians, on the other hand, emphasize the biological and physical characteristics that we share with other organisms.) And, although they can accept that scarcity crippled some preindustrial societies, they argue that the limiting factors in these cases were knowledge and institutions, not resources.[27] Today, our economic and scientific institutions are well-designed to deliver the ingenuity we need to adapt. Third, resource degradation and scarcity are not problems of excessive growth of either population or consumption, but of the failures of government policy and markets. Most importantly, governments must set up economic mechanisms to incorporate the social costs of scarcity—the scarcity's "negative externalities," as economists would label them—in the market prices of resources. Otherwise resources will be overexploited and creative solutions to scarcity undersupplied.[28]

How does this view fare empirically? The story is mixed. Evidence suggests that scarcities of nonrenewable resources, especially metals, can be overcome without undue hardship in modern economies. Repetto writes: "In economic terms, exhaustible resources have not become significantly more scarce over the past century and, by some measures, most have become less scarce."[29] The real prices of metals and minerals have generally declined as new reserves have been located, extraction and refining technologies have improved, demand has been reduced by conservation and production efficiencies, and new technologies have aided resource substitution.[30] This fact has caused some embarrassment for neo-Malthusians. In 1980, Julian Simon wagered Paul Ehrlich and others that the real prices of any selection of resources would decline over any specified period of time. Ehrlich and his colleagues chose several common metals and a ten-year period (1980 to 1990) for the wager. They lost.[31]

But careful analysis of historical long-run data shows that price trends are not always downward. In fact, rather than decreasing linearly, they appear to follow a U-shaped curve, and we may still be in the lower portion of the curve for many ores and minerals.[32] Advanced econometric modeling also suggests metal prices will eventually rise. The economist Robert Gordon and his colleagues project copper prices over the next century assuming very substantial conservation, recycling, and substitution. Although, in their model, scarcity of the metal reduces U.S. national income by only about 0.5 percent, the price of copper-equivalent services rises tenfold and of copper itself fiftyfold. Moreover, the residual economic need for copper can only be satisfied by using prodigious quantities of common rock and freshwater. They write:

> The projected rate of mining copper backstop resources [i.e., obtaining the residual economic requirement for copper from common rock] would require the excavation and processing of about 13 cubic kilometers of rock a year in the United States. This would mean the simultaneous operation of 275 open-pit mines the size of the Bingham Canyon copper mine today, the use of a supply of fresh water equal to 20 percent of the discharge of the Mississippi River, and the generation of electric power equivalent to the entire power production of the world today for this purpose alone. Such operations might have to be multiplied three-fold to allow for the replacement of other geochemically scarce minerals by abundant ones (if that is technically possible).[33]

For renewable resources, such as cropland, freshwater, and forests, the empirical story is also mixed. For instance, although analysts like Ester Boserup have argued that land scarcity induced by population growth can give farmers incentives to raise crop yields, careful studies show the association is weak.[34] Even under the best conditions, it seems unlikely that population growth can boost yields at the pace required by population growth rates in Africa and elsewhere that sometimes exceed 3 percent a year.[35]

Furthermore, induced-innovation theory has lately been challenged. The proponents of the theory, Hayami and Ruttan, claim that land abundance and labor scarcity encouraged American farmers to adopt labor-saving agricultural techniques such as mechanization. But after reviewing the American data using more accurate factor price and quantity estimates, Alan Olmstead and Paul Rhode find that "long-run relative land prices were generally moving in a direction counter to what Hayami and Ruttan claim, and in the wrong direction to explain mechanization in the period before 1910." They conclude that "the evolving structure of American agriculture cannot be explained simply in terms of the relative supplies and prices of a few factors."

They instead argue for a less simplistic theory of agricultural innovation that incorporates settlement patterns, education levels, and social structures as causal variables.[36]

The Distributionist Alternative

Although particularly favored by Marxists and neo-Marxists, the third position in the long debate—the distributionist view—has been adopted by diverse scholars. Like economic optimists, distributionists emphasize how institutional and social arrangements within society, not the availability of natural resources, are the key determinants of prosperity. Their arguments are thus again represented by the arrow across the top of figure 3.2. But, whereas the economic optimists stress the role of markets, distributionists focus on inequalities in the distribution of wealth and power.

A good example of the distributionist view, one to which we will return in later chapters, is James Boyce's study of the factors influencing food production and poverty in Bangladesh.[37] In the decade following its independence in 1971, Bangladesh was often cited as a clear "Malthusian nightmare," in which a climbing population was colliding with rigid physical ceilings to cropland availability and food production.

How does this interpretation fare on closer examination? In terms of cropland supply, it is true that Bangladesh's cropland is heavily used; in general, however, it is not badly degraded, because the annual flooding of the Ganges and Brahmaputra Rivers deposits nutrients that help maintain the fertility of the country's floodplains.[38] Nonetheless, the supply of good cropland has been constrained by flooding (perhaps aggravated by deforestation in the Himalayan watersheds of the region's major rivers);[39] the susceptibility of the country to cyclones; and the construction by India of the Farakka Barrage, a dam upstream on the Ganges River.[40] In terms of demand for land, at about 0.08 hectares per capita, cropland is extremely scarce. The United Nations projects that Bangladesh's current population of 128 million will grow to 180 million by the year 2025.[41] Because virtually all of the country's good agricultural land has already been exploited, this population growth will cut the amount of cropland per capita by almost 30 percent by 2025.

Boyce notes that early European travelers were astonished by the region's great wealth from its rich soils, abundant water, and warm climate. Now most inhabitants are extremely poor. Given the supply and demand pressures on cropland, a simple Malthusian explanation of this poverty has prima facie appeal, but Boyce concludes it is not satisfactory. Although the marginal agricultural product of additions to the labor force may have declined in the 1970s and 1980s, this outcome cannot be attributed simply to land scarcity. Yields of rice per hectare in Bangladesh were among the lowest in the world; in fact, average yields were about one-third of those obtained in China or Taiwan, and an even smaller fraction of those obtained at research stations in Bangladesh. Boyce notes that there was therefore extraordinary potential for increased labor productivity despite the scarcity of land.

Boyce's careful empirical analysis leads him to conclude that population growth actually induced agricultural innovation during the 1970s and 1980s and thus helped to increase agricultural yields. But growth in yields was not fast enough to compensate for the population's increasing food demands. Boyce argues that the country had a critical need for innovation to provide effective control of flood and irrigation waters; water control was the "leading input, or binding technological constraint" on agricultural productivity.[42] But to a large extent, water control was a public good that required institutions to permit and guide collective action. In rural Bangladesh during this period, the necessary institutional innovation was seriously hindered by struggles among social groups over the distribution of power and wealth.

Powerful landlords were unwilling to cooperate with each other because they sought relative advantage. They were reluctant to hire seasonally idle labor for the construction of water-control projects because they feared the potential for unrest when large groups of the poor worked together. Government efforts to mobilize local resources for water control, through the construction of tanks, wells, and irrigation canals, were distorted to benefit large landowners; funds were misappropriated; and projects were badly constructed and poorly maintained because landlords had little direct interest in their success. Landlords sought to control wells to permit monopoly pricing and to gain rights to adjacent cropland. At the same time, poorer groups threatened by the increased economic and political power of landowners with access to the well-water often sabotaged new tubewells.

Boyce argues that the country's distributional inequalities impeded the process of social and technical innovation—especially for water control—that Bangladesh so desperately needed in the 1970s and 1980s. He calls for a massive change in property rights that would weaken rural elites and allow for effective collective action for water control. But he concedes that such institutional changes are clearly unlikely "in the absence of a broad political mobilization of the landless and near-landless majority in the countryside, and the barriers to this are formidable."[43]

Since Boyce conducted his study, Bangladesh's situation has improved. The rate of population growth has dropped sharply, largely because of the village-level activities of family planning nongovernmental organizations (NGOs) (but average fertility still remains well above replacement rate). Some improvements are due to the kind of policies—both national and international—promoted by free-market and free-trade economists. For instance, an export-oriented textile manufacturing boom in urban centers has benefited the whole economy. Moreover, according to Francesco Goletti, "removal of impediments to trade and distribution of irrigation equipment" and the "liberalization of import of irrigation equipment in 1988 has resulted in a wider spectrum of minor irrigation equipment available to farmers."[44] As a result, agricultural productivity has risen: "a boom in agriculture has brought the country close to feeding itself, with food imports of more than 10 million tons now down to 2.5 million tons a year."[45]

Nonetheless, although the country has substantially reduced its overall grain deficit, Goletti notes that "in comparison with other low-income Asian countries, Bangladesh has one of the lowest records in terms of agricultural growth rate." Boyce's analysis therefore remains a valuable explanation of why Bangladeshi underdevelopment persists. More generally, the analyses of Boyce and like-minded distributionists remind us that social and political factors are essential elements of any complete explanation of the relationship between population growth, resource scarcity, and prosperity.

Thresholds, Interdependence, and Interactivity

Meanwhile, as the debate among the three camps described above has continued in recent decades, often without much obvious progress, scientists have been busy with their research. They have developed a far richer understanding of the natural systems surrounding human societies, an understanding that has the potential to affect this debate profoundly. Much of their research has focused on the thresholds, interdependence, and interactivity of complex systems of environmental resources such as climate, oceans, forests, and agricultural lands. The influence of these systems on human society is, at least in part, a function of the systems' intrinsic character and is not, therefore, fully determined by human institutions, policies, and technologies. Consequently, figure 3.3 shows that the thresholds, interdependence, and interactivity of environmental systems have an independent (or exogenous) influence on the physical availability of resources. I believe that this influence is largely negative.[46]

Several decades ago, scientists and laypeople generally regarded Earth's environmental systems as relatively resilient and stable in the face of human insults. But during the last twenty to thirty years, scientists' perceptions have shifted. They now understand that the causal relationships within environmental systems are sometimes best represented by sharply nonlinear mathematical functions. These systems may respond slowly and incrementally to human intervention for a long time and then suddenly change their character. In other words, they exhibit "threshold" effects. The geographer William Clark discusses these effects in interlinked physical, ecological, and social systems:

Typically in such systems, slow variation in one property can continue for long periods without noticeable impact on the rest of the system. Eventually, however, the

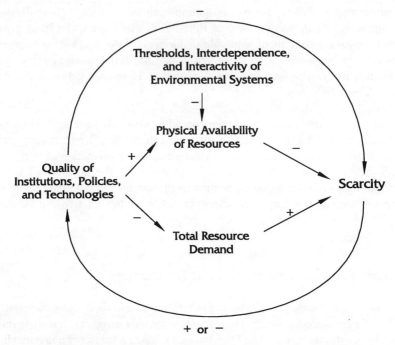

Figure 3.3. Moving the Debate Forward: Ecological Complexity, Social Friction, and Adaptive Failure

system reaches a state in which its buffering capacity or resilience has been so reduced that additional small changes in the same property, or otherwise insignificant external shocks, push the system across a threshold and precipitate a rapid transition to a new system state or equilibrium.[47]

Indeed, some environmental systems are chaotic. In a chaotic system, nonlinear and feedback relationships among the system's elements amplify small perturbations, making the trajectory of its development highly sensitive to minute differences in initial conditions, and making accurate prediction of the system's state more difficult the further one tries to project into the future.[48]

Recent developments in atmospheric science illustrate well this new understanding of environmental systems. A key figure in these developments has been the eminent geochemist Wallace Broecker. He has focused on the operation of the *North Atlantic conveyor*, a cycle of water in the Atlantic in which a northward flow of warm surface water is complemented by a southward flow of dense, cold, deep water. This flow carries a staggering amount of heat energy from the tropics to the North Atlantic—equivalent to about 30 percent of that received by the North Atlantic from the sun—which in turn raises the temperature of adjacent lands by six to eight degrees Celsius.[49] The conveyor appears to be delicately balanced and perhaps susceptible to sudden disruption by human-induced global warming, with potential effects on Earth's entire climate.[50] In 1987, Broecker reflected on recent polar ice-core and ocean-sediment data that suggest Earth has experienced many episodes of sudden climate change, perhaps caused by shutdowns of the conveyor:

> What these records indicate is that Earth's climate does not respond to forcing in a smooth and gradual way. Rather, it responds in sharp jumps which involve large-scale reorganization of Earth's system. . . . We must consider the possibility that the main responses of the system to our provocation of the atmosphere will come in jumps whose timing and magnitude are unpredictable.[51]

Although the historical climate record seems indisputable, there is thankfully no evidence yet of such wholesale reorganizations of Earth's contemporary climate. The Antarctic ozone hole, which appeared in the mid-1970s, is, however, a dramatic example of threshold effects in today's atmospheric systems.[52] The scientific models of ozone depletion used until the 1980s had, for the most part, assumed a rough linear relationship between chlorofluorocarbon (CFC) emissions and ozone depletion. In fact, significant depletion of Antarctic stratospheric ozone was not identified until the mid-1980s, because the computer programs that analyzed satellite data on Antarctic ozone concentrations had been written to discard anomalous results.[53] Atmospheric scientists had not even remotely anticipated the catalytic process that occurs on the surface of stratospheric ice crystals when certain temperature and light conditions interact with particular concentrations of water, nitrogen compounds, and CFCs. If the conditions are right, it turns out, this destruction can occur at lightening speed, stripping the ozone from multikilometer-thick layers of the stratosphere in a matter of weeks.[54] (Recent studies of ozone depletion over the Arctic show how sensitive this process is to initial conditions: accounting for relatively small-scale variations in concentrations of ozone-destroying chemicals within the stratosphere improves predictions of total ozone depletion by 40 percent.[55])

The Antarctic ozone hole was startling evidence of how environmental systems can respond nonlinearly to human inputs, of the capacity of humankind to affect significantly the ecosystem on a global scale, and of our inability to predict exactly how environmental systems will change.

Outside of the atmospheric sciences, a parallel evolution of perspective has occurred. Events such as the sudden collapse of the Peruvian anchovy fishery in the 1970s and of the Northwest Atlantic cod stock in the late 1980s show that threshold effects and chaotic behavior are not limited to the global atmosphere.[56] Ecologists, in particular, now generally realize that metaphors of stability, equilibrium, and balance are not appropriate to describe complex, interdependent systems of organisms. Instead, metaphors of anarchy, flux, and constant turmoil are more apt.[57] Field studies of prairie grass communities and mathematical analysis of Dungeness crab populations show chaotic dynamics, with wild, unanticipated booms and crashes in population size.[58]

The tasks of predicting and managing environmental systems are thus vastly harder, especially when human impacts on these systems are rising.[59] The renowned ecologist C. S. Holling summarizes the problem:

> Any of the realistic representations of the key processes [governing natural populations and systems] show the existence of thresholds, limits, and other non-linearities. As a consequence, each process can show population-density regions of negative feedback control, other regions of positive feedback destabilization, and still other regions of neutral influence. Once the models incorporate three or more population variables or species, together with realistic representations of the key processes, a very wide range of complex population behaviors is produced. Even in the simplest models, multiple stable states are the rule, not the exception, and behavior can range from extinctions, to stable limit cycles, to boom-and-bust flips between stability regions, even to chaotic behavior.[60]

Unfortunately, the prediction and management of environmental systems— and often, in consequence, the avoidance of severe resource scarcity—is complicated by several factors additional to the threshold effects, multiple equilibria, and chaotic behavior recently identified by scientists. Three such factors are particularly important: extreme events, the ramifying character of scarcities in interdependent environmental systems, and interactions among human impacts on these systems.

First, even if the basic features of an environmental system (such as the mean values of key variables describing its character) change only slowly and linearly, the frequency of events within the system that are judged to be extreme—by prevailing social and technological standards—can increase sharply. For example, although a slow two or three degree warming of mean global temperature might not seem too significant, in itself, for agricultural production, it could produce a large increase in the frequency of crop-devastating droughts, floods, heat waves, and storms, even if it does not force the climate system to a completely new equilibrium. T. M. Wigley notes that severe social impacts of environmental change can result "not so much from slow fluctuations in the mean, but from the tails of the distribution, from extreme events." Because the probability distributions for most climate variables describe a bell curve, he calculates that "a change in the mean by one standard deviation would transform the 1-in-20 year extreme to something that could be expected perhaps 1 year in 4, while the 1-in-100 year extreme becomes a 1-in-11 year event."[61]

Such extreme events can have especially pernicious effects on society. Martin Parry argues, for instance, that extreme weather is more likely to exhaust the social buffers that underpin farming systems. Once these buffers of labor, capital, and social structure are gone, and once farmers abandon their lands, a sustained improvement in weather will not quickly return these lands to cultivation. It takes a much longer spell of good weather to restore the social buffers than it does for a series of extreme events to deplete them.[62]

Second, environmental systems—from Earth's climate, to regional fisheries, soils, and forests—are dynamic and interdependent. Overextraction of (or damage to) one resource in such a system can produce ramifying effects and scarcities throughout the surrounding ecological system.[63] Forests, for example, not only provide wood for fuel, construction, and paper. They also reduce the amplitude of variation of the hydrological cycle by slowing runoff of rainwater and by absorbing and releasing some of it through transpiration; they stabilize soils and reduce erosion; they absorb and fix atmospheric carbon dioxide that otherwise might contribute to global warming; and they provide a habitat for diverse organisms. In turn, each of these functions helps sustain other parts of the ecological system. Thus, the loss of forests can generate much more than just a scarcity of wood for a local community: it can also generate scarcities of soils, of rainfall, of sustained and manageable river flow for hydropower and transportation, and of reservoir and irrigation capacity (because these systems become plugged with silt). If forest loss is widespread enough, it can diminish the biodiversity we need for our medicines and industries, and it might boost climate change. Some of these problems will induce yet other shortages: for instance, the silt that washes into the sea can smother coral reefs and thereby damage local fisheries.[64]

Third, the dynamic and interpendent character of environmental systems also means that multiple human impacts on these systems can interact to produce synergistic outcomes. An agricultural region may, for example, be simultaneously stressed by degraded soil and changes in precipitation caused by regional deforestation or climate change. The total effect on crop output of these interacting impacts can be much greater than the sum of their separate effects.[65] Scientists recently discovered a striking example of interaction effects in certain lakes in northwestern Ontario. The combination of a warming climate with acid rain has increased the penetration of ultraviolet-B (UV-B) radiation into lake water. The researchers conclude that much of the damage to aquatic life in these lakes that was originally attributed solely to acidification might actually be attributable, at least in part, to increased exposure to UV-B.[66]

In recent years, this more sophisticated understanding of how environmental systems work—one that takes into account the characteristics discussed above—has percolated out of the scientific community into the policy-making community. It has also subtly influenced the broader public's view of environmental problems. Progressive, incremental degradation of environmental systems seems less tolerable than it once was, because we now realize that we do not know when and where we might cross a threshold, with complex, unpredictable and perhaps highly undesirable results.

Social Friction and Adaptive Failure

With the important contribution to this long debate of geochemists, ecologists, and other scientists, we arrive at the present. The three original, ideologically hardened camps are still easily identifiable in the scholarly literature and popular discussion, although new arguments, many creative and nuanced, are starting to blur the boundaries of the debate.[67] Unfortunately, for the most part, neither economic optimists nor distributionists have taken full account of recent findings about the thresholds, interdependence, and interactivity of environmental systems. And many (but not all) neo-Malthusians have simply folded these findings into their generally alarmist story about human destruction of the planet's ecosystem.

None of these three camps, I believe, fully recognizes a particularly important implication of the scientists' findings. As I will explain in chapter 6, thresholds, interdependence, and interactivity boost the need for new and more sophisticated institutions and technologies within societies affected by resource scarcity. In other words, these ecosystem characteristics mean that societies must be able to supply more social and technical ingenuity to adapt to rising resource scarcity.

Can all societies meet this rising need for ingenuity? In chapter 6, I show that severe scarcities also sometimes stimulate competition among powerful groups and elites to protect their narrow interests. This competition, which I call *social friction*, can impede the supply of the institutions and technology—the supply of the ingenuity—needed to alleviate the underlying scarcity. In terms of figure 3.3, therefore, this means that the correlation between scarcity and the quality of institutions and technology, which is positive according to induced innovation theorists, is sometimes negative (I have therefore added a negative sign to the arrow across the bottom of the figure). Scarcity, put simply, can hinder institutional and technological adaptation. Rather than inspiring the wave of ingenuity predicted by economic optimists, environmental scarcity instead sometimes reduces the supply of ingenuity available in a society.

This possibility is largely overlooked by most analysts to date, yet it is implicit in some of their findings. For instance, although James Boyce does not make the point directly, it is clear from his research that worsening scarcities of land and water in Bangladesh sharply aggravated the struggles between landlords and peasants that disrupted innovation in water institutions. In chapter 6, I identify some of the key social and institutional conditions that can combine with severe scarcity to produce such adaptive failure. It turns out that distributionists like Boyce are right to emphasize social imbalances in wealth and power. But I believe they do not, in general, recognize a central reason why these imbalances matter. Highly unequal social arrangements make it much more likely that environmental scarcity will cause severe social friction. Such arrangements, in other words, often interact with severe scarcity to generate destructive social competition that impedes technological and institutional adaptation.

My argument about how scarcity can disrupt ingenuity supply and adaptation is, I believe, the main contribution of this book to the long debate described above. It is an explicit attempt to move the debate forward, because it allows us to synthesize the three seemingly irreconcilable positions discussed in the first half of this chapter. Neo-Malthusians emphasize physical causes of scarcity and poverty: population size and growth, the resource-consumption rate per capita, and the quantities of natural resources available to a society. Economic optimists and distributionists emphasize social factors, but they differ on which social factors are important: economic optimists stress market failures and bad economic policies and institutions, whereas distributionists emphasize social structures and political behavior, especially the skewed distribution of wealth and power among social classes and groups.

The argument here integrates both physical and social variables. Social improvements such as better markets and less unbalanced wealth distribution often alleviate the negative effects of scarcity. But a society's capacity to make these improvements—to deliver the required social ingenuity—will be partly determined by scarcity itself, which is powerfully influenced by the society's physical context.

More generally, although the behavior of social systems is not fully determined by their physical context, it is not independent of this context either. The political scientist Daniel Deudney notes that during the twentieth century most explanations of social behavior have taken the form of "social-social" theory; in other words, these theories have posited social causes of social behavior.[68] However, once we recognize that environmental systems often exhibit complex, nonlinear, interactive behavior, and that environmental scarcity can undermine adaptive responses, we must reintroduce nature into our explanations of social behavior. We need theories that are, at least in part, "nature-social" theories.[69]

A focus on ingenuity supply also helps us rethink the neo-Malthusian concept of strict physical limits to growth. The limits a society faces are a product of both its physical context and the ingenuity it brings to bear on that context. If a hypothetical society were able to supply infinite amounts of ingenuity, then that society's maximum sustainable population and rate of resource consumption would be determined by biological and physical laws (such as the second law of thermodynamics). Because infinite ingenuity is never available, the resource limits societies face in the real world are more restrictive than this theoretical maximum. And because the supply of ingenuity depends, in part, on many social and economic factors and can therefore vary widely, we cannot determine a society's limits solely by examining its physical context, as neo-Malthusians do. Rather than speaking of limits, it is better to say that some societies are locked into a race between a rising requirement for ingenuity and their capacity to supply it.

If a country loses the race—if, in other words, a gap develops between ingenuity requirement and supply—social dissatisfaction will rise, with increasing stress on marginal groups, including those in ecologically fragile rural areas and urban squatter settlements. A serious ingenuity gap will cause major social changes like constrained agricultural and economic productivity and large population movements. These changes boost dissatisfaction and undermine regime legitimacy and coercive power, raising the likelihood of widespread and chronic civil violence. Violence further erodes the society's capacity to supply ingenuity, especially by causing human and financial capital to flee. Countries with a severe ingenuity gap therefore risk entering a downward and self-reinforcing spiral of crisis and decay.

Although many analysts might reach a different conclusion, I believe we will see an increasing bifurcation of the world into societies that can maintain an adequate supply of ingenuity in the face of rising scarcities and those that cannot. Future resource crises and the social hardships that accompany them will therefore be regional rather than global. We may see, for example, falling grain prices and regional food surpluses in Western countries occurring simultaneously with civil strife in parts of Africa and Asia that is caused partly by environmental scarcity.

As scarcities become more serious in some regions, poor countries will need immense amounts of human ingenuity in order to adapt and prosper, and their citizens will sometimes need to exhibit great tolerance, generosity, and commitment to the commonweal. But scarcities will often make tolerance, generosity, and cooperation less abundant, not more so. The pushing and pulling of powerful groups as they struggle to protect their interests will often weaken poor societies' capacities to produce and deliver the ingenuity they need.

In this chapter, I have offered a simplified and somewhat idiosyncratic account of the two-century debate over the relationship between population growth, resource scarcity, and prosperity. Neo-Malthusians, economic optimists, and distributionists have been the main parties to this debate, which has become repetitive and sterile. Protagonists often seem to talk past each other. More recently, however, atmospheric scientists, ecologists, and other scientists have helped us better understand important physical characteristics of environmental systems, including their thresholds, interdependence, and interactivity. In this book, I make the additional point that environmental scarcities can sometimes hinder adaptive institutional and technological change.

In the next chapter, I provide a more detailed account of the sources, nature, and global manifestations of environmental scarcity.

Appendix

How to Read a Systems Diagram

Diagrams using causal arrows—which researchers often call *systems diagrams*—are common in this and subsequent chapters. In many cases their interpretation is straightforward, but occasional care is needed.

In almost all cases in this book (the exception being figure 4.1 in chapter 4), if two variables are linked by an arrow and there are no plus or minus signs associated with the arrow, then the reader should assume that the variables exhibit a positive correlation. In other words, an increase in the value of the variable at the start of the arrow (the cause) produces an increase in the value of the variable at the end of the arrow (the effect), and a decrease in the value of the variable at the start produces a decrease in the value of the variable at the end. The variables, in other words, change their values in the same direction.

In diagrams such as those in this chapter, where plus and minus signs are associated with the causal arrows, the plus sign means that the two variables linked by the causal arrow have a positive correlation. A minus sign, however, indicates that they have a negative correlation, which means an increase in the value of the variable at the start of the arrow produces a decrease in the value of the variable at the end, and vice versa. With a negative correlation, the variables change their values in opposite directions.

Complex combinations of positive and negative correlations within a systems diagram require careful interpretation, especially when feedback loops are involved. A useful general rule is that an even number of minus signs in any feedback loop produces a positive feedback and an odd number of minus signs produces a negative feedback. Positive feedbacks are self-reinforcing cycles: a change in the value of a variable in the loop produces a string of consequences that causes the same variable to change its value even more in the same direction. Such spirals of reinforcement can be vicious or virtuous (that is, variable values can change in directions that are harmful or beneficial), but they are inherently unstable. Negative feedbacks, on the other hand, are self-correcting cycles: a change in the value of a variable in the loop produces a string of consequences that ultimately counteracts the original change.

A good example is provided in figure 3.3. The top and bottom arrows in the figure represent possible relationships between the quality of institutions, policies, and technologies in an economy and the degree of resource scarcity. Although it is generally acknowledged that the worse the institutions, policies, and technologies, the greater the scarcity (represented by the minus sign associated with the top arrow), it is not so clear whether greater scarcity has a beneficial or harmful effect on institutions, policies, and technologies. The conventional wisdom in economics (represented by the induced-innovation school) is that the effect is beneficial, which means that the lower arrow should have a plus sign associated with it and that the feedback would be negative. In other words, if bad institutions, policies, and technologies contribute to scarcity, the scarcity itself can provide counteracting incentives to fix the institutions, policies, and technologies. However, I argue in this book that scarcity's effect is sometimes harmful, which would imply a minus sign on the lower arrow. If I am right in certain circumstances, the implications are serious, because the feedback becomes positive: scarcity reinforces the institutional, policy, and technological failures that contributed to scarcity in the first place.

4

Environmental Scarcity

As WE HAVE SEEN in previous chapters, natural resources can be roughly divided into two groups: nonrenewables, like oil and minerals, and renewables, like freshwater, forests, fertile soils, and Earth's ozone layer. A nonrenewable consists of a *stock*, which is the total quantity of the resource available for consumption. A renewable resource has both a stock and a *flow*, which is the incremental addition to, or restoration of, the stock per unit of time.[1] Surprisingly, many of the participants in the long debate over the relationship between resource scarcity and prosperity have not highlighted this critical distinction between renewables and nonrenewables.

Experts often draw an analogy between the stocks and flows of resources and money in a bank: they note that a renewable resource's stock is the resource's capital or principal, which generates a flow of interest or income that can be tapped for human consumption and well-being. For example, the topsoils on the American Great Plains are capital that can be used to grow grain. A "sustainable" farming economy can be defined as one that leaves these soils—this capital—intact and undamaged so that future generations of Americans will enjoy an undiminished stream of income in the form of food products. If the natural decay of crop residue adds about 0.25 millimeters of topsoil to farmed land a year (or about 3.25 metric tons/hectare), then sustainable farming should not produce an average soil loss greater than this amount.[2] If farming does cause greater loss, then the underlying stock of topsoil is depleted in quantity or degraded in quality.[3]

Renewable resources can be further divided—again roughly speaking—into two groups: those that provide goods and those that provide services. Ocean fisheries supply fish that are a good, while the stratospheric ozone layer renders a service by protecting life from high levels of ultraviolet radiation. Some renewables provide both goods and services: forests supply timber (a good) while also maintaining regional hydrological cycles (a service).

Three Sources of Scarcity

Resource scarcity is an omnipresent feature of our existence. As we have seen in the previous chapter, scarcity can stimulate useful institutional and technological change. In this book, however, we are mainly concerned with scarcity of renewables that is so severe that it has the potential to seriously undermine human well-being. It can arise in three ways: through a drop in the supply of a key resource, through an increase in demand, and through a change in the relative access of different groups to the resource. I call these respectively *supply-induced*, *demand-induced*, and *structural* scarcities.

A simple pie metaphor illustrates these three kinds of scarcity. Supply-induced scarcity gets worse when the resource pie shrinks because it has been depleted in quantity or degraded in quality. Demand-induced scarcity rises when, for example, a growing population divides a static resource pie into smaller slices for each individual. Structural scarcity is aggravated when some groups get disproportionately large slices of the pie while other groups get slices that are too small.

Unfortunately, analysts tend to focus on only one type of scarcity at a time. For example, ecologists and environmentalists often focus on *environmental change*, a term that refers only to a human-induced decline in the quantity or quality of a renewable resource—that is, to worsening supply-induced scarcity. And, as I showed in chapter 3, neo-Malthusians and economic optimists accent supply-induced and demand-induced scarcities while generally overlooking the political economy of resource distribution. The term *environmental scarcity*, however, allows us to incorporate in one analysis the three distinct sources of scarcity and to study how they interact with and reinforce each other. I discuss these interactions in detail in the next chapter.

Demand-induced scarcities arise only with resources that are (to use the economists' term) *rivalrous*. A good or resource is rivalrous when its use by one economic actor reduces its availability for others. Examples are fisheries, cropland, forests, and water. Structural scarcities arise primarily with resources that are *excludable*, which means that property rights or other institutions can be used to prevent access to the resource by some actors. Cropland is usually excludable, and structural scarcities of cropland are readily apparent in many societies, as we will see in later chapters. However, some renewables, like high-seas fisheries, are too dynamic to be physically controlled and therefore remain nonexcludable.

A resource that is rivalrous yet nonexcludable—again like high-seas fisheries—is often called an *open-access* or a *common-pool* resource. Because property rights are weak, such resources are vulnerable to excessive degradation and depletion. Some renewables, such as forests, have physical characteristics that permit the assignment of clear property rights; nonetheless, they are often open access because of historical norms and laws governing their exploitation. Other resources, especially those that provide services like the climate and hydrological cycles, are neither rivalrous nor excludable.[4] For the most part, my discussion in this and later chapters assumes we are dealing only with *prototypical* resources that are both rivalrous and excludable; my argument can be easily generalized, however, to other types of resources.[5]

Factors Producing Scarcity

The three kinds of environmental scarcity are produced by many factors that are causally related in complex ways. I discuss below the key factors and relationships producing supply-induced scarcity and then review briefly the factors behind demand-induced and structural scarcities.

Figure 4.1 shows that any human-caused increase in supply-induced scarcity is the product of three factors: the total human population in the region, the use per capita of each technology available to that population (where the range of technologies is represented in the figure as $Tech_1 \ldots Tech_n$), and the amount of resource consumption or degradation produced by each unit of use of these technologies.[6] Use per capita of each technology, in turn, is influenced by available natural resources, including nonrenewables and renewables, and by *ideational* factors, including institutions, social relations, preferences, and beliefs. These ideational factors also influence fertility rates and therefore population size. (I use the adjective "ideational" to emphasize that things like institutions and social relations are products of the human mind.)

The figure shows that a society's technological activity can feed back to affect its ideational factors. Resource depletion and degradation can also influence ideational factors, for example by prompting or impeding institutional reform. Finally, the amount of consumption or degradation of a renewable resource arising from a technology's use is influenced by the sensitivity of the region's ecosystem to the use of that technology (a factor that incorporates the ecosystem's complex threshold and interactive responses to human perturbations).[7]

The example of fisheries depletion illustrates figure 4.1. The total depletion of a given fishery is a function of the size of the human population consuming fish from the fishery, the type of fishing technologies used by this population, the use per capita of these technologies, and the technologies' impact on the fishery per unit use. The kinds of fishing technology deployed—whether they are, for example, hand-cast nets or offshore trawlers—and their use per capita will be influenced by such ideational factors as the population's level of scientific and technical knowledge and the social and economic status of the fishing communities. The kinds of technology and their use per capita will also be influenced, of course, by the availability of fish. Finally, the technologies' impacts on the fishery will depend in part on the sensitivity of the fishery ecosystem as a whole. If the fishery is close to a threshold point, then sustained overfishing could cause it to collapse suddenly.

Sometimes renewable resources will be depleted or degraded not by direct consumption but by technological activities that indirectly harm the resource. For example, heavy pollution by factories and the clearing of coastal mangrove swamps to build aquaculture pens often have immense indirect effects

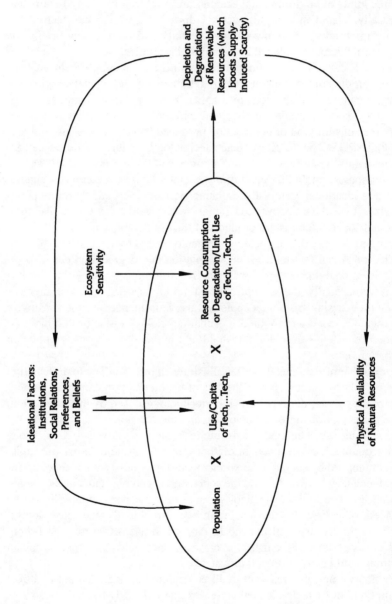

Figure 4.1. Determinants of Supply-Induced Environmental Scarcity

on the survival and reproduction of inshore fisheries. Economists call such indirect effects the *negative externalities* of these technological activities, because they are costs borne not by the economic actors using the technologies but by other actors in the society.

Over the short and medium terms, the range of technologies in figure 4.1 does not vary much. It is a result of the economy's current capital stock (including its machinery, factories, and infrastructure), which embodies the society's prevailing level and type of technology. Over the long term, as this capital stock turns over, the range of technologies varies as a function (in part) of the availability of natural resources and certain ideational factors, including beliefs about the nature of the physical world held by knowledge-elites in the society and also the society's general willingness to invest in capital, research, and development.

We can see that the ideational factors at the top of the diagram are particularly important: they make up a broad and complex social and psychological context. This context includes the pattern of wealth and power distribution within the society; the economic, political, and legal incentives to produce and consume material goods (including the system of property rights and markets); family and community structures; perceptions of the probability of long-run political and economic stability; historically rooted patterns of trade and interaction with other societies; and metaphysical beliefs about the relationship between humans and nature.[8]

Ideational factors help determine the kind of physical activities pursued in a given society. They also help determine a society's vulnerability and adaptability when faced with serious environmental scarcity.[9] Without a full understanding of them, we cannot begin to grasp the nature of the relationship in a given society between human activity and the scarcity of renewable resources, nor can we grasp why some societies respond better to this scarcity than others.[10] In general, recognition of the role of ideational factors distinguishes simplistic environmental determinism from sophisticated accounts of interactions between societies and their environments.[11]

Many of these factors also affect demand-induced and structural scarcity. Demand-induced scarcity is a function of population size multiplied by per capita demand for a given resource; an increase in either population or per capita demand increases total resource demand. For example, the number of people living in an arid region might go up, which, all other things being equal, will increase total demand for water; or a constant number of inhabitants might instead demand on average more water for new agricultural technologies (such as irrigation). In both these cases, if only a constant and limited flow of water is available, water scarcity will increase.

Both population size and per capita demand are influenced by a range of ideational factors, from relations between genders (which affect fertility rates) to economic preferences (which affect demand for resources). This influence was nicely illustrated by a recent debate over the role of population growth and resource scarcity in the conflict between the Miskito Indians and the Nicaraguan government during the Sandanista period.[12] Bernard Nietschmann argued that the Nicaraguan state's need for resources to sustain the country's economic and agricultural development caused environmental degradation to spread from the Pacific to the Atlantic coast of the country. As this happened, indigenous Miskitos in the east came into sometimes violent conflict with the central government. Sergio Diaz-Briquets responded that the Sandinistas expropriated Miskito lands because of ideology not scarcity. The Atlantic coastal region was largely ignored by the Nicaraguan state under former president Somoza. Following the revolution, the Sandinistas had ample newly expropriated land to distribute to their followers; but the new government—guided by Marxism—saw the Miskitos as a backward people with a competing worldview and a precapitalist mode of production, whose land was needed for a state-directed strategy of economic development. The gap between the two views can be bridged by noting the influence of ideology (and, in consequence, of preferences) on resource demand: the Marxist ideology of the Sandinista regime boosted the state's appetite for land resources.

Increased population size and increased per capita demand for a given resource can have dual effects on environmental scarcity: they both increase total demand for the resource, and they can both decrease supply by contributing to the resource's depletion or degradation. Growing populations and greater per capita resource demand can thus simultaneously boost demand-induced and supply-induced scarcity.

The third kind of environmental scarcity—structural scarcity—is caused by unequal distribution that concentrates a resource in the hands of some groups and subjects the rest to greater than average scarcity. Each society has, for example, rules and laws (once again, ideational factors) that define the limits and nature of ownership of things such as farmland. These property rights affect how resources are distributed among different groups in the society, and they often change as a result of large-scale development projects or new technologies that alter the relative values of resources.[13]

Chapter 5 shows that these three kinds of environmental scarcity can operate singly or in combination and can produce a variety of negative social effects, including constrained agricultural and economic productivity, increased migration, sharper social segmentation, and disrupted institutions. These social effects are often interlinked and will, under certain circumstances, generate violent conflict.

The Physical Trends of Global Change

The remainder of this chapter provides a brief survey of the impacts of human activity on the earth's renewable resources. I focus on nine physical trends that are observable in the global human-ecological system: human population growth, rising energy consumption, global warming, stratospheric ozone depletion, rising cropland scarcity, tropical deforestation, rising scarcity of freshwater, decline of fish stocks, and loss of biodiversity.[14] For each trend, I identify our best understanding of the current situation at the global and, where appropriate, regional levels. I also identify the likely trajectory of the trend over the next decades. (Except where indicated, the following statistics are the best available as of mid-1997.)

The following pages are intended to provide a general context for the specific discussion of environmental scarcity and violence in later chapters. In many parts of the developing world, environmental scarcities—especially of soil, water, and forests—are worsening quickly. Because about half of the people on the planet depend on local renewable resources for some aspect of their day-to-day livelihood, these worsening scarcities have an immediate and intimate impact on the well-being of a substantial fraction of humankind. In fact, in many developing countries, serious environmental scarcities directly or indirectly affect a large majority of the population.

The first two trends in the above list of nine play a role on the left side of figure 4.1: population growth is a driving force behind both supply- and demand-induced scarcity; rising energy consumption is a reasonable surrogate indicator of rising material consumption in human societies and therefore of changes in the figure's "use per capita of technology" variable. The remaining seven trends are often grouped together under the rubric "global change." They are all large-scale human-induced changes in the availability of renewable resources. These changes are similar because they are all long-term and hard to reverse. Nonetheless, they differ greatly in their present human consequences. On one hand, depletion and degradation of cropland, water, fuelwood, and fish are today harshly affecting hundreds of millions of people in the developing world. On the other, despite the profile in the West of global warming and ozone depletion, these two problems are not yet having clearly identifiable, significant effects on people's well-being.

These seven environmental changes also differ greatly in spatial scale. Loss of cropland, forests, water supplies, fish stocks, and biodiversity, for example, physically manifest themselves as local and regional problems, although they appear all over the planet and are often powerfully influenced by global institutions and economic relations. In contrast, global warming and ozone depletion involve genuinely global physical processes. Lastly, these environmental changes differ in time scale: for instance, while a region can be deforested in only a few years, and severe ecological and social effects may be noticeable almost immediately, human-induced greenhouse warming will probably develop over many decades,[15] and it may not have truly serious implications for humankind until half a century or more after the signal is first detected.[16]

Many of these seven trends are causally interrelated. For example, deforestation can change local hydrological cycles that, in turn, affect water scarcity. Global warming may eventually contribute to deforestation by moving northward the optimal temperature and precipitation zones for many tree species, by increasing the severity of windstorms and wildfires, and by expanding the range of pests and diseases.[17] The release of carbon from these dying forests would, of course, reinforce global warming. And the increased incidence of ultraviolet radiation resulting from the depletion of the ozone layer may damage phytoplankton at the base of the ocean food chain, thereby affecting regional fisheries.

In my discussion below, I generally avoid great statistical detail, because it would imply an unjustifiable and misleading level of precision about the values of the many variables (such as fertility rates, regional energy consumption rates, total cropland supply, and the like) underlying these trends. The present and, especially, the future values of these variables are uncertain, sometimes highly uncertain. Three factors affect this uncertainty. The first is the quality of our theories about the physical and social processes that determine the values of the variables. Demographic theory, for instance, gives us a fairly firm grasp of the determinants of population growth, permitting reasonably accurate projections of this growth, at least for thirty years or so.[18] In contrast, the timing, rate, and climate impacts of global warming are largely unknown, mainly because of serious gaps in theoretical knowledge about the roles of clouds and the oceans in this warming. Moreover, as I discussed in chapter 3, many ecosystem variables are influenced by complex chaotic, non-linear, and interactive processes; even if these processes were understood in theory (which invariably they are not), their outcomes would remain almost impossible to predict with any useful degree of precision.

The second factor is the quality and quantity of the data available on the current values of the underlying variables and on the processes determining their values. For example, reasonably detailed data are available on the annual catch and sustainable yields of some regional marine fisheries, but, for the most part, data on regional degradation of cropland are either unobtainable or of extremely poor quality. Similarly, our estimates of the number of plant and animal species on the planet range from 5 million to well over 30 million, which makes predictions of biodiversity loss highly imprecise. The third factor is lack of knowledge about both the ability and the willingness of humans to change the social, economic, and technological processes that contribute to environmental stress. This lack of knowledge produces uncertainty about future trajectories of all nine trends discussed here. For example, one of the reasons that expert predictions of future energy consumption vary widely is that we know little about people's willingness to accept reductions in energy consumption that affect their lifestyles.

In sum, for some of the nine trends, uncertainty arises mainly from an inadequate understanding of the physical processes affecting them. For others, uncertainty arises more from a lack of understanding of social processes, such as the evolution of key ideational factors. We can safely say, however, that no matter how much research is devoted to understanding these nine trends, policymakers cannot escape significant uncertainty surrounding estimates of their future directions. For this reason, they should not demand precise estimates before making decisions about major environmental problems, because that strategy will simply delay policy decisions indefinitely.

Population Growth

Figure 4.1 shows that population size can be a key force driving supply-induced scarcity. Sometimes population growth does not damage the environment, but often this growth—in combination with prevailing social structures, technologies, and consumption patterns—makes environmental degradation and depletion worse.[19] In the 1960s, certain commentators, especially Paul Ehrlich, rang the alarm on global population growth, which at the time was over 2 percent per year.[20] (Although this may not seem like a frightening figure, it implies that the earth's population will double every thirty-five years.) Ehrlich and others claimed that skyrocketing human numbers would mean critical shortfalls of food, space, and other resources; huge, violent cities without work for masses of poor; and greater misery for future generations of people.

Professional demographers, however, have long assumed that developing countries would pass through a "demographic transition" similar to that experienced by today's developed countries during the nineteenth and twentieth centuries. In this transition, a decline in a population's mortality rates is eventually followed by a compensating decline in fertility rates.[21] Demographers concluded that this transition results from increased material prosperity—especially better nutrition and sanitation—and certain social changes, such as higher literacy rates, the emancipation of women, and increased access to contraceptives.[22] Because mortality and fertility rates do not fall simultaneously, total population grows during the period when fertility rates exceed mortality rates.

Following the Second World War, mortality rates in most developing countries fell rapidly, and now even countries like India are approaching life expectancies at birth of close to sixty-five years. More recently, especially beginning in the 1970s, average fertility rates began dropping sharply in many of these countries, with rates often falling from six or seven children per woman to three or four. The easiest part of fertility reduction tends to occur first: it is more difficult to convince mothers to forgo the last one or two children to bring family size down to replacement rate. Nonetheless, the observed fertility decline and the range of countries affected have far exceeded demographers' most optimistic predictions. They have repeatedly revised downward their projections of developing countries' future populations; for example, since

1990 the UN has changed its "medium" projection of the 2025 population for Bangladesh, a country long regarded as having an intractable population problem, from 235 million to 180 million (Bangladesh's current population is around 128 million).

Demographers now realize that lower fertility rates are often due less to higher material standards of living than to the spread of "modern" ideas via radio and television—ideas about lifestyle, family size, and women's status.[23] This fact may explain why, in recent years, many developing countries that have not seen dramatic increases in per capita wealth have nevertheless seen rapid declines in fertility rates. Moreover, there is evidence that the speed of decline may accelerate with time.

The latest United Nations medium projections suggest the total human population will grow from the current 6.0 billion to about 8 billion in 2025 and 9.4 billion in 2050 (the UN's "low" projections, which are not implausible given recent fertility declines, are 7.5 and 7.7 billion respectively).[24] Although the rate of global population growth has dropped from 2.1 percent to about 1.3 percent over the last two decades, the human population is still expanding by about 80 million a year (growth peaked in the late 1980s at about 87 million a year). In fact, demographers estimate that growth will average about 80 million people a year during the entire four decades from 1980 to 2020. Moreover, about 50 percent of the anticipated growth in the developing world's population will result from "demographic momentum": the age structure of today's populations in developing countries, especially the large number of girls still to reach reproductive age, guarantees a much larger population in the future even if all these countries immediately make widely available the best family planning technologies.[25]

Over 90 percent of today's population growth is occurring in developing countries, which means that, crudely speaking, the ratio of poor people to rich in the world is rapidly rising. In 1950, the ratio was about two to one; today, with a world population of about 6.0 billion, the ratio is about four to one; and in 2025, with population around 8 billion, it will be almost six to one.[26] (Although rapid economic development in many countries means, in general, that the world's poor are becoming wealthier, the rich are becoming wealthier, too—in some case even faster than the poor; consequently, this rough dichotomy of the world into rich and poor remains appropriate.)

Regional population growth rates diverge widely. Western Europe's population will grow very little, if at all, by 2025. But China's population will increase by 16 percent, North America's by 20 percent, and South America's by 32 percent. The populations of North Africa, South Asia, and Central America will grow by a third to a half, and the population of sub-Saharan Africa will almost double. Africa will expand its share of the global population most quickly, increasing from 12 percent in 1990 to a projected 18 percent by 2025. South Asia will remain home to a quarter of the world's population.[27]

At the level of individual countries, the progress of the demographic transition in China and India is particularly interesting, because these countries today encompass almost 40 percent of the world's total population. China's one-child policy has produced a sharp drop in population growth, but often at the cost of coercion and human-rights violations. The policy is followed more closely in urban areas than in the countryside, where the authority of the state is weaker. China's growth rate is currently about 0.8 percent, which means the country still adds over 10 million people to its population a year.

In India, fertility rates have fallen much more quickly in the south of the country than in the north. Especially along the Ganges—in the country's Hindi heartland—large families are still common. Family-planning programs have generally not been popular, and until recently the Indian government has not had an effective strategy for reducing population growth. Yet the slow but steady process of development has lowered fertility rates even along the Ganges, with average family size now down to around four children in that region. By the mid- to late-1990s, the country's annual population growth rate had fallen to about 1.5 percent, but its population still expanded by around 15 million people a year. Indeed, in 1997, more than 30 percent of the world's birth's occurred in India.[28]

Elsewhere in the world, Latin America is generally well along in its demographic transition, with fertility rates dropping fast from Bolivia to Mexico. Fertility rates have fallen more slowly in much of sub-Saharan Africa, especially in West Africa. Nonetheless, the last decades have seen striking progress in some African countries, such as Kenya, that have traditionally had some of the highest fertility rates in the world. Rates remain relatively high in some Islamic countries of the Middle East, which puts severe strain on renewable resources (especially water and land) in countries like Egypt and Jordan.

In sum, events in much of the world suggest that we have turned the corner on the human population explosion. This news has been accompanied by a spate of revisionist articles declaring that the population issue is no longer a concern.[29] Yet a number of factors suggest that this revisionist optimism is premature. Fertility rates still remain high in a number of poor countries: currently thirty-three countries, including twenty-five in Africa, have rates of six children per woman.[30] In countries where fertility rates have dropped quickly, demographic momentum ensures populations will continue to expand, at a minimum, for two to three decades. In fact, at least seventy-four countries—including Nigeria, Syria, and Honduras—will probably double their populations during this period.[31] It is very unlikely, therefore, that we will see a global population below 7.5 billion in 2025; in other words, the world's total population will increase by at least a quarter in the next twenty-five years.

Moreover, in many countries, populations are now so large that even small annual growth rates, in percentage terms, mean large absolute increments to total population (as we have seen in China and India). With increasingly restricted opportunities to migrate internationally, these increments must be absorbed and employed largely within the countries that generate them. When the demographic transition occurred in Europe in the nineteenth and early twentieth centuries, much of the economically surplus population emigrated to the New World. But a similar escape valve is, for the most part, no longer available to today's developing countries (all the same, there will be increased migration from poor to rich regions, as discussed in the next chapter).

In the absence of opportunities for easy external migration, much of the developing world's surplus population is moving into cities; combined with the natural growth of the population already living there, these cities are expanding so rapidly that they are threatening to become, and in some cases have already become, unmanageable. The potential instability of cities (discussed in chapter 7) is magnified by the age structure of their populations. The demographic transition has produced a *youth bulge*, which means these cities' populations have a disproportionately large number of young people compared to other age groups. In Africa, for example, 44 percent of the population is under fifteen years of age. Underemployed, urbanized young men are a particularly volatile group that can be easily mobilized for radical political action.

Finally, there are serious reasons to question whether some countries—including Egypt, Pakistan, India, and China—have the natural resources and economic capacity to sustain their populations indefinitely. Even when their population growth ends, the task of employing, feeding, housing, and raising the standard of living of their, by then, immensely expanded populations will have only just begun. And far into the future, these countries' populations will exact a huge toll on underlying environmental resources.

Energy Consumption

Total human *primary* energy consumption in 1990 was roughly equivalent to 8.8 billion metric tons of oil, an amount that would fill a huge cube just over two kilometers long on each side.[32] During the past two decades, humankind's primary energy consumption has climbed steadily by 2 to 4 percent a year, with short pauses only in the early 1980s and 1990s.[33]

In many developed countries, per capita energy consumption is thirty or more times that in developing countries. But per capita consumption in developed countries has not increased rapidly in the last fifteen years as the energy intensity of production (the amount of energy used per unit of GDP) has generally declined. In contrast, in many developing countries, per capita consumption is rising very fast with the expansion of industrialization, electrification, and transportation networks. Combined with growing populations, this energy intensification will, in some cases, boost the total energy consumption of developing countries more than twice as fast as that of developed countries.

Currently, oil makes up 38 percent of global *commercial* energy consumption; coal, 30 percent; natural gas, 20 percent; hydropower about 7 percent; and nuclear power, 5 percent. As accessible and cheap petroleum reserves are depleted, these percentages will change. In the first decades of the next century, many experts predict that oil consumption will drop, while natural gas, nuclear power, nonconventional sources (such as solar, wind, and tidal power), and perhaps coal will fill the gap.[34] Around 60 percent of the world's population depends, at least in part, on *noncommercial* sources of energy for cooking and heating. These traditional fuels include wood gathered from forests, and twigs, branches, and straw gathered from grasslands and fields. In large areas of the world, especially Sahelian Africa, the Indian subcontinent, and China, these forms of energy are increasingly hard to find, and gatherers have to walk many kilometers for the day's fuel.[35]

The level of global energy consumption in coming decades will depend on a wide array of factors, including whether energy prices are adjusted to reflect the costs of pollution and global warming to our societies, whether new technologies allow more efficient production and use of energy, and whether international agreements are achieved to restrict releases of carbon dioxide. Despite this uncertainty, experts have tried to estimate future primary energy demand. In 1981, for instance, the International Institute for Applied Systems Analysis (IIASA) published low and high estimates suggesting global energy demand in 2025 would be between 16 and 26 billion metric tons of oil equivalent (between two and three times present demand). In 1985, Jose Goldemberg and other researchers proposed that a dramatic effort at energy conservation could cut this figure to less than 9 billion metric tons.[36]

In 1993, the World Energy Council (WEC) published four scenarios for primary energy demand, each using different assumptions about economic growth, energy intensity of production, energy efficiency, technology transfer, and institutional improvements. The predicted energy demand in 2020 for these scenarios range from 11.3 to 17.2 billion metric tons of oil equivalent. The lower estimate involves assumptions that are probably unrealistic, but it is the only estimate that keeps carbon dioxide emissions at roughly the 1990 level.[37] A 1992 study by the MITRE Corporation suggests that global commercial energy demand in 2025 will be about 13 billion metric tons of oil equivalent, which is roughly in the middle of the WEC range. This study also estimates that oil shortages will begin around 2030 or sooner, because of the depletion of oil resources.[38]

In 1995, the WEC and IIASA published a joint report that extended the time horizon of the 1993 WEC estimates to 2050. Although they acknowledged the inherent uncertainty in such long-range predictions, they judged that world economic output would increase by three to five times by 2050 and that global demand for energy services would rise by as much as ten times. But because energy intensities will continue to decrease, primary energy requirements would rise by only one-and-a-half to three times (to 14 to 25 billion metric tons of oil equivalent).[39]

Finally, some authorities argue that the WEC and others have underestimated the growth of energy demand in developing countries over the next thirty years. Though such studies are probably right to assume that energy efficiency will rise in these countries, they are probably wrong in their estimates of the overall growth of energy use. Churchill argues, for example, that "growth rates in the demand for energy in developing countries of between 5 and 7 percent are quite possible for sustained periods in the next thirty years."[40] If so, total primary energy consumption—and the environmental costs of carbon emissions and other pollution—will be considerably greater than that suggested by the WEC, IIASA, and MITRE estimates.

Global Warming

Human activities, especially consumption of fossil fuels and hydrocarbons, release a number of gases (mainly carbon dioxide, chlorofluorocarbons, methane, and nitrous oxide) that impede the escape of infrared radiation (heat) from the surface of the earth to space. In the crudest terms, we can say that the more of these gases present in the atmosphere, the higher the mean temperature at the surface of the planet.[41] In fact, if it were not for the naturally occurring greenhouse effect, the current average temperature of the planet would be about thirty-three degrees Celsius lower than it is now, and the earth would not be able to support most of the life currently present. However, the scientific story is much more complicated than this, because there are countless ill-understood positive and negative feedbacks that may accentuate or diminish human perturbations of the global heat balance. For instance, scientists are uncertain to what extent increased cloud cover caused by global warming will trap further heat (a positive feedback) or reflect sunlight (a negative feedback).

Over the last few years, though, a consensus has developed among the experts: assuming no major changes in the trend of human emission of greenhouse gases, we will likely see a global warming between one and three and one-half degrees Celsius by 2100, with a "best estimate" of two degrees warming.[42] This may not seem like much of an increase, except when we realize that the earth has warmed only about five degrees since the coldest period of the last ice age, around 18,000 years ago. Moreover, the predicted rate of warming during the next hundred years will "probably be greater than any seen in the last 10,000 years."[43]

Already, global mean surface air temperature has risen by between 0.3 and 0.6 degrees Celsius since the late nineteenth century, and the last decade has seen a number of the warmest years on record.[44] Nonetheless, it is too early to say that this increase represents the emergence of a global warming signal from the noise of natural climate variation. Moreover, climate scientists have only recently begun to understand the important counteracting effect on global warming of human emissions of sulfate aerosols that reflect some sunlight back into space, especially over heavily industrialized areas. On balance, however, "evidence suggests a discernible human influence on global climate."[45] This evidence converges from numerous research programs, including large-scale computer modeling of the global atmosphere, analysis of ice-core and sedimentary materials for data on past climates, analysis of ocean circulation and sea-temperature data, and measurement of Earth's temperature changes by satellites from space and by ground stations around the world.

What might be the impact of two degrees warming in the next hundred years? At the moment, the spatial resolution of even the most sophisticated atmospheric models is too low to give us confidence in predictions about precipitation patterns, storm frequency, and soil moisture for specific regions. However, we can say that temperature increases in high latitudes will be much greater than the mean; that sea levels will rise about five centimeters per decade, principally from thermal expansion of seawater; that seasonal temperature differences in high latitudes will decrease because winters will become warmer; that extremely hot days will be more common; and that hydrological cycles will become more vigorous.[46] These changes will affect agricultural production in both the developed and developing worlds (an issue I will discuss further in chapter 5), especially if they increase the incidence of extreme events, such as droughts, floods, and heat waves. Moreover, as we saw in the last chapter, the impact of global warming on food production might be multiplied if other critical agricultural resources—including cropland and freshwater supplies—are already depleted or degraded.

Stratospheric Ozone Depletion

In the last chapter, I described the hole in the stratospheric ozone layer over the Antarctic, and the dramatic effect that this hole has had on scientists' and policymakers' appreciation of threshold effects in ecosystems. But the ozone hole is not just a matter of metaphysical interest. Each year it contributes to the general depletion of ozone over a wide area of the southern hemisphere. During the southern spring (in September and October), the hole forms inside a circular pattern of wind called the *circumpolar vortex*; as summer approaches, this vortex breaks up, and ozone-depleted air moves northward from Antarctica. Although Antarctica's pattern of chemical and atmospheric events is not exactly replicated over the Arctic, scientists have found disturbing evidence of many of the necessary conditions for rapid depletion there, too. In addition, while the situation over the South Pole is perhaps most dramatic, stratospheric ozone depletion has occurred around the planet as CFCs have moved into the upper atmosphere.

In 1995, the World Meteorological Organization (WMO) and several other organizations completed a comprehensive assessment of ozone depletion.[47] They noted that the maximum concentration of ozone-destroying chlorine and bromine compounds was expected to occur in the troposphere (near the planet's surface) in 1994, thanks to various international agreements limiting emissions of these compounds.[48] Concentrations will peak in the stratosphere some three to five years later, because it takes a number of years for these compounds to migrate from the surface of the earth to the stratosphere.

Averaged across the whole planet, total statospheric ozone loss has been about 5 percent since the mid-1960s (this figure includes the contribution of the Antarctic ozone hole). But such aggregate figures understate mid- and high-latitude losses. Ozone levels are currently decreasing by about 4 to 5 percent per decade at midlatitudes in the northern and southern hemispheres, with much larger losses in the winter and spring than in the summer and fall.[49] In 1992 and 1993, "springtime depletions exceeded 20 percent in some populated northern midlatitude regions, and the levels in the Antarctic ozone hole fell to the lowest values ever recorded."[50] (Materials ejected by the Mount Pinatubo eruption in 1991 probably aggravated the severity of depletion during these years.)

Although chlorine and bromine concentrations in the stratosphere will soon decline, these substances will continue to do their damage for many decades, because they persist in the stratosphere as catalysts of ozone destruction for up to fifty years.[51] Unfortunately, scientists' numerical models of ozone depletion—based on current understandings of atmospheric chemistry—have often underestimated depletion trends, making the trajectory of the ozone layer's recovery difficult to predict. The WMO's comprehensive assessment, however, estimates that ozone losses will peak in the late-1990s at about 12 to 13 percent at northern midlatitudes in the winter and spring, at 6 to 7 percent at northern midlatitudes in the summer and fall, and at about 11 percent at southern midlatitudes on a year-round basis.[52]

Lower levels of ozone in the stratosphere permit more harmful ultraviolet (UV) radiation to reach the surface of the earth from space. Satellite observations show that, since 1972, the amount of UV radiation has increased an average of 6.8 percent per decade in the northern hemisphere and 9.9 percent per decade in the south.[53] Research suggests that, on average, a 1 percent decrease in stratospheric ozone produces about a 1.6 percent increase in the incidence of carcinogenic UV radiation on the surface of the earth, which in turn produces about a 2.7 percent increase in nonmelanoma skin cancer rates.[54] But the increasing occurrence of skin cancer should perhaps be the least of our concerns: increased UV radiation may have deleterious effects on crops, forests, amphibians, ocean phytoplankton (which are at the bottom of the ocean foodchain), and human and livestock health.[55] Research results on these effects are still preliminary.

Although greenhouse warming and ozone depletion have caught the Western public's attention over the last decade, certain terrestrial and aquatic environmental trends—such as rising cropland scarcity, tropical deforestation, rising freshwater scarcity, and depletion of fish stocks—deserve equal attention. Such problems will probably, in fact, interact with and multiply the effects of atmospheric change; and they merit immediate concern because they are already seriously threatening the well-being of many developing societies.

Cropland Scarcity

Currently, total global cropland amounts to about 1.5 billion hectares, which is roughly twice the area of the lower forty-eight states in the United States (an additional 3.25 billion hectares are classifiable as pasture or rangeland). Optimistic estimates of total arable land on the planet, which includes both current and potential cropland, range from 3.2 to 3.4 billion hectares, but most of the best land has already been exploited. What is left is usually less fertile, not sufficiently rain-fed or easily irrigable, infested with pests, in regions of endemic human disease, or harder to clear, plow, and plant.

Experts generally describe a country as "land scarce" when 70 percent or more of arable land is under production. In Asia, which includes four of the world's five most populous countries, about 82 percent of all arable land is cultivated. Although the percentages are lower in Africa and Latin America, the poor quality of much of the remaining land suggests that the previously high rates of cropland expansion cannot be maintained.[56] In some areas of Africa and Latin America—especially the Sahel, the semiarid regions of East and Southeast Africa, southern Mexico, Central America, and the Andean Highlands—land scarcity is already critical. The bulk of remaining potential cropland in these continents, and the world's largest remaining reserves of untapped agricultural land, lie under the rain forests of the Congo and Amazon basins. But these lands are generally fragile and easily degraded: their soils are thin and readily eroded by tropical rains, and the soil organic matter oxidizes quickly in the heat. They are also two of the world's main repositories of biodiversity.

For developing countries during the 1980s, cropland grew at just 0.26 percent a year, less than half the rate of the 1970s. More importantly, arable land per capita dropped by 1.9 percent a year.[57] In the absence of a major increase in arable land in developing countries, experts anticipate that the world average of 0.26 hectares of cropland per capita will fall below 0.20 hectares by the year 2025, given the current rate of world population growth.

Experts commonly use a threshold of 0.07 hectares of land per capita to indicate absolute land scarcity. (Absolute thresholds such as this one are always contentious, because they depend on assumptions about prevailing resource-use technologies, capital availability, and other inputs to production. Still, they are useful benchmarks for gauging the severity of resource scarcity.) In 1990, Egypt was already well below the threshold, at about 0.055 hectares per capita, and by 2025 population growth alone will push diverse countries such as Kenya, Bangladesh, and Israel far under the threshold. Average figures tell only a very limited story, however, because the inequalities in land distribution that exist in every society mean that some weaker and marginal groups will be subjected to much harsher scarcity than the averages reveal. In large areas of the developing world, tens of millions of marginalized peasants already subsist on extraordinarily small, and often fragmented, plots of low-quality land. Over 70 percent of all rural households in developing countries are either landless or nearly landless.[58]

Around the world, tracts of land are being lost each year to a combination of problems, including encroachment by cities, erosion, depletion of nutrients, acidification, compacting, and salinization and waterlogging from over-irrigation.[59] The geographer Vaclav Smil, who is generally very conservative in his assessments of environmental damage, estimates that 2 to 3 million hectares of cropland are lost annually to erosion, perhaps twice as much land goes to urbanization, and at least 1 million hectares are abandoned because of excessive salinity. In addition, about one-fifth of the world's cropland is suffering from some degree of desertification (which includes wind erosion and changes in soil moisture).[60] Taken together, he concludes, the planet will have lost about 100 million hectares of arable land between 1985 and 2000, which is about the area of California and Texas combined.[61]

Data on cropland area at the regional level are surprisingly poor. Efforts to estimate total cropland area are hindered by steep slopes, complex terrains, terracing practices, and underreporting by peasants and farmers trying to avoid agricultural and land taxes. Accounting for such factors can produce major revisions in cropland estimates. Recently, for example, many Chinese experts boosted their figure for the country's total cropland from under 100 million hectares to 120 to 140 million hectares.[62] Needless to say, such revisions dramatically effect judgments about a country's ability to feed itself.

Also unavailable are good comparative, cross-national data on soil degradation. The most comprehensive are displayed on three large soil degradation maps (commonly called the GLASOD maps) produced in 1990 by the International Soil Reference and Information Center and the United Nations Environment Programme, in collaboration with over 250 soil and environmental scientists from around the world.[63] Although the data on these maps are highly aggregated and for some regions questionable, they do provide a useful overall impression of the extent and type of regional soil damage.[64] They show that some degree of degradation (mainly caused by water erosion) affects 38 percent of the world's current cropland, with particularly serious impacts in Africa (65 percent of the land affected), Latin America (51 percent), and Asia (38 percent). The maps show that there is no clear correlation between population density and soil degradation. In general, regions of the world that originally had the best soil now carry the highest population densities; but high population density sometimes promotes careful land husbandry—as in the Netherlands—which actually reduces soil damage.

Tropical Deforestation

The total area of closed tropical forest on earth, which means forest where the branches of the trees largely obscure the ground when viewed from the air, is estimated to be around 1.2 billion hectares, or about the area of the United States and Mexico together. If forest is more generously defined to include all lands with a minimum tree crown cover of 10 percent, the total area is about 1.8 billion hectares.[65] Estimates of tropical deforestation vary widely, however, because there are different kinds and degrees of forest degradation, and it is often unclear whether a particular hectare should be counted as deforested. Furthermore, forests frequently recover through planting and natural regeneration, which also tends to blur category boundaries. Finally, satellite images are far less precise than commonly thought in allowing researchers to determine the extent of forest damage. The images usually have to be supplemented with detailed ground inspections.[66]

Despite these difficulties, recent estimates by the UN Food and Agriculture Organization (FAO) suggest that the already high rate of global tropical deforestation of the early 1980s has increased even more. In the early 1980s, the world was losing 11.3 million hectares of tropical forest annually. By 1991 the FAO put the figure at 17 million hectares.[67] The annual average tropical forest loss during the 1980s was 15.4 million hectares, or about 0.8 percent of total tropical forest cover per year; particularly affected were easily accessible moist deciduous forests and rain forests. During the single decade of the 1980s, an area of tropical forest nearly three times the size of France was converted to other uses.[68]

Between 1960 and 1990, Asia lost nearly a third of its tropical forests, while Latin America and Africa lost almost a fifth.[69] Today, three countries alone— Brazil, Indonesia, and Malaysia—account for over half of the world's tropical rain forest loss.[70] Other countries experiencing high rates of deforestation include Costa Rica, Cameroon, India, Myanmar, the Philippines, Thailand, and Vietnam. The damage to tropical forests is, in fact, more alarming than these statistics suggest, because they do not give a good account of widespread frag-mentation and degradation of tropical forests that can severely affect the resil-ience and biodiversity of forest ecosystems.

When accused in the early 1990s of permitting high deforestation rates, the Brazilians responded that the FAO figures were inflated in their case. They noted that the rate of deforestation in Brazil dropped dramatically after 1988 because of changes in domestic policy. Yet more-recent reports suggest that logging and land-clearing in the Amazon basin have surged again.[71] Given the unreliability of the data and the susceptibility of deforestation rates to policy decisions, it is hard to predict the state of the world's forests decades into the future. But it seems safe to say that in twenty to thirty years most of the re-maining virgin tropical forests in Southeast Asia, South Asia, and Central America will be gone, and the remainder will be concentrated in the Congo and Brazil.

The Philippines provides a good example of the speed and extent of regional tropical forest loss in recent decades. After the Second World War, about half the area of the Filipino archipelago was forested. By the mid-1980s, logging and the encroachment of farms had reduced the virgin and second-growth for-est from about 16 million hectares to 6.8 to 7.6 million hectares.[72] At the turn of the twentieth century, the Philippines had about 10 million hectares of vir-gin forest; now less that a million hectares remain, and it seems certain that almost all of this will be gone by early in the twenty-first century. The logging industry boomed in the 1960s and 1970s and, following the declaration of martial law in 1972, President Ferdinand Marcos handed out concessions to huge tracts of land to his cronies and senior military officials. Pressured to make payments on the foreign debt, the government encouraged log exports to the voracious Japanese market. Numerous companies were set up with ex-clusive opportunities to exploit forest resources, and they rarely undertook reforestation. Despite the regime change in the Philippines and the more ag-gressive concern for the environment of the Aquino and Ramos governments, rates of deforestation have remained very high. Efforts to replant wide areas have generally failed, because of corruption and inefficiency in the agencies charged with the planting; moreover, the hilly areas where forest degradation is most critical have very thin soils, and they are continually stressed by the migration of landless peasants from lowland areas.

Scarcity of Freshwater

Scarcity of freshwater will be one of the chief resource issues of the twenty-first century.[73] The water-scarcity crisis is starkest when framed in terms of rising demand, although water depletion and pollution—that is, supply-induced scarcity—is also a critical problem. Reduced water quality has a direct effect on human health: about 250 million new cases of waterborne disease are reported every year, causing about 10 million deaths.[74]

In 1999, humans will withdraw about 4,250 cubic kilometers of freshwater a year from various sources (mainly rivers), returning about 1,700 cubic kilometers to these sources, often in polluted condition.[75] (For comparison, the total flow over Niagara Falls every year is about 90 cubic kilometers.) This consumption is growing at a rate of 2 to 3 percent a year. Total river resources at any one time amount to about 2,000 cubic kilometers, but because of the constant cycling of water between the atmosphere and surface of the earth, the annual quantity available from rivers is probably closer to 40,000 cubic kilometers.

Although these aggregate figures seem to indicate abundance, there are great differences in water availability among regions. Many areas—including much of Europe, large parts of the United States, the Ganges basin in India, and the northwestern provinces of China—are using virtually all of their locally generated river runoff. In a number of arid developing countries, quick population growth threatens to reduce water availability below 1,000 cubic meters of water per capita per year, a benchmark regarded by many experts as about the "minimum necessary for an adequate quality of life in a moderately developed country."[76] Once again, however, such averages are deceiving, because they hide the large disparities in water access that exist in all societies. In general it is safe to say that as average water availability drops below 1,000 cubic meters in a developing region, a significant fraction of the society's population will confront serious scarcity problems. Irrigated agriculture will be restricted; residents of urban squatter settlements and slums will often have insufficient water for basic hygiene; and rural families will often have to walk far from their villages to find water at streams and ponds.

Table 4.1 identifies regions where water crises are very likely in the next decades as a result of population growth. The possibility of greenhouse-induced climate change introduces some uncertainty into these estimates, because climate change would shift precipitation patterns and therefore the overall water supply. Some arid regions—especially in coastal areas—might no longer face water shortages, whereas other, predominantly interior regions could suffer prolonged drought. Despite this uncertainty, the Middle East and parts of Africa are of particular concern with respect to water scarcity: these regions' populations are still expanding rapidly, and water is already extremely scarce.[77] Taking the world as a whole, the number of people living in countries with water stress or chronic water scarcity in 1997 was about 430 million; by the year 2025, using the UN's medium population projections, the number is expected to rise to 3 billion, or over a third of the planet's population (using the low projections, the figure is 2 billion).[78]

Water has long been a source of contention among certain groups and societies. Some experts suggest that international disputes over river water, in

TABLE 4.1
Water Availability in 1995 and in 2025

	Per Capita Water Availability 1995 (m^3/person/year)	Projected per Capita Water Availability 2025 (m^3/person/year)
Africa		
Algeria	527	313
Burundi	594	292
Comoros	1,667	760
Egypt	936	607
Ethiopia	1,950	807
Kenya	1,112	602
Libya	111	47
Malawi	1,933	917
Morocco	1,131	751
Rwanda	1,215	485
Somalia	1,422	570
South Africa	1,206	698
Tunisia	434	288
The Americas		
Canada	98,667	79,731
United States	9,277	7,453
Barbados	192	169
Haiti	1,544	879
Asia/Middle East		
Bahrain	162	104
Cyprus	1,208	947
Iran	1,719	916
Israel	389	270
Jordan	318	144
Kuwait	95	55
Oman	874	295
Qatar	91	64
Saudi Arabia	249	107
Singapore	180	142
Yemen	346	131

Source: Tom Gardner-Outlaw and Robert Engelman, *Sustaining Water, Easing Scarcity: A Second Update* (Washington, D.C.: Population Action International, 1997). Water availability in 2025 was estimated using the United Nations' medium population projections, obtained from United Nations Population Division, *World Population Prospects: The 1996 Revision, Demographic Indicators 1950–2050*, Diskettes 1–4 (New York: United Nations, 1996).

Note: The table lists selected countries where population growth will drive annual per capita water availability to 1,000 cubic meters or less per person by 2025. Figures for the United States and Canada are provided for comparison.

particular, could become more frequent in coming decades. For instance, the Nile River runs through nine countries, and downstream nations—especially Egypt and the Sudan—are vulnerable to upstream water diversion because of their dry climates and dependence on irrigated agriculture. Other African rivers are shared by several countries; for example, the Zambezi and the Niger flow through eight and ten countries respectively, and the Senegal has been at the center of a serious clash between Mauritania and Senegal (as we shall see in the next chapter). Depletion of aquifers may also be a source of disputes: Egypt and Libya, for example, see the shared Nubian aquifer as a vital future source of water for huge agricultural zones. In the Middle East, some experts believe that the desire to secure the waters of the Jordan, Litani, Orontes, and Yarmuk Rivers contributed to tensions preceding the 1967 Arab-Israeli war.[79] There is also strong disagreement between Syria and Turkey over Euphrates water.

Although the potential for conflicts among countries over shared water resources receives much attention in the popular media, I argue in chapter 7 that water scarcity rarely causes interstate wars. Rather its impacts are more insidious and indirect: it constrains economic development and contributes to a host of corrosive social processes that can, in turn, produce violence within societies.

Decline of Fish Stocks

The FAO has estimated that the maximum sustainable yield of the world's marine and freshwater fisheries is 100 million metric tons. Total world fish production has quintupled since 1950, from 20.75 to 101.27 million metric tons in 1993 (the current U.S. annual catch is about 6 million metric tons).[80] Marine fishers caught about 78 percent of the 1993 total; inland fishers caught an additional 7 percent; and marine and inland aquaculture raised about 16 percent. Of the approximately 86 million metric tons of fish caught from marine and inland fisheries, about 57 million metric tons went to human consumption (and is therefore commonly called *food fish*) and the remainder to products such as fish meal.

As we approach the limit of sustainability, there is widespread evidence—from Maine, to Newfoundland, to Southern India—of regional overexploitation. Many fisheries are also suffering from eutrophication, coastal pollution, and the destruction of mangrove swamps and other nursery grounds (often to build prawn farms and aquaculture pens). Tropical fisheries, especially in Southeast Asia are being ravaged by a combination of dynamite and cyanide fishing. Furthermore, scientists are only just beginning to understand that many large fisheries undergo complex, decade-long regime changes, often in synchrony in widely separated parts of the planet's oceans. These large swings in productivity are not well understood but are probably related to global climate changes, in particular El Niño oscillations in the South Pacific.[81]

As early as 1987, the FAO commented: "The time of spectacular and sustained increases in fisheries catches is over. . . . Almost all important stocks of demersal species are either fully exploited or overfished. Many of the stocks of more highly valued species are depleted. Reef stocks and those of estuarine/littoral zones are under special threat from illegal fishing and environmental pollution."[82] In a 1995 report, the FAO concludes that about 69 percent of the world's conventional species are "fully exploited, overexploited, depleted, or in the process of rebuilding as a result of depletion." The FAO goes on to note that "this situation is globally non-sustainable and major ecological and economic damage is already visible."[83]

To maintain current per capita human fish consumption (about thirteen kilograms per year), the world will have to produce about 91 million metric tons of food fish by the year 2010.[84] Because it is unlikely that the quantity of food fish caught from marine and inland fisheries will exceed 60 million metric tons annually, the remaining 31 million metric tons will have to come from aquaculture. This figure implies a doubling of aquaculture production—from its 1993 level of 16 million metric tons—in just over fifteen years; although such expansion may seem improbable, it requires a rate of growth no greater than that of the last decade. Maintaining an annual food fish production of 60 million metric tons from wild fisheries, given that these fisheries are already under severe stress, will require much greater use of nonconventional species, of fish now caught for animal feed, and of currently discarded fish. Even with such measures, however, the world's excessively large and increasingly sophisticated fishing fleets are likely to push most regional fisheries beyond the limits of sustainability. In some cases, this pressure will cause fisheries to collapse; once again, such events will most severely affect marginal communities, especially artisanal and small-scale fishers along the coasts of developing countries.

Loss of Biodiversity

Loss of biodiversity is a good general indicator of the damage humankind is inflicting on Earth's renewable resource systems. As noted above, the estimates of the number of species on the planet cover a wide range, from 5 to more than 30 million. The current best estimate for the number known to science is 1.75 million.[85] The recent and monumental *Global Biodiversity Assessment* produced a consensus estimate of 13.6 million species in total, suggesting that "only 13 percent of the species on Earth have yet been described."[86]

The wide range of estimates is largely due to great uncertainty about species diversity in the tropical forest regions. Experts assume that these forests contain a vast repository of genetic information, the majority of it contained in insects and microbes not yet identified or catalogued. The world's biodiversity is a priceless resource for the development of new crops, medicines, and a wide array of industrial products from paints to lubricants. As tropical forests are destroyed, much of this genetic information is lost. Moreover, ecosystem simplification (that is, the reduction of biodiversity in croplands, planted forests, and other managed ecosystems) to obtain higher yields of products like grains and wood tends to reduce ecosystem stability and the availability of services such as soil nutrients and pest control.[87] These services have to be replaced, often at great expense, with chemical substitutes.

In the last 600 million years, five great episodes of extinction have afflicted life on the planet. The most severe occurred at the end of the Permian period, 240 million years ago, when 77 to 96 percent of all marine animal species vanished.[88] The better-known episode of extinction occurred when the dinosaurs disappeared—probably because of the impact of a huge meteorite or comet in the region of the Yucatan peninsula—at the junction of the Cretaceous and Tertiary periods, 65 million years ago. In all five cases, the number of animal species was more severely reduced than that of plant species. Recovery to the preexisting level of biodiversity took 10 to 100 million years.

Today, with the rapid loss of tropical forests and other species' habitats around the planet, *both* plant and animal species are disappearing at an extraordinary rate. Harvard entomologist E. O. Wilson has calculated conservatively that the global loss from tropical deforestation alone could range from four to six thousand species a year, a rate ten thousand times greater than the natural background rate of extinction prior to the appearance of human beings.[89] Wilson estimates that current tropical deforestation at about 1 percent per year is producing a yearly 0.2 to 0.3 percent decrease in the number of species in these regions. Using species-area models based on island biogeography, the *Global Biodiversity Assessment* similarly concludes that "recent rates of deforestation . . . translate into a rate of extinction of about 0.25 percent per annum."[90] Although this figure should be regarded as only a crude estimate, the "current extinction rates are dramatically higher than background extinction rates."[91]

Current extinction rates can also be estimated by comparing the estimated life span of average species in well-known taxa. For example, the fossil record suggests that average mammal species existed for about 1 million years prior to the arrival of humans; documented extinctions during the last century suggest an average mammalian species life span of ten thousand years; and recent species-by-species studies suggest a current figure of one hundred to one thousand years.[92] A recent report by the World Conservation Union lends support to this assertion: 25 percent of mammal species are threatened, as are twenty-four of twenty-six mammalian orders. Rates are even higher in regions, such as the Philippines and Madagascar, where species are unique and geographically contained.[93]

There is some controversy surrounding such alarming conclusions, because the actual number of recorded extinctions of plant and animal species since A.D. 1600 is only about eleven hundred. However, the *Assessment* concludes that "whatever the uncertainties may be about the scale of extinctions, what is clear is that many species will be reduced to small and fragmented populations in the near future."[94]

Loss of habitat to loggers, human predation, urban growth, and pollution all contribute to this crisis. If we add the stress of climate change, an estimate of a 25 percent reduction in planetary biodiversity in the next one hundred years is plausible. Such a loss would rival four of the five previous mass extinctions on earth. From both a moral and practical point of view, it could be the single greatest calamity human beings inflict on the planet. As the *Assessment* notes, "we have been more successful in simplifying than in reconstructing complex ecosystems. Our lack of success in ecosystem restoration suggests that great caution should be exercised in reducing biodiversity through management practices because of the potential loss of goods and services in the long term."[95]

In this chapter I have identified the three main sources of environmental scarcity—including reduced supply, rising demand, and skewed distribution—and I have presented a model of the main variables and causal relationships that produce these scarcities. I discussed the sources of uncertainty surrounding our estimates of present and future environmental scarcity. And finally, I sketched some of the ways in which this scarcity manifests itself at the regional and global levels. In the next chapter, I show how the three sources of scarcity can interact in particularly pernicious ways, and I examine some of the key social effects of this scarcity, ranging from constrained economic productivity to weakened states.

5

Interactions and Social Effects

THE ENVIRONMENTAL PROBLEMS described in the previous chapter are large-scale, long-term, and inadequately understood. They strike directly at our most intimate links to the biosphere, such as our ability to obtain the food and water we need for survival. Many people have a strong intuition that these problems will affect social stability, and some analysts have given voice to this intuition.[1] But sensational claims about "water wars," "food wars," and "environmental refugees" in the popular literature are—almost without exception—simplistic and flawed, largely because they are not based on a sturdy foundation of clear concepts, variables, and empirically grounded generalizations. In this and the following two chapters, I therefore propose a detailed model of the links between environmental scarcity and violent conflict. I illustrate and support this model with evidence drawn from our research project and others. Taken together, these chapters should give analysts and policymakers a tool kit of concepts and generalizations that they can use to analyze, explain, and sometimes predict connections between environmental scarcity and violence around the world.

Interactions

In the last chapter, I introduced the concepts of supply-induced, demand-induced, and structural scarcity. These three kinds of environmental scarcity often interact, and two patterns of interaction are particularly common: *resource capture* and *ecological marginalization*. Figures 5.1 and 5.2 diagram these patterns.

Resource capture occurs when a fall in the quality and quantity of a renewable resource interacts with population growth to encourage powerful groups within a society to shift resource distribution in their favor. This shift can produce dire environmental scarcity for poorer and weaker groups in the society. Ecological marginalization occurs when unequal resource access joins with population growth to cause migrations to regions that are ecologically fragile, such as steep upland slopes, areas at risk of desertification, tropical rain forests, and peri-urban squatter settlements. High population densities in these areas, combined with a lack of knowledge and capital to protect local resources, cause severe environmental damage and chronic poverty.[2]

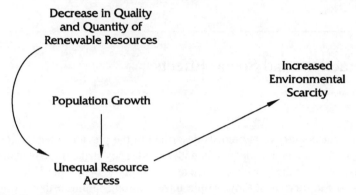

Figure 5.1. Resource Capture

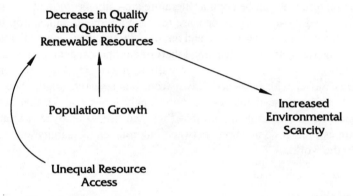

Figure 5.2. Ecological Marginalization

Resource Capture

One motivation behind resource capture—as we will see in the case of the Jordan River basin—can be a powerful group's fear of the disadvantage that rising scarcity might produce. Another motivation, more obvious in the example of the Senegal River basin below, is greed. As critical resources become more scarce, prices rise, which can open up opportunities for fast profits from speculation on resources. It also becomes easier to corner the market on key resources—that is, to capture such a significant fraction of the resource pool that monopolistic profits can be extracted. Both of these motivations arise most obviously with resources, such as cropland and forests, that are easy to privatize and divide into saleable units (that are, in economists' terms, *excludable*).

The concept of resource capture is similar to, but narrower than, the political economists' concept of *rent-seeking* behavior. In general, rent-seeking refers to attempts by individuals and groups to maximize economic "rent" by manipulating the laws and institutions governing the disposition of factors of production in an economy. *Rent* is the economic return from a factor in excess of the amount needed to keep it in its present use; that is, it is the return above the factor's *opportunity cost* (which is determined by its most profitable alternative use).[3] Rent-seeking does not necessarily involve natural resources, whereas resource capture—as I use the term here—does. Moreover, resource capture describes the behavior of powerful groups, usually elites, in a social system; these groups are motivated to capture resources by rising supply-induced and demand-induced scarcity. Rent-seeking, on the other hand, is not necessarily a problem associated with such groups and does not necessarily involve such motivations: it often happens at the local level, and large numbers of people can be involved, such as petty landlords and officials; in addition, it can occur independently of changes in the degree of resource scarcity.

The water shortage on the West Bank of the Jordan River provides an example of how population growth can combine with high consumption of a scarce local resource to promote resource capture. In the early 1990s, Israel's average annual supply of renewable freshwater was about 1,950 million cubic meters (mcm).[4] Israeli demand, including that of settlements in the West Bank and Golan Heights, was about 2,150 mcm. The annual deficit of about 200 mcm was (and still is) covered by overpumping aquifers. As a result, water tables in some parts of Israel and the West Bank have dropped. This decline has caused the exhaustion of some wells and the infiltration of seawater from the Mediterranean.[5] At the same time, Israel's population is expected to increase from the present 6.0 million to around 7.5 million in the year 2020.[6] Based on this projected expansion, the country's water demand by 2020 is conservatively estimated at 2,800 mcm.[7]

Sixty percent of Israel's annual sustainable supply of water, or about 1,200 mcm, comes from groundwater, and the rest from river flow, floodwater, and wastewater recycling. Two of the three main aquifers on which Israel depends lie principally underneath the West Bank, although their waters drain into Israel. About 475 mcm, or about 40 percent of the groundwater Israel uses (and about a quarter of its sustainable supply) originates in this territory.

To protect this important source, the Israeli government strictly limited water use by Jewish settlers and Arabs on the West Bank. But there was a stark differential in water access between the groups: on a per capita basis in the early 1990s, settlers consumed about four times as much as Arabs. Of the 650 mcm of all forms of water annually available there, Arabs were allowed to use only 125 mcm. Israel restricted the number of wells Arabs could drill in the territory, the amount of water Arabs were allowed to pump, and the times at which they could draw irrigation water. During the period of occupation after

1967, Arabs were not permitted to drill new wells for agricultural purposes, although the Mekorot (the Israeli water company) drilled more than thirty wells for settlers' irrigation. The area of irrigated Arab farmland on the West Bank dropped from 27 percent of the total cultivated area to 3.5 to 6.0 percent.[8]

Arab agriculture in the region also suffered because some Arab wells became dry or saline as a result of deeper Israeli wells drilled nearby. These Israeli water policies, combined with the confiscation of agricultural land for settlers as well as other Israeli restrictions on Palestinian agriculture, encouraged many West Bank Arabs to abandon farming and move to towns. There, they have become either unemployed or day laborers within Israel (when the borders to Israel are not closed for security reasons).

The links between these processes and unrest in the West Bank and Gaza are unclear; many political, economic, and ideological factors operate. But it is reasonable to conclude that water scarcity and its economic effects contributed to the grievances behind the *intifadah* in these territories.

Events in the Senegal River valley in 1989 also illustrate resource capture. The valley demarcates the border between Senegal and Mauritania in West Africa. Senegal has fairly abundant agricultural land, but much of it suffers from high to severe wind and water erosion, loss of nutrients, salinization because of over-irrigation, and soil compaction caused by intensification of agriculture.[9] In the early 1980s, the country had an overall population density of thirty-eight people per square kilometer and a population growth rate of 2.8 percent (giving a doubling time of about twenty-five years).[10] In contrast, except for the Senegal Valley along its southern border and a few oases, Mauritania is largely arid desert and semiarid grassland.[11] In the 1980s, its population density was very low at about two people per square kilometer, but the growth rate was 2.9 percent. This combination of factors led the FAO and two other organizations to include both Mauritania and Senegal in a 1982 list of "critical" countries whose croplands could not support their projected populations without a large increase in agricultural inputs, such as fertilizer and irrigation.[12]

Under normal conditions during this period, the broad floodplains fringing the Senegal River supported productive farming, herding, and fishing based on the river's annual floods. But during the 1970s, a serious drought and the prospect of a chronic food shortages encouraged the region's governments to seek international financing for the high Manantali Dam on the Bafing River tributary in Mali and the Diama salt-intrusion barrage near the mouth of the Senegal River between Senegal and Mauritania. These dams were designed to regulate the river's flow to produce hydropower, expand irrigated agriculture, and provide riverine transport from the Atlantic Ocean to landlocked Mali, which lies to the east of Senegal and Mauritania.

The plan had unfortunate and unforeseen consequences. In the context of critical land scarcities elsewhere in the region, land values sharply increased along the river in areas where high-intensity agriculture was to become feasible. The elite in Mauritania, which consists mainly of white Moors, then rewrote the country's legislation governing land ownership, effectively abrogating the rights of black Africans to continue farming, herding, and fishing along the Mauritanian riverbank.[13]

There has been a long history of racism by white Moors in Mauritania toward their non-Arab, black compatriots. In the spring of 1989, the killing of Senegalese farmers by Mauritanians in the river basin triggered explosions of ethnic violence in the two countries. In Senegal, almost all of the seventeen thousand shops owned by Moors were destroyed, and their owners were deported to Mauritania. In both countries, several hundred people were killed and the two nations nearly came to war.[14] The Mauritanian regime used this occasion to activate the new land legislation, declaring the Mauritanians who lived alongside the river to be "Senegalese," thereby stripping them of their citizenship; their property was seized. About seventy thousand black Mauritanians were forcibly expelled to Senegal, from where some launched raids to retrieve expropriated cattle. By 1993, diplomatic relations between the two countries had been restored, but neither had agreed to allow the expelled population to return or to compensate them for their losses.

We see here the interaction of two sources of human-induced environmental scarcity. Degradation of land resources and population pressures helped precipitate agricultural shortfalls, which in turn encouraged a large development scheme. These three factors together raised land values in one of the few areas in either country offering the potential for a rapid move to high-intensity agriculture. A powerful elite then changed property rights and resource distribution in its favor, which produced a sudden increase in resource scarcity for an ethnic minority, expulsion of the minority, and ethnic violence.

Ecological Marginalization

The Philippines offers a good illustration of ecological marginalization. Unequal access to rich agricultural lowlands combined with population growth to cause migration to easily degraded upland areas; erosion and deforestation contributed to economic hardship that spurred insurgency and rebellion.

Spanish and American colonial policies in the Philippines left behind a grossly unfair distribution of good cropland in lowland regions, an imbalance perpetuated since independence by a powerful landowning elite.[15] From the 1960s into the 1980s, green-revolution technologies greatly increased lowland production of grain for domestic consumption, and of cash crops—like sugar, coconut, pineapple, and bananas—that helped pay the country's massive external debt. This increased production raised demand for agricultural labor on large farms, but not enough to compensate for a population growth rate often over 2.5 percent. Together, therefore, unequal land access and population growth produced a surge in agricultural unemployment.

With insufficient rural or urban industrialization to employ this excess labor, wages experienced unrelenting downward pressure.[16] Economically desperate, millions of poor agricultural laborers and landless peasants migrated to shantytowns in already overburdened cities, such as Manila; millions of others moved to the least productive and often most ecologically vulnerable territories, such as steep hillsides.[17] In these uplands, settlers used fire to clear forested or previously logged land. They brought with them little money or knowledge to protect their fragile ecosystems, and their small-scale logging, production of charcoal for the cities, and slash-and-burn farming often caused horrendous environmental damage, particularly, water erosion, landslides, and changes in the hydrological cycle.[18] (Erosion rates in some upland regions exceed three hundred metric tons per hectare per year, which is well over twenty times the sustainable rate.) This damage set in motion a cycle of falling food production, clearing of new plots, and further land degradation. There are few new areas in the country that can be opened up for agricultural production, so even marginally fertile land is now hard to find in many places, and economic conditions remain desperate for many peasants.[19]

The situation in the Philippines is not unique. Jeffrey Leonard notes that ecological marginalization occurs with striking regularity around the planet, affecting hundreds of millions of people in places as diverse as the Himalayas, Indonesia, the Sahel, El Salvador, Honduras, and Brazil. Over time, this process "causes environmental degradation and intractable poverty to become more and more closely intertwined in particular geographic areas with fragile environmental conditions. The world's poorest people are thus increasingly clustered in two types of areas: remote and ecologically fragile rural areas and the edge of growing urban areas."[20]

Moreover, resource capture and ecological marginalization are often intimately linked. Frequently, in fact, one leads to the other. The history of Chiapas, Mexico, for example, is a chain of multiple yet discrete instances of these two processes.[21] This chain has most harshly affected the state's rapidly growing population of indigenous peoples and campesinos. As population pressures have mounted on agricultural land (see fig. 5.3), elites and wealthy farmers have often taken control of the best land and have perverted land reform and redistribution policies. Many peasants affected by these depredations have migrated from the state's Central Highlands to the periphery of the Lacandon Rain Forest, in the state's southeast corner. There, they have cleared new land, only to be forced—either by the quick depletion of soil nutrients or by more land seizures by wealthy farmers—to move deeper into the vulnerable forest.

In recent decades, the agricultural frontier in Chiapas has closed, partly because of ever-greater restrictions on expansion into the Lacandon. During the

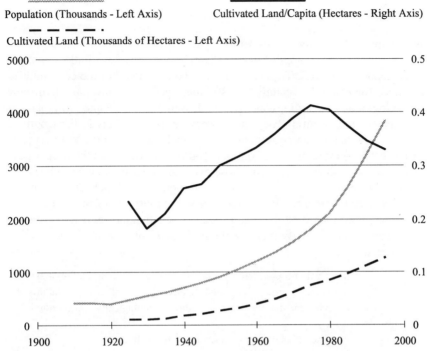

Population (Thousands - Left Axis)   Cultivated Land/Capita (Hectares - Right Axis)

Cultivated Land (Thousands of Hectares - Left Axis)

Figure 5.3. Decline in Cultivated Land per Capita in Chiapas, Mexico. *Sources*: Thomas Benjamin, *A Rich Land, a Poor People* (Albuquerque: University of New Mexico Press, 1989), 225, fig. 4, and 231, fig 5; Instituto Nacional de Estadística, Geografía e Informática, *Anuario Estadística del Estado de Chiapas, Edición 1991* and *Edición 1994* (Mexico, D. F.: Instituto Nacional de Estadística, Geografía e Informática, 1991 and 1994); Instituto Nacional de Estadística, Geografía e Informática, *VII Censo Ejidal* (Mexico, D.F.: Instituto Nacional de Estadística, Geografía e Informática, 1994); Coordinación General de Estadística, Geografía e Informática, *Chiapas Básico 1987* (Coordinación General de Estadística, Geografía e Informática, 1987); and George Collier, Personal Communication, 25 May 1995.

period of economic reform in the 1980s, these processes combined with the loss of agricultural subsidies and credits for small producers to sharply aggravate economic hardship and, in turn, the grievances of poor peasants. Economic reform also weakened the political control of the PRI (the Partido Revolucionario Institucional, the Mexican ruling party), which improved the opportunity for insurgent groups to challenge the regime. Eventually, as we will see in chapter 7, this simultaneous rise in grievance and opportunity produced the Zapatista insurgency.

Social Effects

Environmental scarcity and its various patterns of interaction—including resource capture and ecological marginalization—may cause countless changes
in developing societies. These changes can be beneficial for the communities
affected; for example, scarcity can stimulate people to develop useful new
technologies and institutions, as I will discuss in the next chapter. But many of
the changes are harmful. They range from sharp reductions in the length of
time rural Africans can cook their food as fuelwood becomes scarce (which
means they are more likely to contract food-borne disease) to the deeper poverty of Asian inshore fishermen whose once-abundant grounds have been destroyed by dynamite fishing and industrial pollution. Which of these many
negative social effects can link environmental scarcity to violent conflict?

Research has identified five main social effects that can, either singly or in
combination, substantially increase the probability of violence in developing
countries:

- constrained agricultural productivity, often in ecologically marginal regions;
- constrained economic productivity, mainly affecting people who are highly dependent on environmental resources and who are ecologically and economically
  marginal;
- migration of these affected people in search of better lives;
- greater segmentation of society, usually along existing ethnic cleavages; and,
- disruption of institutions, especially the state.[22]

These effects are often causally interlinked, sometimes with feedback relationships. For example, the migration caused by falling food production can reduce the amount of labor available for work in fields, which further disrupts
food production. Or, economic problems can lead to the flight of people with
wealth and education, which in turn eviscerates universities, courts, and institutions of economic management, all of which are crucial to a healthy
economy.

It is important to emphasize that environmental scarcity is not a sufficient
cause of any of these five social effects. Scarcity always interacts with other
factors to produce these effects. Therefore, we must be acutely sensitive to
what I call *contextual factors*, which are unique to each socio-ecological system and influence the strength of the linkages between scarcity and its social
effects. These contextual factors include the physical characteristics of a given
environment, such as its sensitivity to human perturbations (see chap. 3), and
also ideational factors unique to the society in question, including its institutions, social relations, and culture (see chap. 4).[23]

Analysts who doubt that environmental scarcity is an important cause of
social hardship often suggest that it is contextual factors—especially failed

institutions and policies—that ultimately explain events like poor harvests, large migrations, and worsened intergroup cleavages. In their minds, environmental scarcity is at most an aggravator of already existing problems or a trigger that releases accumulated nonenvironmental pressures. But this skepticism betrays a simplistic understanding of causation in our natural and social worlds. It suggests a naive, almost dichotomous view: if environmental scarcity, in itself, cannot be shown to be a sufficient cause of certain social hardships, then something else must be the cause. Yet a more accurate view of environmental scarcity's role is that it often acts as a deep, underlying stressor of social systems, and it produces its effects by interacting with contextual factors unique to the society.

Because issues of causal role are at the heart of much of the debate surrounding the impact of environmental stress on society, I consider them further in this chapter's appendix. Now, however, I turn to the five negative social effects that can link environmental scarcity to violent conflict.

Agricultural Productivity

Reduced or constrained agricultural productivity is often mentioned as potentially the most worrisome consequence of environmental change. Many poor people in developing countries spend more than half their income on food and are, therefore, acutely vulnerable to food price increases caused by production shortfalls. Figure 5.4 presents some of the causal connections between environmental change and agricultural output frequently proposed by researchers. This figure is not exhaustive: it focuses only on the consequences for agriculture of supply-induced environmental scarcities (that is, the depletion and degradation of environmental resources); moreover, the interaction of environmental and agricultural variables is far more complex than the figure suggests.[24] Finally, no one region or country exhibits all the indicated processes: some processes, such as the effects of water shortages on food output, are obvious in many areas, but others, including the effects of global warming, are not clearly discernible anywhere.

The effects of global warming may not yet be clear, but figure 5.4 identifies some that could eventually be important.[25] Coastal cropland in countries such as Bangladesh and Egypt is vulnerable to storm surges. Such events could become more frequent and harmful to crop output, because global warming will cause sea levels to rise and might intensify storms. The greenhouse effect will also change precipitation patterns and soil moisture; although this may benefit some agricultural regions, others will suffer. Lower precipitation will most severely affect regions that already have degraded and eroded soils, because lost rooting depth makes plants particularly vulnerable to drought.[26]

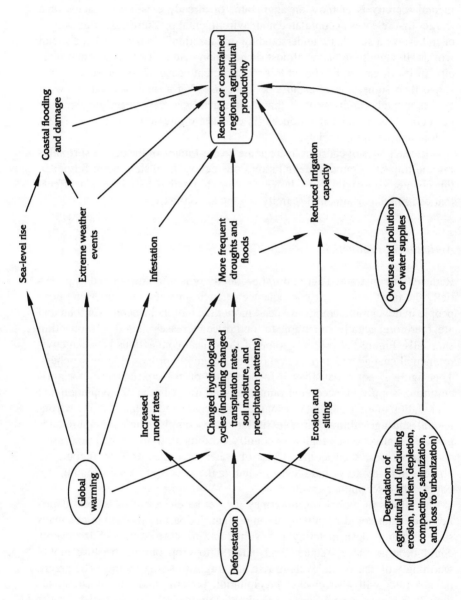

Figure 5.4. Possible Effects of Environmental Change on Agricultural Productivity

Many plants grow faster and larger in a warm environment rich in carbon dioxide, and they often use water more efficiently.[27] But optimistic estimates of greatly increased crop yields in a warmer, carbon-rich world have usually been based on laboratory experiments under ideal growing conditions. In addition, these estimates have generally ignored the influence on yields of more frequent extreme climate events caused by global warming (especially droughts and heat waves), increased pest infestation, and the decreased nutritional quality of crops grown in a carbon-enriched atmosphere.[28]

An important recent study of the impact of greenhouse warming on agriculture by Cynthia Rosenzweig and Martin Parry takes many of the above factors into account. It suggests that a doubling of atmospheric carbon dioxide concentration, and the resulting climate changes, will cause only a small drop in the world's total crop output. However, the differential impacts will be large: the researchers conclude that "developing countries are likely to bear the brunt of the problem."[29]

Figure 5.4 also identifies some of deforestation's possible effects on food output. Logging and land-clearing can accelerate erosion, change regional hydrological cycles and precipitation patterns, and decrease the land's ability to retain water during rainy periods. The resulting flash floods damage irrigation works while plugging reservoirs and irrigation channels with silt. These changes can seriously affect crop production. For example, when the government of the Philippines and the European Economic Community commissioned an Integrated Environmental Plan for the still relatively unspoiled island of Palawan, the authors of the study found that only about half of the thirty-six thousand of irrigated farmland projected within the Plan for 2007 would actually be irrigable because of the hydrological effects of decreases in forest cover.[30]

Finally, Figure 5.4 highlights the effects of worsening scarcities of cropland and water on agricultural production. As we have seen in the upland Philippines, these scarcities often have grievous impacts on peasants and farmers in ecologically marginal rural areas.[31] Nonetheless, aggregate data on food output suggest that many countries have adjusted to scarcity by boosting inputs of labor, capital, and ingenuity. In particular, beginning in the 1960s, the "green revolution"—which combined higher-yielding grains with the intensive use of irrigation, chemical fertilizers, and pesticides—sharply raised agricultural output.[32] In many poor countries, this package of technologies has more than compensated for increasing land scarcity, often allowing food production to exceed population growth, with multiple benefits to local economies.[33]

Between 1965 and 1986, global cereal production increased at 3 percent a year, meat and milk output increased 2 percent annually, while the rate for oil crops, vegetables, and pulses was 2.5 percent.[34] In the 1980s alone, total food production in the developing world increased by 39 percent; even in Africa, it increased by a third. About one hundred developing countries saw some growth in total food output, while thirty saw increases of 40 percent or more.[35] Exports from developed countries with huge agricultural surpluses often alleviated regional shortfalls in food production in the developing world. Based on this past experience, we might conclude that developing countries have sufficient capacity, with intermittent assistance from Northern grain exporters, to respond to worsening land and water scarcities in the future.[36]

But highly aggregated statistics, such as those above, are often misleading. In the 1980s, food output per capita dropped in seventy-five countries. This group included three-quarters of African, almost two-thirds of Latin American, and half of Asian countries. Fifteen countries saw a drop of at least 20 percent in food output per person.[37] More importantly, aggregate figures hide wide disparities in food availability among and within developing countries. At the end of 1980s, for example, twenty-five poor countries could not provide sufficient food calories for the health, growth, and productive work of their populations.[38] Even if adequate food is available on average in a country, distributional problems, poverty, and disparities in access to natural resources often produce wide differences in food consumption within their populations. Because of a combination of production and distributional problems, some 840 million people around the world—about 15 percent of the world's population—currently suffer from chronic hunger (down from 920 million, or 24 percent of the world's population, in the early 1970s).[39] Although both the percentage and absolute number of hungry people have fallen globally in the last twenty years, Latin America, South Asia, and especially sub-Saharan Africa have not shown improvements in these statistics. Around the world, 34 percent of the world's children are malnourished; about eleven thousand die every day from malnutrition or related problems; and tens of millions of children suffer sickness and learning disabilities because of deficiencies of micronutrients like iron, vitamin A, and iodine.

Moreover, even some aggregated agricultural statistics do not seem as promising as they once were. The rate of increase in global agricultural production has dropped in the last thirty years: from 3 percent per year in the 1960s, to 2.3 percent in the 1970s, and to 2 percent in the period from 1980 to 1992. Growth in global cereal production has shown an even steeper decline: from 3.6 percent per year in the 1960s, to 2.6 percent in the 1970s, to 1.6 percent from 1980 to 1992.[40] Because this rate is only barely ahead of global population growth, world grain output per person has shown little increase since the mid-1970s.[41] The annual variability of world grain output appears to have increased, perhaps because of the wide use of crop monocultures that are vulnerable to pests and diseases.[42]

Many agricultural experts are especially troubled by declines in the growth rate of agricultural yields (that is, the growth rate of food output per hectare of land). Yields of maize, rice, and wheat in developing countries increased more than 100 percent between 1961 and 1991. Asian wheat yields rose from

0.5 metric tons per hectare to 2.5 tons; Chinese rice yields increased from 2 tons to 6 tons. Recently, however, the annual rate of growth of yields in East and Southeast Asia has slowed: for example, the rate for rice in Southeast Asia has fallen from 3.2 percent in the 1970s to 1.6 percent in recent years. Chinese rice yield growth rates have dropped more than 50 percent.[43] These declining growth rates suggest that some developing countries, especially in East Asia, have already reaped a large proportion of the green revolution's potential benefit.

Complex contextual factors, particularly institutions, play a big role in determining whether developing countries can respond effectively to the effects of land and water scarcity on agriculture. These factors include the society's prevailing land-use practices, land distribution, and market mechanisms within the agricultural sector.[44] Market mechanisms are especially relevant today, because many developing countries are relinquishing state control over markets (including agricultural markets), reducing government spending, and lowering restrictions on foreign investment.

As we saw in chapter 3, induced-innovation theorists argue that, if the institutional and market setting is appropriate, scarcities will stimulate technological change that boosts food output. Population growth and land scarcity expand the agricultural labor force and produce innovation-generating changes in resource and product prices. Thus, Ester Boserup claims that "the growth of population is a major determinant of technological change in agriculture."[45] Population growth can also aid conservation by allowing a society to use labor-intensive soil conservation practices that would otherwise be impossible, such as terracing and the construction of extensive soil-retaining levees. Induced-innovation and like-minded theorists often suggest that the green revolution was spurred by market forces, in particular by shifts in the prices of rice and of key inputs to rice production (like land, fertilizer, and labor).[46]

Unfortunately, many societies—most notably in Africa—do not have the crucial institutional prerequisites or the capital to permit such smooth adjustments.[47] In the absence of these prerequisites, local and regional scarcities of land and water have a harsh impact, especially on marginal groups. The groups often find themselves caught in a vise between rising scarcities on one side and failed institutions and policies on the other. Moreover, induced-innovation theorists have often interpreted the lessons of the green revolution too simplistically: the revolution was produced by a conjunction of price signals with enlightened political leadership, long-standing programs of scientific and technical training, and a network of new agricultural research institutions supported by American foundations and government agencies.[48] A particular geopolitical context in the 1950s—a perceived competition between the Communist bloc and the West, in which rice production was believed to be key to winning the hearts of poor Asians—also spurred this program of innovation.[49] The green revolution actually shows that technological adaptation to scarcity involves not just market forces, but an exceedingly complex interplay of these forces with nonmarket actors, institutions, and context.

In any case, technological fixes such as the green revolution are not panaceas. As indicated above, the marginal returns to green-revolution inputs (such as fertilizer) have recently diminished in some developing countries, especially in East and Southeast Asia. Anne Booth notes that in Java "many paddy farmers, especially those operating well-irrigated land, are now applying the maximum amount of fertilizer and it is unlikely that substantial further yield increases can be obtained with current varieties."[50] Unfortunately, there is no new generation of revolutionary technologies waiting in the wings to keep food output rising. Genetic engineering is helping scientists develop nitrogen-fixing, salinity-resistant, and drought-resistant grains, but the widespread use of such crops in the developing world is at least one, and probably two, decades in the future.[51] The use of biotechnology to develop new plants began only recently, and the course of this research will be long and painstaking. The diffusion of the resulting technologies to farmers in developing countries will also take time.

The constraints imposed by regional scarcities of land and water will be much more evident as countries' food needs soar and as they reach the limits of potential gains from current green-revolution technologies. Projections of the developing world's future needs are sobering. Increased per capita consumption of grain combined with population growth will boost total developing-country annual consumption of grain from 875 million metric tons in the late 1980s to 2.35 billion tons by 2030; world consumption will rise from 1.68 billion tons to 3.3 billion tons.[52] Africa is already experiencing a chronic shortfall in food production. In the early 1990s, the shortfall was 12 million tons annually; by the year 2000, some experts estimate, it will reach 50 million tons; and by 2020, without major changes in resource management, 250 million tons.[53]

What can be done? All regions of the world, especially developing regions, can benefit from improvements in efficiency and reductions in wastage in agricultural production; Vaclav Smil estimates that an additional 2.5 to 3 billion people could be fed through efficiency gains and changes in diets alone.[54] Cropland expansion is possible in some areas, most notably in tropical Africa and the Amazonian basin, but very little unexploited land (or water) is available where a large fraction of the world's population growth will occur, in China, South Asia, Southeast Asia, and the Middle East. Moreover, in these same regions much cropland has been lost or degraded by erosion, nutrient depletion, salinization, waterlogging, or urban encroachment.[55]

The higher output needed to satisfy increased food demand in the face of limited land resources will, therefore, have to come mainly from higher yields. Many countries will have to boost their agricultural production by 2 percent or more per year well into the next century to avoid huge food imports. By 2030, grain yields in developing countries will need to average nearly 7 metric tons per hectare (about today's yield on U.S. corn farms). Yet the current world average is only 2.8 tons,[56] and many farmers in countries like India and Pakistan do not reach half this average. Nonetheless, in much of South Asia and in parts of Africa the full implementation of existing green-revolution technologies could double or triple yields.[57] These gains could, for quite a while, more than compensate for the effects of cropland scarcity (water scarcity is another matter, because green-revolution technologies rely upon heavy irrigation). In the countries in East and Southeast Asia that have already exploited much of the green revolution's potential, land and water scarcity might seem more immediate problems; but many of these countries are now wealthy enough (if they can quickly recover from their current economic crisis) to compensate for deficits by importing food.

Assuming that developing countries have access to the necessary foreign exchange or financial aid, food imports might seem a reasonable way to compensate for production shortfalls, even over an extended period. But a dependence on external agricultural regions will make importers vulnerable to vagaries of climate, economics, and politics in the exporting countries. Moreover, as the redundancy of food-growing regions is reduced, the likelihood of a sudden global shortfall increases.

A recent major effort to project world food output and consumption to the year 2020 took many of the above factors into account. The researchers suggested that, although the aggregate global supply and demand picture is relatively good, "many regions will experience virtually no improvement in food security." Most dramatically, according to these projections, population growth ensures that "there will be very little reduction in the number of malnourished children" in the developing world as a whole; the number will actually increase in sub-Saharan Africa and parts of South Asia.[58]

Ultimately, it is institutional factors that largely determine whether or not countries and their agricultural systems respond effectively to rising scarcities of land and water. If institutions fail in Africa, the continent's vast undeveloped resources of land and water will not be tapped and its agricultural systems will remain grossly inefficient. If institutions fail in South Asia, the full potential of green-revolution technologies will not be exploited. And no matter how wealthy the countries in East and Southeast Asia become, if their institutions fail, the benefits of their wealth and of increased food imports will not reach the groups in their societies affected by land and water scarcity. In all these cases, if institutions fail, supply-induced and demand-induced scarcities of land and water will hit food production hard in some subregions, and the worst affected will be those who are already economically and ecologically marginal. In the next chapter, therefore, I address directly the issue of scarcity's effects on institutional adaptation or, as I term it, the supply of social ingenuity.

Economic Productivity

If we are interested in environment-conflict linkages, perhaps environmental scarcity's most important negative social effect is the constraint it sometimes imposes on economic development. We should note, however, that because of resource capture and ecological marginalization, the main result of demographic and ecological stress is not so much generalized economic hardship as an increase in the wealth gap between those elites that take advantage of the opportunities scarcity offers and those marginal groups that suffer the brunt of scarcity.

Figure 5.5 shows some ways that scarcity might negatively affect economic wellbeing, especially of less advantaged groups. Again the figure focuses solely on the effects of supply-induced scarcities. It shows that environmental degradation or depletion might influence economic productivity directly or indirectly via other social effects, such as changes in agricultural productivity. (Thus the node labeled "reduced or constrained regional agricultural productivity" represents all the causal processes indicated in figure 5.4 and discussed above.) Once more, while no developing countries exhibit all causal links indicated in figure 5.5, most exhibit some.

A great variety of environmental stresses could affect wealth production. Hypothetically, for example, increased ultraviolet radiation caused by ozone depletion could eventually raise the rate of disease in humans, with serious economic results over the long term.[59] Although we have yet to see clear evidence of this particular effect, there is nonetheless abundant evidence of a strong link between other kinds of environmental scarcity and economic productivity. For instance, logging for export markets often creates short-term economic gain for the exporting country's elite, but the resulting deforestation can depress the economy's longer-term productivity. Increased runoff damages roads, bridges, and other valuable infrastructure, while the extra siltation reduces the transport and hydroelectric capacity of rivers. As forests are destroyed, wood becomes scarcer and more expensive, and it absorbs an increasing share of the household budget for the poor families that use it for fuel.

Agriculture is the source of a large share of the wealth generated in developing societies. Per Pinstrup-Andersen notes that "in most low-income developing countries, growth in the agricultural sector, whether through food or non-food agricultural commodities, is the most effective and often the only viable lead approach to sustainable economic growth and poverty alleviation."[60] Consequently, if environmental scarcity constrains agricultural production, as suggested above, it may have a large effect on a country's overall economic development. Some experts believe that the economic relief brought by the green revolution within many poor countries will be short-lived. Jeffrey Leonard writes: "Millions of previously very poor families that

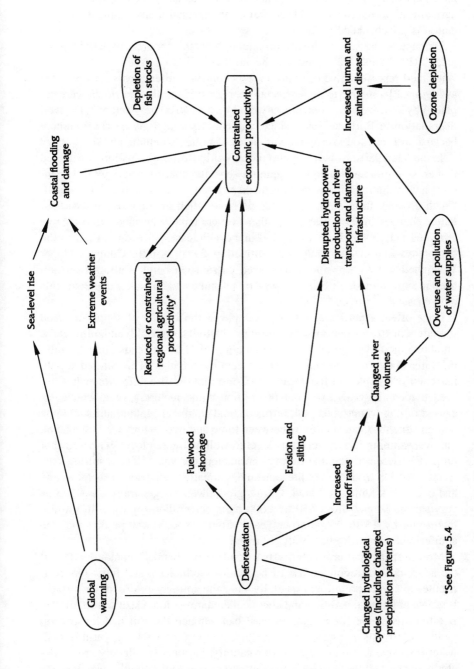

Figure 5.5. Possible Effects of Environmental Change on Economic Productivity

have experienced less than one generation of increasing wealth due to rising agricultural productivity could see that trend reversed if environmental degradation is not checked."[61]

Damage to the soil is already producing a harsh economic impact in some areas. The Magat watershed on the northern Filipino island of Luzon—a watershed representative of many in the country—suffers gross erosion rates averaging 219 metric tons per hectare per year; if the lost nutrients were replaced by fertilizer, the annual cost would be over $100 per hectare.[62] Dryland degradation in Burkina Faso reduces the country's GDP by nearly 9 percent because of fuelwood loss and lower yields of millet, sorghum, and livestock.[63]

In the late 1980s, Robert Repetto of the World Resources Institute estimated that erosion in upland Indonesia annually cost the country's agricultural economy nearly half a billion dollars in discounted future income.[64] He noted: "With erosion, farm output and income have fallen in some regions without major changes in farm practices; other farmers have been induced to change cropping patterns and input use; and in extreme cases, erosion has led to the complete withdrawal of land from cultivation. Farmers in the Citanduy Upper Watershed grow corn, upland rice, and cassava on better soils. As erosion becomes more severe, rice is replaced by peanuts; and on nearly depleted soils only cassava is grown."[65]

Gaza offers a particularly stark example of the impact of supply-induced scarcities of freshwater on agricultural productivity, on health and, ultimately, on economic development.[66] The population of Gaza depends almost totally on water drawn from an aquifer underneath the territory. This limited supply has been overexploited for decades.[67] Consumption of aquifer water has exceeded recharge rates by about 60 million cubic meters a year, which has caused falling water tables, salt intrusion, and chemical contamination.[68] In its natural state the Gaza aquifer is between three and five meters above sea level, but overpumping has reduced this level to well below sea level, with a further drop of between fifteen and twenty centimeters per year.[69] The resulting salt-water intrusion from the Mediterranean has already been detected as far as one and one-half kilometers inland. Gaza's groundwater is generally classified as very saline, ranging from 650 to 3,600 parts per million (ppm), with salinity increasing by 15 to 20 ppm per year.[70] Some experts now predict that the aquifer will eventually be totally salinized.

Moreover, agricultural activity has resulted in chemical contamination of the acquifer.[71] Unregulated use of pesticides, herbicides, and fertilizers contributes to severe pollution, especially since the aquifer is close to the surface. Because of both salinization and chemical contamination, Gaza's groundwater is often unsuitable for irrigation, as it can damage the soil and lower crop yields.[72] Citrus is a significant agricultural crop in the territory, yet it is both water-intensive and intolerant of high salinity. Farmers are already seeing declining crop quality and yields in many areas due to the regular use of high-salinity irrigation water.[73]

TABLE 5.1
Potability of Groundwater in the Gaza Strip

	Acceptable Concentration[a] (ppm)	Gaza Concentration (ppm)
Total dissolved solids	500	1,200–3,200
Sodium (Na$^+$)	20	300–1,100
Chloride (Cl$^-$)	250	400–1,500
Calcium (Ca^{+2})	36	40–120
Sulfate (SO$_4^{-2}$)	250	50–400
Magnesium (Mg^{+2})	30	40–120
Bicarbonate (HCO$_3^-$)	225	300–700
Potassium (K$^+$)	4	6–10
Nitrate (NO$_3^-$)	45	40–140
Fluoride (F)[b]	1.5	0.4–2.9

Source: Hisham Zarour, Jad Isaac, and Violet Qumsieh, "Hydrochemical Indicators of the Severe Water Crisis in the Gaza Strip," in *Final Report on the Project Water Resources in the West Bank and Gaza Strip: Current Situation and Future Prospects* (Jerusalem: Applied Research Institute in Jerusalem, 1994).
[a] World Health Organization standard levels.
[b] Fluoride figures drawn from Zaher Kuhail and Zaki Zoarob, *Potable Groundwater Crisis in the Gaza Strip, 1987–1994* (UNRWA and Palestinian Health Authority, 1994), 11.

According to one relatively optimistic analyst, 50 percent of Gaza's drinking-water supply is "murky," and 23 percent is not potable at all.[74] The Applied Research Institute in Jerusalem (ARIJ) is far more pessimistic, maintaining that Gaza groundwater is simply not fit for human consumption. A water-quality survey conducted by ARIJ in 1992 identified concentrations of several key substances that far exceed generally accepted levels for potability (see Table 5.1). A similar study conducted between 1987 and 1994 by the United Nations Relief Works Agency and the Palestinian Health Authority determined that every one of Gaza's sixty drinking-water wells exceeded acceptable levels for at least two tested contaminants.[75]

Anthropologist Anna Bellisari argues that the routine consumption of contaminated or saline water by Gaza Palestinians contributes to deterioration of the overall health of the population:

The water crisis is very costly to Palestinians not only in the agricultural and industrial sectors, but especially in terms of public health, which depends largely upon adequate, safe supplies of domestic water. Water shortages and pollution are responsible for a major portion of the acute and chronic infections widespread throughout the Occupied Territories, and are likely to cause permanent health damage to a large segment of the population.[76]

This conclusion is supported by a recent World Bank report, which suggests that inadequate and contaminated water supplies contribute to the high frequency of gastrointestinal and parasitic infections found in Gaza.[77] There are no studies that provide decisive proof, but this preliminary evidence suggests a causal link between scarce and contaminated drinking water and Gaza's high levels of infant mortality, infectious disease, hypertension, and other health-related problems, all of which retard economic development.

Environmental scarcity can affect development even in fast-growing economies, although its effects may be obscured by the sheer momentum of economic growth and by aggregate figures that do not reveal differences in growth rates across a country's regions. For example, a team of Chinese researchers led by Mao Yushi, a member of the Chinese Academy of Social Sciences and the director of the Unirule Institute of Economics in Beijing, has examined the combined effect of supply-induced environmental scarcities on China's economic output.[78] The main burdens the team identifies are lost water and timber resources as a result of deforestation; higher human morbidity and mortality and reduced industrial output because of water and air pollution; and reduced crop output resulting from soil erosion and desertification. The team calculates the current cost at more than 18 percent of China's gross domestic product. Mao writes: "The final outcome [of the studies] is quite stunning. On an annual basis, economic losses to China as a result of environmental degradation equal 380.2 billion yuan. This figure represents 18.8 percent of China's total national income (2022.3 billion yuan in 1992)." Although China's economy is booming, much of the new wealth is concentrated in the coastal provinces that are able to trade with the Pacific Rim. Many other parts of the country, especially the central and northern interior, remain extremely poor. Their economic development is constrained in part by their poor transport links to the coast and in part by severe and worsening scarcities of land and water.[79] As we will see below, the increasing wealth gap between the interior and the coast is driving huge and potentially destabilizing migrations within the country.

Unfortunately, as the China team found, gauging the actual economic cost of environmental depletion and degradation is not easy. Current national income accounts do not incorporate measures of resource loss. Repetto comments: "A nation could exhaust its mineral reserves, cut down its forests, erode its soils, pollute its aquifers, and hunt its wildlife to extinction—all without affecting measured income."[80] For example, in the case of agriculture in Indonesia, he notes that the country's national income accounts "significantly overstate the growth of agricultural income" in the highlands.[81] "Thus despite apparently healthy growth, upland farming on Java has been on a treadmill: each current increment in production is offset by an equal but unrecorded loss in soil productivity."[82] Such inadequate measures of economic wealth and productivity reinforce the misperception that there is a policy trade-off between economic growth and environmental protection; this misperception, in turn, encourages societies to generate present income at the expense of their potential for future income.

Migration

Some commentators have suggested that environmental scarcity will produce vast numbers of *environmental refugees.*"[83] Sea-level rise, they claim, will drive people back from coastal and delta areas in Egypt and Bangladesh; spreading desert will empty Sahelian countries as their populations move south; and coastal fishermen will leave their depleted fishing grounds for cities. But there are two reasons why the term *environmental refugee* is often misleading. First, it implies that environmental disruption is the clear and dominant cause of certain refugee flows; and second, it suggests that people will move out of their homelands in vast and sudden waves. But I show in this book that environmental factors only produce their effects in complex interaction with other social and physical variables. And environmental scarcity rarely manifests itself in such a sharp and hurtful way that people are suddenly compelled to leave.

Many experts on migration emphasize the importance of both *push* and *pull* factors in the decisions of potential migrants. *Push* factors are defined as characteristics of the current place of residence, such as low economic development, that encourage people to leave. *Pull* factors are characteristics of a potential home that attract people to go there. Migration experts use these concepts to help distinguish refugees from migrants: while refugees are motivated mainly by push factors, migrants are motivated by a combination of both push and pull factors. Astri Suhrke argues that environmental problems are more likely to produce migrants than refugees, because such problems usually develop gradually, which means that the push effect is not sharp and sudden and that pull factors can therefore clearly enter into potential migrants' calculations.[84]

I believe, however, that this push/pull distinction is not helpful. For one thing, it encourages analysts to try to determine the relative causal weights of factors in the sending and receiving areas. In debates among migration analysts, one often hears claims that push factors are more important than pull factors, or vice versa. These analysts appear to assume, implicitly, that the relative importance of push and pull factors can be construed in additive terms—that, for example, 40 percent of the motivation in a particular case of migration is due to push factors, whereas 60 percent is due to pull factors.

But the real motivator of migration is the gap between the potential migrants' current level of satisfaction and the level they expect to attain in a new land (see fig. 5.6). The larger the gap, the greater the incentive to migrate. And

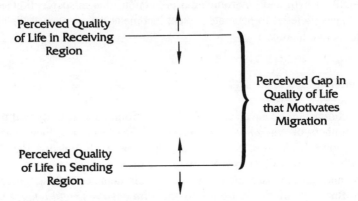

Figure 5.6. Factors Motivating Migration

this gap is not determined by an additive function of push and pull factors but by the relationship between the perceived quality of life in the home region and that in the receiving region.[85] Anything that constrains or depresses the perceived quality of life in the home region, and anything that augments the perceived quality of life in the receiving region, increases the size of the gap.

The distinction between additive and relational models of migration is crucial in this book. Analysts who are skeptical about the importance of environmental scarcity as a cause of migration often argue that people's main motivation to move is not environmental scarcity in the home region but rapid economic development in the receiving region. For example, in the case of China, many analysts suggest that rapid economic growth in coastal regions, not environmental stress in the interior, explains the massive migrations from the country's interior to its coast. A push/pull model encourages this kind of argument, because China is not experiencing sharp and sudden environmental deterioration in the interior that is clearly stimulating population movement. Where is the environmental push, these skeptics ask? All the action, they point out, appears to be on the coast—that is, on the pull side.

Environmental scarcity is having a subtle, yet powerful effect, nonetheless. As we have seen above and in chapter 2, water and land scarcity in China's interior inhibits economic development. Thus, while the coast grows at 12 percent or more annually, the interior grows at only 4 to 5 percent, and the economic gap between the two grows exponentially. Skeptics might argue, in response, that this is a naturally self-limiting process: as wage levels rise on the coast and remain depressed in the interior, industries will eventually have incentives to move inland.[86] But industries will be less inclined to take advantage of cheap labor if key resources, especially water, are of uncertain availability in the interior.

A focus on the gap between the sending and receiving region allows us to keep such processes in the forefront of our analysis. Land and water scarcity in China, and other environmental scarcities in developing countries around the world, often do not have a dramatic push effect on migration. Rather, their impact is slower and in some ways more insidious. These scarcities constrain economic development. The affected regions may still grow economically, but they do not grow nearly as fast as they would in the absence of severe scarcity. Their residents are therefore naturally drawn to places that are economically booming or that offer greater opportunity. Environmental scarcity is, without doubt, a significant cause of today's unprecedented levels of internal and international migration around the world.

The Bangladesh-Northeast India region in South Asia is a good illustration. Over the last forty years, land scarcity has caused millions of people to move from East Pakistan or Bangladesh to the Indian states of Assam, Tripura, and West Bengal. Of course, people have been moving around this part of South Asia in large numbers for centuries, but in recent decades the movements have increased in size.

Detailed data are scarce, because both India and Bangladesh manipulate their census data for political reasons, and the Bangladeshi government avoids admitting there is large out-migration, because the question causes friction with India. But by piecing together demographic information and experts' estimates, we conclude that migrants from Bangladesh have expanded the population of neighboring areas of India by 12 to 17 million, of which only 1 or 2 million can be attributed to migration induced by the 1971 war between India and Pakistan that created Bangladesh. We further estimate that the 1991 population of the state of Assam was boosted by at least 7 million people to a total of 22 million.[87]

Scarcity of cropland has strongly contributed to this migration, but only one of the three sources of scarcity—demand-induced scarcity brought about by rapid population growth—appears to be a direct and major cause. Supply-induced scarcity (that is, cropland degradation and depletion) is a secondary cause because, as noted in chapter 3, annual floods help mitigate land degradation by adding nutrients to the soil. When questioned, migrants often identify the flooding as the proximate cause of their movement, but in many cases flooding causes people to move because population growth has already critically limited per capita access to land. As for structural scarcity, although land distribution is highly unequal, this distribution has changed little since an initial attempt at land reform immediately following East Pakistan's independence from the British.[88] Consequently, population growth appears to be the consistent driver behind rising land scarcity in Bangladesh in recent decades, and therefore behind the huge movements of people out of the country. This growth has produced a wide gap between current satisfaction for Bangladeshis and their perceived potential satisfaction elsewhere: the country's population density is over nine hundred people per square kilometer, whereas the density in neighboring Assam is under three hundred.[89]

We must note contextual factors that are key to a full explanation of this case. Within Bangladesh, these factors include inheritance practices that cause families to divide cropland into smaller plots with each generation. As we saw in chapter 3, contextual factors also include national and community water-control institutions that have sharply limited agricultural output and kept peasants from gaining full benefit from some of the most fertile land in the world.[90] In receiving areas of India, politicians have often encouraged Bangladeshi migration to garner votes. Furthermore, in the Ganges-Brahmaputra region, the concept of nation-state is often not part of the local culture. Many people think of the region as "greater Bengal," and borders do not figure heavily in the calculations of some migrants, especially when there are receptive family, linguistic, and religious groups across the frontier.

Although such contextual factors are important, they cannot obscure the fact that land scarcity in Bangladesh, arising largely from population growth, has been a powerful force behind migration to neighboring regions.[91]

Social Segmentation

Severe environmental scarcity can aggravate divisions or *segmentation* among ethnic, religious, and linguistic groups.[92] Constrained agricultural productivity, constrained economic productivity, and large migrations (the three social effects of environmental scarcity discussed above) can precipitate social segmentation, which can in turn disrupt institutions (the fifth social effect, discussed below).

Scarcity sharpens distinctions between winners and losers—between groups that profit from scarcity and those that are hurt. It encourages competition among groups for control of resources critical to survival and prosperity, and it encourages resource-dependent groups to turn inward and to focus on narrow survival strategies.[93] This insularity reduces interactions among these groups and between them and the state. Segmentation in turn erodes civil society, which is the dense network of nonstate associations and organizations (including religious groups, community-service organizations, and, by some accounts, political parties) that mediates between the individual and the state.[94] As a result, society is less able to articulate effectively its demands on the state. Segmentation also reduces the density of *social capital*—the trust, networks, and norms of reciprocity generated by vigorous, crosscutting exchange among groups.[95]

The South African case is a good example of these processes.[96] Apartheid concentrated millions of blacks in some of the country's least productive and most ecologically sensitive territories, where population densities were further

TABLE 5.2

Comparison of Population Densities within Rural South Africa, 1991

	Population Density (Persons/Square km)		
	South Africa	White Areas	Former Homelands
Cropland and Pastureland	21.28	6.17	108.70
Cropland	133.33	39.37	625.00

Source: Adapted from Development Bank of South Africa, *South Africa's Nine Provinces: A Human Development Profile* (April 1994): 99.

increased by high natural birth rates. In 1980, rural areas of the Ciskei homeland had a population density of eighty-two people per square kilometer, whereas the surrounding rural areas of Cape Province had a density of two. (Table 5.2 provides 1991 density figures for white and black areas in South Africa as a whole.)

The black populations in these "homelands" were forced to subsist on local cropland, water, and fuelwood. High population densities, low capital availability, and the lack of resource-management skills severely degraded this resource base and made it impossible for homeland residents to adopt environmentally sound resource-use practices. Corrupt and abusive local elites often captured the best local resources, which marginalized weaker groups to the most ecologically sensitive parts of the homelands. As a result, wide areas of these territories were completely stripped of trees for fuelwood, grazed down to bare dirt, and eroded of top soil. A 1980 report concluded that nearly 50 percent of Ciskei's land was moderately or severely eroded, and nearly 40 percent of its pasturage was overgrazed.[97]

In the decade from the mid-1980s to mid-1990s, especially with the collapse of apartheid's notorious "influx control" laws that limited black migration to the cities, environmental scarcity in the homelands contributed to an annual migration of up to 750,000 blacks to the country's urban areas.[98] These migrants settled on marginal lands in the cities: on hillsides, in river valleys, or close to industries. Severe population pressures in these areas damaged and depleted local streams, community cropland, and fuelwood stocks. The concentration of many people on a declining urban resource base, in the context of weak local governments, again caused resource capture: powerful warlords—local leaders who controlled their own paramilitary forces and owed "only nominal allegiance to any higher authority"—secured community support in part by controlling basic environmental resources, such as land and water.[99] Resource capture multiplied warlord power and wealth, permitting extraction of surpluses in the form of taxes, rents, and levies.[100]

Segmentation occurred as communities withdrew into themselves to protect access to these resources. It often took the form of divisions among ethnic groups (in particular, between Zulu and Xhosa), among family-based clans, and among residents of townships, informal settlements, and work hostels. As resources were degraded within their territories, warlords often tried to maintain power by pointing to resources in neighboring townships and informal settlements and mobilizing their communities to seize them. This mobilization often set in motion a cycle of appalling violence among African communities. "Squatters are mobilized to fight for access to resources in neighboring townships, and township youth organize military style units to defend their areas and counter-attack squatter areas."[101] These processes further exacerbated intergroup segmentation and broke down social networks, weakened community norms, and eroded trust, resulting in a loss of the society's social capital. The apartheid state often actively manipulated ethnic divisions to promote its local interests, especially during the tumultuous transition period to a post-apartheid regime.

Disrupted Institutions

In many developing societies, the four social effects described above are likely to tear the fabric of legitimized, accepted, and authoritative institutions that guide and pattern social behavior.[102] Dropping agricultural output can weaken rural communities and institutions by causing malnutrition and disease and by encouraging people to leave; constrained economic productivity corrodes confidence in the national purpose and weakens the tax base; mass migrations of people into a region can disrupt labor markets, shift class relations, and upset the often institutionalized balance of economic and political authority among ethnic groups; and social segmentation can prevent the reform and development of new community-based institutions.

   Research suggests that one institution in particular, the state, is key. The multiple effects of environmental scarcity appear likely to weaken the state in some poor countries. As we will see in the next chapter, weakening of the state reduces the ability of society to generate and deliver the social and technical ingenuity it needs to respond to environmental scarcity. And as we will see in chapter 7, weakening of the state also raises the probability of civil violence by shifting the balance of power from the state to potential challenger groups.

   Joel Migdal defines the state as "an organization, composed of numerous agencies led and coordinated by the state's leadership (executive authority) that has the ability or authority to make and implement the binding rules for all the people as well as the parameters of rule making for other social organizations in a given territory, using force if necessary to have its way."[103] In keeping with much contemporary scholarship, this definition assumes the state is a single, rational entity. Much like a corporation, the state is a cohesive actor that manages its income and expenditures in order to best attain its goals. Unlike other actors, though, the state oversees a clearly delineated territory and is often sufficiently powerful to determine the rules governing behavior in its social environment.

The above definition, although a good starting point, leaves two matters unsettled. First, the boundaries of the state are unclear. For example, in the realm of environmental policy, nongovernmental organizations (NGOs) now provide many important services to the state and carry out key functions traditionally performed by the state.[104] Astute analysts of politics in developing countries regard NGO activity as often central to effective governance. When and where do we include these organizations within our concept of the state? More generally, scholars of the state now widely acknowledge the indistinct nature of the boundary between the state and civil society. Some important scholarship currently focuses on the circumstances under which the relationship between the state and civil society is either mutually empowering or mutually debilitating.[105] Many scholars now argue that state strength is enhanced by a vigorous civil society that instills habits of trust, reciprocity, and civic engagement in the populace; that provides information to the state on the interests, desires, and concerns of social groups; and that collaborates with the state on the local implementation of state policies.[106]

Second, Migdal's definition of the state does not give us a clear idea of how to define or measure state capacity; the words *ability* and *authority* in the definition carry a heavy, yet ill-defined burden. States with high capacity are generally thought to exhibit a number of characteristics, including some degree of autonomy from outside interests, the ability to influence these interests to achieve state goals, and internal organizational coherence. Yet the literature provides remarkably little additional guidance on this issue.

To aid our research on the links between environmental scarcity and violence, therefore, we developed a set of indicators of state capacity.[107] These indicators, which are listed in table 5.3, are best thought of as variables describing certain properties of a given state and its components. The components include the executive, legislative, and judicial branches; the police and military; the government bureaucracy; and key institutions of financial management, such as the central bank. The indicators are divided into two groups: the first group relates to intrinsic characteristics of the state and/or its components; the second to relations between the state and society as a whole. There are four of each, and all are at least in principal *operationalizable* (that is, measurable) using qualitative or quantitative measures.

The variables listed in table 5.3 determine the ability of the state to get its way—that is, to convince, cajole, or coerce recalcitrant groups within society. The state can pursue three possible strategies: moral suasion (for which legitimacy is important), bribery and cooptation, and outright coercion. Fiscal resources are key to the latter two (and not irrelevant to the first): money is

TABLE 5.3
Indicators of State Capacity

Indicators of the State's (or Its Components') Intrinsic Characteristics

---

Human Capital	The technical and managerial skill level of individuals within the state and its component parts.
Instrumental Rationality	The ability of state's components to gather and evaluate information relevant to their interests and to make reasoned decisions maximizing their utility. (Note that *utility* may be locally defined; i.e., it may reflect the narrow interests of the component and not the broader interests of the state or society.)
Coherence	The degree to which the state's components agree and act on shared ideological bases, objectives, and methods; also, the ability of these components to communicate and constructively debate ideas, information, and policies among themselves.
Resilience	The state's capacity to absorb sudden shocks, to adapt to longer-term changes in socioeconomic conditions, and to resolve societal disputes sustainably without catastrophic breakdown. The opposite of *brittleness*.

Indicators of the Relations between the State (or Its Components) and Society

---

Autonomy	The extent to which the state can act independently of external forces, both domestic and international, and co-opt those that would alter or constrain its actions.
Fiscal Resources	The financial capacity of the state or of a given component of the state. This capacity is a function of both current and reasonably feasible revenue streams as well as demands on that revenue.
Reach and Responsiveness	The degree to which the state is successful in extending its ideology, sociopolitical structures, and administrative apparatus throughout society (this refers to both geographic reach and reach into the socioeconomic structures of civil society); the responsiveness of these structures and apparatus to the local needs of the society.
Legitimacy	The strength of the state's moral authority; i.e., the extent to which the populace obeys its commands out of a sense of allegiance and duty, rather than as a result of coercion or economic incentive.

---

needed for side payments to obstructionist coalitions, and it is needed to build the coercive apparatuses of the police and army.

Obviously there are causal relations among some of the variables listed in the table. The level of human capital, for example, will influence instrumental rationality. The level of fiscal resources will affect autonomy, legitimacy, reach/responsiveness, and human capital, while at the same time being partly a consequence of these factors. However, while there may be correlations and causal relations linking these variables, they measure different things. It is easy to imagine them moving independently of each other.

It is also important to note that responsiveness is not the inverse of autonomy; in other words, a highly responsive state is not necessarily one of low autonomy. Loss of autonomy implies the state reacts almost reflexively to the interests and wishes of powerful elites and interest groups; the opposite of autonomy is thus reactivity. Responsiveness, on the other hand, implies that the state knows what is going on at the local level and takes this information into consideration when arriving at its policies; it is thus closely associated with reach, which is why they are combined into one variable.

Although analysts can use the indicators in table 5.3 to judge the capacity of a given state as a whole, they also offer us a useful way to disaggregate this capacity. We can apply most of the indicators to individual components of the state (we cannot, of course, apply coherence to individual components, because coherence is, by definition, a characteristic of the state as a whole). The kind and degree of state capacity often varies across these components. Moreover, state capacity is usually not *fungible*: it usually cannot be reallocated or moved from one component to another at will. For example, while the judiciary of a given state may be relatively legitimate, the executive branch may not be, and the executive cannot accrue to itself, at will, the judiciary's legitimacy.

This set of conceptual tools has allowed our researchers to identify links between rising environmental scarcity and declining state capacity. They have found four separate and often simultaneous effects.[108]

First, environmental scarcities increase financial and political demands on the state. For example, to deal with severe water scarcity, the Chinese government must spend huge sums on new infrastructure such as wells, dams, canals, pipelines, and irrigation systems; and it must build large facilities to control industrial and municipal pollution.[109] In addition, analysis of diverse cases—including those of South Africa, Pakistan, and the Philippines—shows that environmental scarcities expand marginal groups that need help from government by constraining rural economic development and by encouraging people to move into cities where they demand food, shelter, transport, energy, and jobs.[110] As J. D. Kasarda and A. M. Parnell note, rapid population growth in cities contributes to "high rates of unemployment and underemployment, . . . soaring urban poverty, insufficient shelter, inadequate sanitation, inadequate or contaminated water supplies, serious air pollution and other forms of environmental degradation, congested streets, overloaded public transportation systems, and municipal budget crises."[111] In response, governments come under pressure to introduce subsidies of urban services; these subsidies drain revenues, distort prices, and cause misallocations of capital.

Second, resource scarcities affect the state via their effects on elites. On one hand, scarcities threaten the incomes of elites that depend on resource extraction. These elites often compete among themselves for shrinking resource rents; they may turn to the state for compensation, or they may act to block institutional reforms that would distribute more fairly the costs of rising scarcity.[112] Scarcities also aggravate competition among political elites that derive their power from rival political institutions. Thus, evermore critical water scarcity in China is opening up sharp divisions between Beijing and the provinces and among the provinces themselves.[113] The management of such conflicts requires immense amounts of state attention, time, and money.

On the other hand, as discussed previously, environmental scarcities generate opportunities for powerful coalitions of elite members to capture windfall wealth. Scarcities can boost the economic power of small elite groups (or what I call, in the next chapter, *narrow distributional coalitions*). As they become more powerful, these groups are increasingly able to ignore state dictates. For example, Philip Shenon of the *New York Times* notes that critical land scarcity in the booming southern Chinese province of Guangdong creates "huge profits from land sales." These profits "tend to overwhelm any fear of the central government. With the prospect of millions of dollars in profits on even a small plot of land, developers and corrupt officials are often willing to take the risk of ignoring instructions from Beijing."[114]

Such individuals and groups can become powerful enough to shirk taxes on their greater wealth and to penetrate the state to make it do their bidding. In particular, they often lobby to change the property rights and other laws governing the use of scarce resources such as water, land, and forests. These groups have a great incentive to pursue such change: the state is usually able to generate large economic rents by expanding the range of permissible uses of resources and by granting monopolistic access to resources. In many societies, these rent-seeking elite groups influence the state through bribery, kickbacks, and other forms of corruption.[115]

Third, such predatory behavior by elites often evokes defensive reactions by weaker groups that directly depend on the resources in question. The struggle for resource control between powerful and weak groups, and among weak groups themselves, worsens social segmentation, which in turn debilitates civil society and erodes the trust-building processes that civil society promotes. The loss of trust, of information flows from society to the state, and of private implementation of state policies reduces the reach and responsiveness of the state at the local level. The state's failure to meet local needs then depresses its legitimacy.

Fourth and finally, if resource scarcity affects the economy's general productivity, tax revenues to local and national governments can decline. In the state of Bihar, India, for instance, severe cropland scarcity and fragmentation induced by population growth have contributed to a steep fall in land taxes received by the state government.[116] Such a revenue decline hurts elites that benefit from state largesse and reduces the state's capacity to meet the increased societal demands arising from environmental scarcity.

We see, therefore, that environmental scarcity can affect a number of the indicators of state capacity in table 5.3. It can directly constrain a state's fiscal resources, and by encouraging predatory behavior by elites, it can reduce state autonomy. Rivalry among political elites reduces coherence, and competition among groups over resources weakens civil society. The conjunction of these four changes, in turn, hinders state responsiveness by reducing its ability to supply efficient markets, clear property rights, and an effective judicial and police system. Environmental scarcity can also boost financial and political demands on the state and increase grievances of marginal groups. A widening gap between rising demands on the state and the state's actual performance, in turn, erodes state legitimacy, further aggravates conflicts among elites, and sharpens disputes between the elites and the masses. As the state weakens, the social balance of power can shift in favor of groups challenging state authority.

Indonesia provides a good illustration of how some of these processes operate in the real world.[117] Charles Barber shows that the proliferation of local conflicts over forests depresses the legitimacy, coherence, and reach of the Indonesian state at the local level. A number of factors have produced these conflicts. Worsening local scarcities of forest resources have severely affected the well-being of communities traditionally dependent on forests and have also provoked increasingly aggressive rent-seeking behavior by elites and capitalist interests. Simultaneously, rapid sociopolitical change in Indonesia has created activist groups ready to challenge the state and the rent-seeking behavior of elites; this change has also provided avenues of protest, and audiences for protest (often overseas), that were previously unavailable. And finally, the Indonesian state has a generally low capacity to generate and deliver new and reformed institutions at both the local and national levels. This low capacity is, in turn, a function of several things: institutional inertia arising from the historical origins of the modern Indonesian state; the state's efforts to undermine traditional community institutions (often referred to as the *adat* system); and, once again, rising scarcities of natural resources that leave the state with fewer resources to co-opt and bribe potential opponents. Barber believes this convergence of factors raises grave questions about the Indonesian state's ability to manage the many political and economic stresses the country will face in coming years.

In this chapter I have shown how the main sources of environmental scarcity interact to produce resource capture and ecological marginalization. I have also discussed five negative social effects that arise from environmental scarcity. In the next chapter, I address a central, still unresolved question: why is it that some societies adapt reasonably well to environmental scarcity and other do not? If we can answer this question, we will be much better able to predict which societies are most vulnerable to turmoil and violence.

Appendix

The Causal Role of Environmental Scarcity

Debate about whether and how environmental scarcity contributes to social phenomena such as economic decline, migration, and violence often centers on the specific causal roles of scarcity.[1] This appendix provides some conceptual tools for a closer analysis of the nature of the relationship between cause (environmental scarcity) and effect (the intermediate social effects discussed in this chapter or the violent conflict discussed in chapter 7).[2] I consider here seven variables that can be used to characterize this causal relationship: necessity, strength, proximity, exogeneity, multicausality, interactivity, and nonlinearity.

Necessity is a dichotomous variable: something is either a necessary cause of a given type of event, or it is not. Environmental scarcity is clearly not a necessary cause of social stress and violent conflict, because such stress often occurs in situations of resource abundance. Unlike necessity, the *strength* of a cause can vary along a continuum, from weak to "sufficient."[3] Causal *proximity* can also vary along a continuum from distant to proximate. We commonly think of proximity in terms of causal distance in time or space. But proximity is really a function of the number of intervening causal steps or variables between the cause and its effect; the larger the number of intervening variables, the lower the causal proximity.[4] The characteristics of proximity and causal strength are sometimes conflated, because a distant cause is often assumed to be weak. But intervening variables do not necessarily weaken the link between a cause and its effect.

The causal independence of a variable, or its *exogeneity*, can similarly vary along a continuum from fully exogenous to fully endogenous. Many analysts assume that environmental scarcity is no more than a fully endogenous intervening variable linking political, economic, and social factors—factors that include a society's specific institutions and political-economic policies—to social stress and conflict (see the first diagram in figure 5.A1). Environmental scarcity does not have any independent role as a cause of this stress and conflict. By this view, environmental scarcity may be an important indicator that political and economic development has gone awry, but it does not merit, in and of itself, intensive research and policy attention. Instead, we should devote our resources to the more fundamental political and economic factors.

But the cases reviewed in this book highlight three reasons why this view is not entirely correct (as illustrated in the second and third diagrams in figure

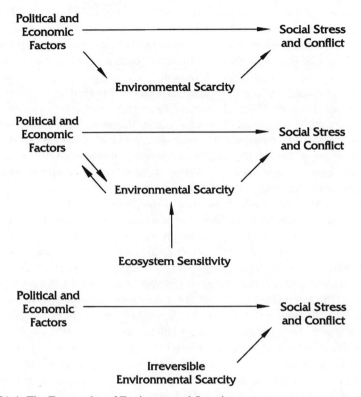

Figure 5A.1. The Exogeneity of Environmental Scarcity

5A.1). First, as we saw in the Senegal and Jordan basins, environmental scarcity can itself be an important force behind changes in the politics and economics governing resource use. In both cases, scarcity caused powerful actors to strengthen in their favor an inequitable distribution of resources. Second, as discussed in chapter 4, ecosystem sensitivity is often an important variable contributing to environmental scarcity, and this sensitivity is, at least in part, an external physical factor that is not a function of human social institutions or behavior. The depth of soils in the Filipino uplands and the vulnerability of Israel's aquifers to salt intrusion are not functions of human social institutions or behavior. Third, in many parts of the world, environmental degradation has crossed a threshold of irreversibility. Even if enlightened social change removes the original political, economic, and cultural causes of the degradation, it will be a continuing burden on society. Once irreversible, in other words, environmental degradation becomes an exogenous variable.[5]

The degree of *multicausality* of the processes producing social stress and conflict also varies. If environmental scarcity contributes to stress and conflict, it almost always operates with other political, economic, and cultural causes. Analysts who are skeptical about environmental scarcity as a cause of social stress often conflate the characteristics of multicausality and causal strength by assuming that if many factors are involved, each must be relatively weak.[6]

Interactivity is a dichotomous variable: the relationship between two causes of an event can be either interactive or additive. Interaction is a common feature of environmental-social systems. In an interactive system of causes of a specific social event, none of the causes is sufficient but all are necessary; thus, causal strength and interactivity are linked because no single cause can produce the event itself. But beyond this statement, it is meaningless to claim that a given cause in an interactive system is stronger—or should be given more weight in the analysis—than another.[7]

Finally, the degree of *nonlinearity* of the mathematical function describing the relation between a cause and effect can vary from high to low. As we have seen in chapter 3, systems with highly nonlinear functions can exhibit unanticipated "threshold effects" and chaotic behavior in response to small perturbations. This is a key characteristic of many environmental-social systems.

Academic and lay discussions of environment-conflict linkages are usually larded with imprecise causal verbs like *aggravate, amplify,* and *trigger.* These fuzzy, "folk" concepts are useful in everyday explanations of physical and social events, but they are not always helpful for research. We can clarify them a bit, however, using the above distinctions.

A claim that an environmental factor amplifies the effect of other causes of conflict implies that the factor interacts with the other causes to multiply their impact. In contrast, a claim that the factor aggravates the impact of the other causes seems to suggest the factor's effect is added to that of others. A trigger of conflict is always a proximate cause, and usually an unnecessary and insufficient one too. The term also implies that the system responds nonlinearly to the factor in question: that is, the factor triggers a disproportionately large response by pushing the system beyond a critical threshold. For instance, stochastic and extreme environmental events—such as cyclones, floods, and droughts—can be important triggers of conflict. They can provide challenger groups with opportunities for action against a state whose buffering capacity has been gradually eroded by civil war, corruption, economic mismanagement, rapid population growth, or deteriorating stocks of renewable resources.[8]

Aggravator, amplifier, and trigger models are popular with skeptics because they seem to relegate environmental scarcities to the status of secondary causes of social stress and conflict. Although these models are often valuable, they offer inaccurate and incomplete explanations of interesting cases. The research discussed in this book shows that environmental stresses can be important contributors to conflict even if causally distant and even if the system is interactive and highly complex.

6

Ingenuity and Adaptation

SOCIETIES may be able to alter the processes linking human activity, environmental scarcity, and violence. If they wish to prevent severe environmental scarcity, they need to understand and act on its precursor ideational and physical variables. If they wish to promote nondisruptive adaptation to scarcity, they need to understand and act on the links between environmental scarcity and its negative social effects, including impoverishment, migrations, and the like. And if they wish to prevent conflict (even though scarcity and its negative social effects may be severe), they need to understand and act on the links between the negative social effects and violence.

I call these *first-*, *second-*, and *third*-stage interventions, respectively. In this book, I do not deal in detail with first-or third-stage interventions. In this chapter, however, I discuss second-stage interventions, because it is around this point—around whether or not societies can adapt to environmental scarcity without undue hardship—that much current debate revolves (as we saw in chapter 3).

Strategies for second-stage intervention fall into two general categories. First, a society can continue to rely on its indigenous resources but use them more sensibly and provide alternative employment to people who have limited resource access. For example, economic incentives like increases in resource prices and taxes can encourage conservation, technological innovation, and resource substitution. Resource redistribution and labor-intensive industries can relieve the effects of skewed access to high-quality resources.

Second, the society might be able to decouple itself from dependence on its own depleted environmental resources by producing goods and services that do not rely heavily on these resources; it could then trade the products on the international market for the resources it no longer has at home (a strategy advocated by many neoclassical economists). Such decoupling might, in fact, be achieved by rapidly exploiting indigenous environmental resources and reinvesting the profits in capital, industrial equipment, and skills to permit a shift to other forms of wealth creation. For instance, Malaysia can use the income from over-logging its forests to fund a modern university system that trains electrical engineers and computer specialists for a high-technology industrial sector.[1]

In this chapter, I focus on the first of these strategies. If either is to succeed, however, a society must be able to supply enough ingenuity at the right places and times. Technical ingenuity is needed to develop, for example, new agricultural and forestry technologies that compensate for environmental loss. Social ingenuity is needed to put in place policies, institutions, and organizations that buffer people from the effects of scarcity and provide the right incentives for technological entrepreneurs.

In the next decades, I argue, the need for both technical and social ingenuity to deal with environmental scarcities will rise sharply. Population growth, climbing average resource consumption, and persistent inequalities in resource access ensure that scarcities will affect many environmentally sensitive regions with unprecedented severity, speed, and scale. Resource substitution and conservation tasks will therefore be more complex, unpredictable, and urgent, driving up the need for technical ingenuity. Moreover, solving these problems through market and other institutional innovations (such as changes in property rights and resource distribution) will require great social ingenuity.

In many cases, scarcities will boost the supply of ingenuity by producing changes in resource prices that, in turn, provide incentives to technological and social entrepreneurs. In other words, necessity will often be the mother of invention. And this increased supply of ingenuity will help alleviate scarcity's severity and social impacts.

Yet analysts often overlook the fact that environmental scarcities can also interfere with ingenuity's supply. Poor countries start at a disadvantage: many are underendowed with the social institutions—including the productive research centers, efficient markets, and capable states—that are necessary for an ample supply of both social and technical solutions to scarcity.[2] Moreover, environmental scarcity sometimes diminishes these countries' ability to create and maintain such institutions; it does so by weakening their states, as we have seen in chapter 5, and by engendering intense rivalries among interest groups and elites.

In some societies, therefore, resource scarcity simultaneously increases the requirement for ingenuity and impedes its supply, producing an *ingenuity gap*. Societies with serious and persistent ingenuity gaps will be far more likely to exhibit the negative social effects—the constrained economic productivity, large migrations, and social segmentation—discussed previously, and they will be correspondingly more vulnerable to serious civil violence.

In its simplest form, therefore, the central question I ask in this chapter is: Can societies be smart enough—can they generate, disseminate, and implement enough of the right kinds of ingenuity at the right times and places—to keep environmental scarcity from negatively affecting their well-being? I do not have precise measures for ingenuity; the argument here is heuristic and illuminative, not quantitative. But I believe researchers can eventually operationalize the key variables and specify the general shapes of the key functions. In time, on the basis of measurable data, we should be able to predict when and where ingenuity gaps will appear.

The Nature and Role of Ingenuity

Economists have long debated which factors determine economic well-being and wealth production. An increasingly influential group of theorists in this debate, whose work is variously called *new economic growth theory* or *endogenous growth theory,* argues that ideas are a factor of economic production in addition to capital, labor, and land.[3] Ideas have independent productive power. As Paul Romer, one of the leaders of this school, writes: "Ideas are the instructions that let us combine limited physical resources in arrangements that are ever more valuable."[4] Romer and his colleagues also argue that productive ideas are not exogenously given to economic actors but are, at least in part, endogenously generated by the actors and the economic system. (See the appendix to this chapter for a more detailed discussion of modern growth theory and the production function.)

These economists focus mainly on ideas embodied in new technologies. In the following pages, I contend that technological ideas are not the only productive ideas; just as important are ideas about social organization, especially about reforming and building institutions. And I argue that the generation and dissemination of productive ideas is endogenous not just to the economic system but also to the broader social system that includes a society's politics and culture.

What Is Ingenuity?

By ingenuity I mean *ideas* applied to solve practical technical and social problems. It would be helpful if we could eventually develop ways of distinguishing among these ideas by their quality. Romer takes a first step by outlining a crude method for representing the information content of ideas.[5] But a means of distinguishing good ideas from ones that are not so good is not essential to my argument here. For simplicity, I focus only on the aggregate supply of ideas that a society applies to its practical problems. If aggregate supply is inadequate, then we can assume that some of the society's technical and social problems are not solved.

Human ingenuity is usually so abundant that it hardly seems remarkable. It is evident in the practical solutions to the countless mundane difficulties we face as a species. On a daily basis, for instance, an average city receives an uninterrupted and seemingly coordinated supply of thousands of metric tons of food and fuel, tens of millions of liters of water, and hundreds of thousands of kilowatt hours of electricity. Huge quantities of wastes are removed; hospitals provide health services; knowledge is transmitted from adults to children in schools; police forces protect property and personal safety; and hundreds of committees and councils from the community to the city level deal with matters of governance. Of course, the amount of ingenuity needed to run such a system is not the same as the amount required to create it, because at any one time a vast array of routines and standard operating procedures guides people's actions. But the system and its countless elements are the products of the incremental accretion of human ingenuity. They have been created, over time, by millions of small ideas and a few big ones.

Within an economy, ingenuity is a factor of production. It often substitutes for the factors of labor and land by raising their productivity. For instance, the unprecedented growth in global agricultural output over the past fifty years has been produced by a huge expansion in the stock of agricultural ideas embodied in people, institutions, and technologies, and, in contrast, "a modest expansion in the quantities of land and water devoted to agricultural production."[6] Ingenuity usually complements physical and human capital: investments in agricultural machinery and trained agricultural workers are invariably accompanied by increases in the local stock of ideas and instructions.

When we consider how ingenuity can alleviate resource scarcity, we must distinguish between technical and social ingenuity. People need technical ingenuity to address problems in the physical world and social ingenuity for problems in the social world. In industrial societies, resource scarcities are usually seen as technological challenges needing the keen attention of scientists and engineers. But the supply of this technical ingenuity depends on an adequate supply of social ingenuity at many levels of society. Social ingenuity is key to the creation, reform, and maintenance of public and semipublic goods such as markets, funding agencies, educational and research organizations, and effective government. If operating well, this system of institutions provides psychological and material incentives to technological entrepreneurs and innovators; it aids regular contact and communication among experts; and it channels resources preferentially to those endeavors with the greatest prospect of success.

Social ingenuity is thus a precursor to technical ingenuity.[7] Countries experiencing serious environmental scarcity need sophisticated and stable systems of markets, legal regimes, financial agencies, and educational and research institutions to promote the development and distribution of new grains adapted for dry climates and eroded soils, of alternative cooking technologies to compensate for the loss of firewood, and of water conservation technologies. Countries therefore need ingenuity to get ingenuity, which means it is both an input to and output of the economic system.[8]

Social ingenuity is also key to adaptation strategies that do not involve new technologies. For instance, a society might adapt to a higher probability of food shortfalls arising from cropland scarcity by establishing lines of emergency credit and by making advance arrangements for transfers of food from food-producing to food-scarce regions. Such social ingenuity is often provided by competent bureaucrats as they design and implement policy and by astute political leaders as they bargain, create coalitions, and use various inducements to get policies enacted and institutions built. Of course, the ingenuity needed to adjust to resource scarcity is not only produced by people at the top of the social hierarchy: many of the needed ideas are produced at the community and household levels as people learn, for example, how to reform local institutions to solve local collective-action problems.[9]

The Requirement for and the Supply of Ingenuity

I define the *requirement* for ingenuity in response to a given resource scarcity as the amount needed to compensate for any aggregate social disutility caused by the scarcity. It is, in other words, the minimum amount of ingenuity that a society needs to maintain its current aggregate level of satisfaction in spite of the scarcity.[10] This requirement is not an economic constraint in the real world; rather, it is an arbitrary, analytical benchmark against which we can evaluate society's delivery of ingenuity. (Note that society's requirement for ingenuity is distinct from its actual demand for ingenuity. Demand depends on ingenuity's price. Often, this price is the wage to the human capital that generates it; examples include the salary paid to an engineer and the remuneration to a consulting firm. Sometimes ingenuity is bought directly, as when a fee is paid for a license to manufacture a patented product.)

Many people who are optimistic about humankind's ability to surmount resource scarcity implicitly use this benchmark: they argue that, with well-functioning economic institutions like markets, the level of satisfaction in a society over the medium and long run will not decrease despite occasional resource shortages. In other words, these optimists assume that ingenuity will be supplied abundantly and cheaply enough to alleviate any disutility arising from scarcity and that the society will demand at least this amount of ingenuity.[11]

I define the *supply* of ingenuity as the amount actually delivered and implemented by the economic and social system. This amount is determined by the price society is willing to pay for it and by numerous other variables, including availability of financial and intellectual capital, society's capacity to generate practical knowledge, and the willingness of society to undergo social and technological change. Ingenuity is supplied in two temporal stages. The first is the generation of a potential solution to a particular problem; the second is the delivery and implementation of the potential solution.[12] Supply can be hindered by factors operating at either or both stages.

Some Factors Increasing the Requirement for Ingenuity

For many renewable resources, both regionally and globally, population growth and increasing per capita resource consumption are causing a steady increase in the ratio of the consumption of the resource per unit of time to the total amount of the resource available.[13] This consumption/resource ratio is an approximate but useful measure of a resource's scarcity.[14] An increase in the numerator of the ratio means greater demand-induced scarcity (if we take resource consumption to equal resource demand), and a decrease in the denominator means greater supply-induced scarcity.[15] Because of the dual impacts on scarcity of both population growth and rising per capita demand (chap. 4), an increase in the ratio's numerator often produces a decrease in its denominator: in these cases, the greater the total consumption of a resource, the less there remains to consume.

The steady rise in consumption/resource ratios for many renewables has a number of important consequences. Serious scarcities tend to affect larger regions. For example, the cod fishery collapsed across much of the Northwestern Atlantic in the 1980s and early 1990s; water shortages are now chronic throughout the Middle East; and large areas of the interior and western regions of China are affected by erosion and loss of cropland.[16] Serious scarcities also tend to develop faster. Twenty percent of West Africa's forests was logged between 1980 and 1990, and the populations of important species of bottom-dwelling fish off Antarctica were seriously reduced barely a decade after large-scale harvesting began.[17] In general, the increased pace of resource depletion means that societies have less time to adjust their institutions and technologies.

Because humans are now consuming a very broad spectrum of renewable resources at very high rates, serious scarcities can affect many resources simultaneously or in quick succession. This multiplicity of scarcities can make it harder to find relatively abundant resources to substitute for scarce ones.[18] Moreover, substitution often simply propagates scarcity by making the substitutes scarce, too. Around the world, for instance, fishermen have depleted high-value species of fish, and they have moved on to successively lower-value species.[19] The same is true with timber: in heavily exploited forests, loggers have moved from old, large-diameter hardwoods and softwoods to small-diameter softwoods that can be made into products like particle board.

The ingenuity requirement to compensate for scarcities of renewables is generally greater than that for nonrenewables. This difference is not widely recognized: for example, economists generally contend that scarcities of renewables and nonrenewables pose similar economic problems and consequently stimulate similar conservation, substitution, and innovation effects (that is, similar ingenuity responses). To the extent that economists acknowledge a difference, it is in the cause of scarcity: renewables are more often *open access* and therefore tend to be depleted or degraded more quickly and with less effect on market prices.[20]

In chapter 3, however, I noted how renewables are crucially different from nonrenewables. Often, highly interdependent systems of renewables exhibit nonlinear and interactive responses to human perturbations.[21] These characteristics boost the need for ingenuity: societies must be smarter to anticipate sudden or severe changes in the behavior of resource systems and deal with these changes once they occur. Moreover, some renewables, such as water, have properties that are essential to biological survival; although ingenuity can be used to conserve or find more of these resources, substitution of other resources or substances is often not an option (nothing can substitute for water in the tissues of a living organism). Because the options for responding to resource scarcity are therefore restricted, society's need for ingenuity rises. Finally, because systems of renewables are highly interdependent, as I emphasized in chapter 3, the overexploitation of one resource can produce ramifying effects throughout its associated resource systems (overlogging a forest can affect local regional hydrological cycles and fish runs in rivers, for instance). Consequently, an economy not only has to find substitutes for goods and services provided by the overexploited resource itself, it must often find substitutes for the resources that are causally dependent on that overexploited resource.

As consumption/resource ratios rise for many renewables, therefore, it is safe to say that some societies will face an increasingly complex, unpredictable, and urgent decision-making environment that will boost their requirement for social and technical ingenuity.[22] Scientists and engineers will need to respond to increasingly complicated and fast-paced substitution and conservation needs. Politicians, bureaucrats, corporate managers, and community leaders will have to be increasingly clever social engineers to adjust existing institutions and to design, build, and operate new ones that allow technical ingenuity to flourish and that promote nontechnological adaptation to scarcity. People at all levels of society will have to be evermore ingenious and quickfooted to minimize activities that deplete resources, to negotiate bargains among competing groups to diffuse scarcity's costs, and to encourage—perhaps through market mechanisms—the development of new technologies.

To maintain satisfaction as consumption/resource ratios rise, societies will need to run resource systems ever more efficiently. System optimization will often demand tightly coupled and highly complex horizontal and vertical management. (By horizontal management, I mean management that operates at a single level of social organization such as the village or nation-state; vertical management cuts across these levels, integrating, for example, the village, national, international, and biospheric levels.) This management will require great ingenuity.[23] As Kenneth Watt and Paul Craig note, "such a society would be characterized by great efficiency in resource use, very diverse energy and materials sources and pathways through the system, a very large number of types of system components (i.e. occupations), and a rich variety of internal control mechanisms."[24] But even if the requisite ingenuity is supplied, the systems will still be vulnerable to sudden shocks, because many environmental scarcities are interconnected and unpredictable, and because efficiency and productivity requirements will tend to compress the time between events, reduce opportunities for recovery, and increase interactions among system elements.[25]

Furthermore, even if societies manage their resource systems exceptionally well, fundamental physical, biological, and social constraints may make it difficult to fully compensate for the effects of scarcity. These constraints include inescapable time lags that affect a society's ability to mitigate scarcity, like the time needed for a new forest to grow, for a new technology to be disseminated, or for cultural change to take place.[26] As scarcity worsens, ever greater amounts of ingenuity may be required to circumvent these constraints. In some cases, they may make it impossible to maintain aggregate social satisfaction, and the requirement for ingenuity will become, for all intents and purposes, infinite.

Of course, optimists are not daunted by such problems. Humans, they argue, will supply the needed ingenuity. For instance, Aaron Wildavsky, Todd La Porte, and others contend that system accidents and shocks can be prevented by careful organizational design; Dennis Avery argues that developing countries can easily overcome their food production problems; and Thomas Schelling and Jesse Ausubel contend that global warming is not of great concern because technology and wealth are making us less dependent on climate.[27] I therefore now turn to ingenuity supply.

Some Factors Limiting the Supply of Ingenuity

Every generation feels it lives on the cusp of chaos. People invariably believe that change is too rapid and that the world is becoming too complex and unpredictable, yet in the end they often manage well. In fact, the past two centuries have brought major material and social progress for much of humanity, despite rapidly growing populations and sometimes serious resource scarcities at the regional level. Many optimists see no reason why the future should be different from the past. Thus, Julian Simon writes, "there is no physical or economic reason why human resourcefulness and enterprise cannot forever continue to respond to impending shortages and existing problems with new expedients that, after an adjustment period, leave us better off than before the problem arose."[28] While I acknowledge the extraordinary potential of human resourcefulness and enterprise, I nonetheless argue that some societies—especially poor societies—will not be able to supply the unprecedented amounts of ingenuity they will need to solve their emerging scarcity problems.

Many economic optimists implicitly assume that the price elasticity of supply of human ingenuity is nearly infinite, which suggests that an increase in demand for ingenuity will produce an equal increase in quantity supplied with no increase in price.[29] Neoclassical economists have also traditionally assumed that ingenuity—or *technology*, as they usually call it—is available exogenously: it is a free public good that individuals, firms, and organizations access as necessary.[30] These economists do not explicitly address where the technology originally comes from.

Other analysts argue that ingenuity is generated endogenously. There are several distinct perspectives here. Induced innovation theorists, such as the agricultural economists Yujiro Hayami and Vernon Ruttan (chap. 3), propose that changes in factor endowments, notably of land, labor, and energy, are reflected in market price signals. These signals in turn stimulate technological and institutional innovation that loosens constraints on agricultural growth. Similarly, Ester Boserup argues that cropland scarcity induced by population growth increases the input of labor into agricultural production and stimulates land-saving changes in cropping practices.[31] Higher frequency of cropping encourages the evolution of secure private property rights, while infrastructural economies of scale produced by a larger population lead to the growth of markets and labor specialization.[32] Julian Simon further contends that larger populations mean more heads to generate the ideas that help societies overcome resource scarcity.[33]

New economic growth theorists also endogenize the generation of technologies. However, rather than focusing on the stimulus provided by changing factor proportions and prices, or on the idea-generating potential of a larger population, they focus on the relationship between the pool of human capital in an economy or firm and the generation of technology. This emphasis is not incompatible with the propositions outlined above: the induced-innovation theorists stress how population growth and external stimuli produce innovation, whereas the new economic growth theorists stress the intervening processes that crucially involve human capital.

Optimistic views about ingenuity supply have not escaped criticism. David Feeny, for instance, focuses on the supply of social ingenuity in the form of new institutions. He notes that many theorists interpret the Coase theorem to mean that societies will alter their institutions when benefits exceed costs.[34] "Although the authors do not, in general, explicitly state that change will occur whenever the marginal social benefits exceed the marginal social costs (including transaction costs) the lack of attention to the supply side of institutional change leaves that impression." He then gives pointed examples of the "failure to adopt innovations with positive net social benefits," and he concludes that "the supply of institutional change is important; trends in the demand, although necessary, are not sufficient for understanding the path of change."[35]

I discuss here four factors that can limit the supply of social and technical ingenuity: market failure, social friction, shortage of capital, and constraints on science. Constraints on science are, in this model, independent of resource scarcity; market failure, social friction, and availability of capital are sometimes affected by scarcity. Each of these four factors can interfere with either idea-generation or idea-implementation; in either case, they will not only limit the total supply of ingenuity but also limit the rate at which it is supplied. These factors can therefore induce critical time lags between the need for ingenuity and its supply.

Market Failure

Traditional economic models imply that an economy will supply the needed ingenuity if prices accurately reflect the costs of resource use. But prices often do not fully reflect these costs. Not only is ingenuity thereby undersupplied, but low resource prices encourage overconsumption of the resource, which can raise the requirement for ingenuity.

Two types of market failure are important.[36] First, as noted in chapter 4, many resources, especially renewables like hydrological cycles and productive seas, cannot be physically controlled or divided into saleable units for the exclusive use of specific consumers. It is therefore hard to assign clear property rights, and they remain *open-access* resources that are vulnerable to overexploitation.[37] At best, their scarcity is indirectly reflected in the prices of marketable resources that are dependent on them. For example, damage to ocean ecosystems can cause fish prices to rise.

Second, even if property rights are clear, market prices may still not fully reflect the costs of resource use. Resource extraction or use can produce *negative externalities*—such as river siltation from upstream deforestation—that are not incorporated in the resource's price.[38] In addition, economic actors often cannot participate in market transactions in which they have an interest, either because they lack the necessary wealth or because they are distant from the transaction process in time or space. Finally, resource systems are often so complex that our knowledge of their functions and resilience, and of the likelihood of negative interaction and threshold effects, is grossly inadequate. Without good knowledge, it is impossible for either private economic actors or society to price resources accurately.

Unfortunately, even if prices accurately reflect the costs of resource use, ingenuity may still be undersupplied, because it has some characteristics of a public good. Rising resource prices may increase the demand for ingenuity, but ingenuity will be undersupplied if entrepreneurs cannot capture the social benefits of the ingenuity they produce.[39]

These problems are not insurmountable. Societies can try to provide secure, enforceable, and transferable property rights for both resources and ingenuity (thus, the importance of improved systems of intellectual property rights); they can develop economic mechanisms to internalize more of the costs of resource use and to represent the interests of a broader range of parties; they can remove structural impediments to efficient markets, such as subsidies; and they can increase their knowledge of the services and functions of resource systems. But these tasks are not easy. "Getting the prices right" demands copious social ingenuity. Thus, paradoxically, market failures that negatively affect the supply of ingenuity boost the need for ingenuity to alleviate the very same market failures.

Poor countries are particularly disadvantaged because they start with underdeveloped economic institutions. They therefore need more social ingenuity to reform existing institutions and establish new ones. Moreover, modern markets are complicated and fragile social arrangements; getting them working right is not a matter—as many conservative economists would have use believe—of simply reducing government interference in the economy. They are defined and structured by an intricate system of institutions, laws, rights, and norms (what I have previously referred to as *ideational factors*). These include laws governing contracts and credit; laws discouraging price-rigging and the excessive concentration of capital; limits on corporate liability; regulatory regimes for natural monopolies and stock and bond markets; a stable banking system; predictable and restrained macroeconomic policies; a strong and incorrupt judicial system to enforce property rights and contracts; and agreements among levels of government permitting the movement of labor, capital, and other productive resources. Taken together, most of these arrangements increase the expected value of private gains and decrease the expected value of private costs from investment.

The state plays the central role in establishing this system of institutions. It must also provide other supports to an efficient market, including a competent civil service, high rates of literacy, a well-functioning infrastructure of transportation, communication, and irrigation systems, and a relatively egalitarian distribution of wealth. Moreover, the public-good character of ingenuity means that the state must often intervene in the economy to increase ingenuity's supply through research, development, and extension services.[40] The requirement for ingenuity within the state is therefore high: establishing a vigorous market in a developing country "demands accurate intelligence, inventiveness, active agency and sophisticated responsiveness to a changing economic reality."[41]

Social Friction

Severe scarcity can generate *social friction*—fierce competition among narrow interest groups—that impedes the supply of social ingenuity in the form of new and reformed institutions, such as markets.

Mancur Olson's pioneering work helps us understand how.[42] Olson analyzes the abilities of different social coalitions—from unions to farm and manufacturing associations—to provide collective goods for their members despite the tendency of members to free ride. For our purposes, he makes three critical points. First, he shows that small coalitions can generally organize themselves more quickly and pursue their interests with greater force than large groups.[43] They therefore have political power disproportionate to their size, and they can be more nimble, focused, and effective in their lobbying.

Second, Olson notes that this disproportionate power will be particularly acute in "unstable" societies, a category encompassing many developing countries, because large coalitions need time and social stability to establish themselves and grow. The governments of unstable countries are therefore "systematically influenced by the interests, pleas, and pressures" of small coalitions.[44]

Third, small coalitions invariably pursue narrowly defined self-interest and are very unlikely to act on behalf of the commonweal. They are almost exclusively *distributional coalitions*, because they strive to redistribute the wealth in the system rather than to increase it. For all practical purposes, Olson writes, there is "no constraint on the social cost such an organization will find it expedient to impose on the society in the course of obtaining a larger share of the social output for itself."[45]

In previous chapters, we have seen that increased environmental scarcity often exacerbates social segmentation, sharpens cleavages among groups, and provokes vigorous action by groups to protect or enhance their interests, action that includes resource capture and rent-seeking. Building on Olson's arguments, we can assume that small groups or coalitions generally pursue their interests better than large ones, especially in developing countries; those that already have wealth, power, and status because of their position in the social order are particularly advantaged. Furthermore, as we have seen, future resource scarcities are likely to create a more complex, unpredictable, and rapidly changing decisionmaking environment. This environment will accentuate the relative power of small coalitions, since they can more quickly identify their interests and focus their efforts.

Because small coalitions usually have narrow interests, they often act to impede the institution building that reflects the broader interest of society. They hinder efforts to reform existing or establish new social institutions, laws, and behaviors if these efforts encroach on coalition interests, as they often do.[46] This *social friction* makes it harder to focus and coordinate social activities, talents, and resources in response to scarcity. As Olson says, narrow coalitions "interfere with an economy's capacity to adapt to change and to generate new innovations."[47] Thus, the coalitions provoked to action by scarcities will sometimes block solutions to the very same scarcities.[48]

How might narrow coalitions have this effect? One mechanism is particularly important. Increasing social friction affects incentives for political entrepreneurs to produce and deliver the social ingenuity needed for new institutions. Public institutions will be supplied at the socially optimum level only in specific circumstances: the private rate of return to the political entrepreneurs who can create these institutions must approach the social rate of return.[49] The actions of narrow coalitions can raise the private costs and reduce the private benefits of such institution building, which in turn increases the gap between private and social returns and results in a socially suboptimal supply of institutions. Ruttan and Hayami thus note that "the supply of institutional innovation depends critically on the power structure or balance among vested interest groups in society."[50]

I have already discussed several cases in which scarcity-induced social friction impeded the supply of ingenuity. For instance, in chapter 3 we saw that scarcities of cropland and water in Bangladesh—scarcities arising from both skewed resource distribution and population growth—induce some agricultural innovation, but they also inflame existing distributional struggles among coalitions. These struggles in turn have obstructed reform of water-control institutions and the deployment of irrigation technologies.[51] In chapter 5, we learned that huge migrations of South African blacks from environmentally devastated former homelands into the country's urban areas have increased intergroup segmentation and encouraged warlordism. The resulting conflicts, especially in the townships and squatter settlements of Kwa-Zulu-Natal Province, have overwhelmed local institutions and impeded their reform.

The case of Haiti, which I will discuss in detail in the next chapter, offers another example. Paul Wallich notes that over 90 percent of the country has been denuded, leaving it "bereft of natural resources crucial to economic survival." Scarcities of forests and soil exacerbate poverty in rural communities and produce significant profit opportunities for powerful elites. Both these changes deepen divisions and distrust between rich and poor and hinder beneficial change. Thus, for example, the Haitian army and remnants of the notorious *Tontons Macoutes* have ruined some reforestation projects by destroying the projects' tree seedlings. These groups fear that such projects will threaten their control of forest resource extraction, undermine their high profits from wood and charcoal sales, and bring together disgruntled rural people. In general, Wallich argues that "wealthy landowners had little incentive to raise their opponent's standard of living, and peasants saw no reason to improve their husbandry as long as those above them stood ready to extract whatever surplus they might produce."[52]

A similar process occurs with the exploitation of Pakistan's forests.[53] Although deforestation has a long history in the country, rates have been particularly high over the past decade, in large part because of rising demand for fuelwood in both rural and urban areas. Legislation on land management and property rights has failed to ensure firm regulation of the forest industry. In many cases, strong urban and rural groups have appropriated both community and government lands for themselves. As a result, a *timber mafia* is now ravaging Pakistan's dwindling forests.[54] Those groups involved are motivated by opportunities to make huge profits from trade in scarce wood resources. They have acquired leading roles in forest institutions and are deeply entrenched in the state's administrative machinery. During the late 1970s and early 1980s, they used large transfers of state development funds to open up forest areas for exploitation. Road and electrification programs facilitated commercial cutting while reinforcing the political and social control of traditional tribal leaders and Sayyeds (direct descendants of Muhammad) over indigenous populations. Thereafter, the collusion of forest officials, large forestland owners, and contractors allowed timber extraction to proceed with little significant regulation. These groups and individuals have been able both to manipulate legislation to serve their interest and to block changes in the law that would make forest management more participatory and sustainable.[55]

In light of the above discussion and examples, it appears that two characteristics of a society—two contextual factors—will especially influence the degree of social friction caused by environmental scarcity and the extent to which this friction hinders the supply of ingenuity. First, a society will manifest more social friction if its culture encourages selfish individual or group behavior; a "culture of selfishness" causes people to retreat more readily into narrow coalitions as scarcity worsens. For example, Filipino culture encourages cooperation within groups rather than among groups; the resulting isolation of groups from each other—the oft-remarked clannishness of the society—undermines the concept of national welfare.[56] As a consequence, "severe want and poverty do not produce cooperation but rather seem to encourage indifference and greed."[57]

The opposite of a culture of selfishness is a culture of good will, reciprocity, civic-mindedness, and trust. Social theorists acknowledge the importance of these virtues to economic well-being.[58] A culture with strong norms of civic-mindedness can impede the rise of narrow coalitions as scarcity worsens. In fact, scarcity can sometimes lead to greater unity and commitment to the common good, rather than to fragmentation. Thus, Geertz observed that the burden of poverty caused by scarcity of cropland in Java was shared among community members.[59]

Second, if narrow coalitions have already penetrated the state, social friction will have a particularly strong affect on society's capacity to reform and build institutions. As I discussed in chapter 5, such a state will tend to grant monopoly rents to powerful coalitions when they mobilize to defend or enhance their interests.[60] And because acute scarcity makes it easier to establish monopoly control over resources, it increases opportunities for rent-seeking behavior. Once entrenched, these rent-seekers are potent obstacles to institutional reform. The degree of penetration is affected by the broader institutional character of the society. Indian democracy, for example, has encouraged the mobilization of narrow coalitions, yet India does not have strong political parties that can mediate between these coalitions and the state. The result is a state deeply penetrated by narrow coalitions. This "interest group activism in a weak-party democracy has contributed to deceleration of public investment and low economic growth rates."[61]

An examination of specific cases shows that these two contextual factors—the tendency of the society's culture to encourage group selfishness and the autonomy of its state—have a critical influence on whether a society can adapt to severe environmental scarcity. We thus find that the distributionists (chap. 3) are right to emphasize social imbalances in the distribution of wealth and power, although their story is not complete. Highly unequal social arrangements help break down a binding sense of community and boost the probability that the state will be penetrated and controlled by elite interests. Both these developments interact with scarcity to generate social friction; this social friction, in turn, hinders the supply of social and technical ingenuity needed to deal with scarcity.

Much like market failure, social friction that hinders the supply of ingenuity also pushes up the requirement for ingenuity. Increased social friction boosts the complexity of a political and economic situation that may already be highly complex because of scarcity. As Olson says, "the accumulation of distributional coalitions increases the complexity of regulation, the role of government, and the complexity of understandings."[62] Governments, policymakers, and community leaders need more ingenuity to generate solutions to gridlock brought about by these coalitions and to motivate, coopt, coerce, and circumvent obstructionist groups.[63]

Some people will object to the argument in this section. They will assert that conflicts caused by scarcity, rather than interfering with the supply of ingenuity, often generate greater creativity and opportunities for innovation. There are two versions of this response. The more extreme version, common to radical distributionists, is that violent revolution by exploited groups dissolves rigid social relations that obstruct beneficial institutional and economic change. I agree that sclerotic and exploitative social structures can reduce the supply of ingenuity and that, sometimes, severe conflict is needed to change them. But if the state is penetrated by rent-seekers and status quo interests, successful and sustainable institutional reform through conflict usually requires that one of the groups challenging the state win the conflict; once in control of the state, the winning group can reestablish order and build new institutions. If challenger groups cannot win and severe conflict persists within the society, new institutions will not take root. In addition, such conflict usually destroys knowledge and physical assets, producing long-term economic and political debilitation—and a reduced supply of ingenuity—after the conflict ends.

Robert Putnam's well-known book, *Making Democracy Work*, represents a more moderate challenge to my argument here. In it, Putnam contends that "strong" societies make "strong" states: pluralistic competition among diverse social groups strengthens norms of reciprocity, which in turn strengthen social institutions, including the state.[64] I would argue, however, that Putnam is not sufficiently attentive to the range of possible meanings of group association that might exist in the minds of the individuals making up these social groups. As a result, he does not distinguish between types of social competition among groups; most importantly, he does not adequately acknowledge that some types of intergroup competition may be uncivil in ways that are socially destructive.[65] The weaker the feelings of civic-mindedness and of broader community—of feelings of community extending beyond the narrow group—in the minds of individual group members, the more likely that severe social competition among groups (perhaps spurred by environmental scarcity) will rend institutions, debilitate the state, and divide social group from social group.

Putnam does seem to acknowledge that pluralistic competition must be bounded by some tacit understanding of civic responsibility. But in his model, "trust" and norms of reciprocity (that is, social capital) are dependent variables, arising from interactions within the dense network of civic associations that make up a vigorous civil society. In my argument above, on the other hand, these factors—to which I would add a sense of responsibility to the commonweal—are to a large extent independent or exogenous, part of the substrate of culture that influences how a society responds to severe stress. To the extent that trust and a sense of responsibility to the commonweal are not entirely exogenous, environmental scarcity may actually weaken them through the social segmentation processes described in chapter 5. In other words, social segmentation can tear apart the civic networks essential to building and maintaining social trust and good will; in turn, loss of trust and good will removes a critical restraint on the severity and harmfulness of the social competition that arises from greater environmental scarcity.[66]

Capital Availability

The amount of ingenuity supplied in response to scarcity will generally be lower in societies with less financial and human capital. Capital is needed for vigorous research by scientists and engineers into opportunities to mitigate and adapt to scarcity. Access to credit helps private entrepreneurs exploit these opportunities and diffuse useful knowledge through the broader economy. Political entrepreneurs need financial capital to provide selective incentives and side payments to coalitions that block institutional change. And the state needs capital to provide public goods like infrastructure and resource monitoring.

Many societies facing serious resource scarcities are poor; moreover, the often predatory behavior of their elites further reduces general capital availability.[67] Scientific and technical research is therefore not well supported, causing heavy reliance on externally developed and often inappropriate technologies.[68] Efforts to build indigenous research capability in developing societies are hindered by shortages of lab equipment, computers, journals and books.[69] Capital shortages lead to deteriorating or inadequate transportation and communications systems and make it difficult for states to implement new policies in response to scarcity or to enforce laws on resource use. Thus, the Filipino government cannot afford to pay for enough four-wheel-drive vehicles, two-way radios, coast guard ships, and police officers to stop widespread illegal logging along its northern coasts.[70]

Shortages of human capital frequently cripple the supply of ingenuity. In 1980, sub-Saharan Africa had about forty-five scientists and engineers in research and development for every million people, while the figure in developed countries was 2,900.[71] Since then, the situation in Africa has worsened. The United Nations reports that by 1987 nearly a third of Africa's highly skilled labor had left for Europe and that the continent as a whole lost sixty-thousand middle and high-level managers between 1985 and 1990.[72] The experts that remain face surging demands for their expertise. Kenya, for example, suffers from increasingly onerous problems of water scarcity, but in 1993 had only three Ph.D.-level hydrologists.[73] (Nonetheless, compared to other poor countries, Kenya is relatively well-endowed with technical expertise). Africa is not the only developing region to suffer a critical brain drain. In India, 30 percent of graduates of the Indian Institute of Technology in Bombay have emigrated since the early 1970s, as have 45 percent of graduates of the All-India Institute of Medical Sciences.[74]

Increasing resource scarcity can affect capital availability by decreasing savings and by diverting capital to serve short-term needs. Severe scarcity often shortens society's time horizons and may thereby shift funds from savings to consumption; it may also shift investment from long-term adaptation to immediate tasks of scarcity management and mitigation. In the face of agricultural shortfalls caused by soil erosion, for instance, societies will tend to invest first in fertilizer production and imports and only later in research on erosion-resistant crops.

Constraints on Science

Economic and technological optimists have an unrealistic faith in humankind's ability to unravel and manage the myriad processes of nature. There is no a priori reason to expect that scientific and technical ingenuity can overcome all types of scarcity. In fact, four constraints on modern science hinder ingenuity's supply. (A great deal could be said about each of these constraints, but I will touch on them only briefly here.)

First are human cognitive limits.[75] Humans do not have infinite ability to understand and manage the nonlinear, multivariate, and often chaotic processes of ecological-social systems. The relationships in some of these systems are "simply too numerous and complex to be grasped, much less controlled, by the human intellect."[76] We may never be able to foresee the manifold consequences of our adaptation and intervention strategies. These cognitive limits are likely to be more serious when human capital is in short supply, because individual experts and decision makers face a greater load of tasks.

Our ability to supply ingenuity is probably restricted by cognitive features of the human brain that evolved in ecological circumstances entirely different from today's.[77] Bounded rationality and various cognitive shortcuts limit the time we use to search for solutions to problems. These shortcuts appear to work, the sociologist Charles Perrow argues, "because our world is really quite loosely coupled, and has a lot of slack and buffers in it that allow for approximations rather than complete accuracy."[78] Unfortunately, our efforts to alleviate scarcity by increasing the efficiency and output of our resource-use systems often boost complexity and tighten coupling, which places a premium on precise, optimal decisions. In such cases, cognitive shortcuts may be more dangerous than helpful.

A second constraint on science is the escalating cost of research. Scientific research generally becomes more costly as it probes further into nature.[79] Many of the scarcities facing poor countries demand advanced science like molecular biology that they cannot afford, especially when faced with capital shortages. A third constraint arises from the cumulative nature of scientific knowledge: each new discovery must build on a host of earlier ones. The pace of discovery is marked by jumps and lags as scientists make breakthroughs or lose time pursuing fruitless leads. This pace cannot be easily forced, especially in basic science where the work's ultimate practical use is not clear.[80]

A final constraint is science's vulnerability to social turmoil. Science is a fragile social process that requires not only a great variety and abundance of resource inputs, but also a nonhierarchical institutional structure, a dense network of connections between like-minded innovators, and a popular culture that respects and promotes science.[81] Recent developments in Russia show science's sensitivity to social context: the country's upheaval in the 1990s has crippled its vast research establishment and has caused a decline in respect for analytical thought and a sharp rise in occult and antiscience movements.[82] If this book's general argument is correct, and environmental scarcities sometimes contribute to major social disruption, then the science that poor societies need to address their underlying scarcities will often not be available, because of the disruptive influence of these very same scarcities.

Conclusions

In this chapter, I have argued that we should focus on the role of ingenuity if we want to understand the factors that determine whether societies successfully adapt to environmental scarcity. As resource scarcity worsens, the social and technological problems faced by societies generally become more complex, unpredictable, and urgent. These trends raise the requirement for ingenuity. But I have also identified several factors that can constrain ingenuity supply: market failure, social friction, shortages of capital, and constraints on science. Some societies therefore experience a chronic ingenuity gap between their requirement for and their supply of ingenuity; as a result, they are vulnerable to environmental scarcity's harsh social effects described in chapter 5.

Other analysts will contend that standard economic responses to scarcity usually stimulate a sufficient flow of ingenuity to overcome the constraints I identify. Or they will contend that new developments in national and international economies, including increased trade and investment and the vastly increased flow of ideas through expanded communications networks, will provide enough ingenuity when and where poor countries need it. Although not convinced by such claims, I have mainly sought to reframe the tired debate on adaptation to scarcity and to raise some issues deserving further thought and research.

My argument needs careful interpretation. First, the size of the ingenuity gap does not necessarily correlate with the extent of social disutility caused by scarcity. The amount of ingenuity needed to remedy a particular scarcity might be high, while the social disutility caused by the scarcity is low, or vice versa. However, a large ingenuity gap does indicate that the disutility—whatever its degree—will probably endure. Second, and most importantly, an adequate supply of ingenuity is a necessary but not sufficient condition for constant or increased social satisfaction. The social distribution of the ingenuity supplied, how it is applied, and for what purpose it is applied also affect aggregate satisfaction. A full account of the social and economic role of ingenuity therefore requires separate models of ingenuity's social distribution and use.

Although preliminary and limited in power, my argument nonetheless has interesting implications for the debate over intergenerational equity. Economists often note that the costs of conserving natural resources are usually borne in the present while the benefits arrive only in the future. Given that humans generally have a positive discount rate, they claim, it makes more sense for poor countries to invest in economic growth and thereby bequeath greater financial, physical, and human capital to future generations. Their descendants can use this capital to address the resource scarcities they face at that time, assuming the payoff is more immediate. I have argued that extra capital will indeed aid the supply of ingenuity. But there are also real disadvantages to waiting: future generations may have to face scarcities much more complex and urgent than today's, which could sharply raise their need for ingenuity; furthermore, future societies may experience greater social friction due to scarcity, which could impede ingenuity supply. In some societies, the additional capital will probably not, by itself, compensate for this ingenuity deficit.

My analysis consequently puts a premium on prevention of scarcity, not on subsequent adaptation to it. (In the terminology introduced at the beginning of this chapter, we should therefore pursue first-stage policy interventions over second-stage interventions.) The optimism of economists and other adaptationists who have boundless faith in the potential of human ingenuity when spurred by necessity is, I believe, imprudent. We are taking a huge gamble if we follow the path they suggest, which is to wait until environmental scarcities are critical and watch human ingenuity burst forth in response. Should it turn out, in the end, that this strategy was wrong for some societies, there will no turning back. These societies will have burned their bridges, because their soils, waters, and forests will be irreversibly damaged.

In the next chapter, I will show how the harsh social effects produced by severe scarcities—including the impoverishment, migration, social segmentation, and institutional failure discussed in chapter 5—boost grievances and shift the balance of power between challenger groups and the state. These changes, in turn, raise the likelihood of various forms of rural and urban violence.

Appendix _____

Can Poor Countries Attain Endogenous Growth?

WITH EDWARD BARBIER

In recent years there has been a vigorous debate about the role of technological innovation in long-term economic growth. At the debate's forefront are new theoretical models in economics that have been termed *endogenous* or *new* growth theory.[1] A key feature of these models is that technological innovation—the development of new technological ideas or designs—is endogenously determined by private and public sector choices within the economic system rather than being exogenously available to the system (as assumed in more conventional neoclassical growth models). This endogenous innovation overcomes diminishing returns to physical capital, thus allowing per capita accumulation of capital and economic growth to be sustained at a positive rate indefinitely.[2] In other words, if public and private sector investments in human capital and innovation are "optimal" then it is possible for an economy to attain a perpetually constant rate of growth in output and consumption.

The current debate over the role of innovation in economic growth has fostered empirical investigations across countries and regions to determine the extent to which long-term economic growth rates fit the predictions of endogenous growth or neoclassical growth theories.[3] The cross-country comparisons of growth rates have pointed to an important issue for analysts: Why is it that the long-term economic growth rates of poor countries as a group are not catching up with those of rich countries?

According to the endogenous growth school, the answer is fairly straightforward. Poor countries fail to achieve higher rates of growth because they fail to generate or use new technological ideas to reap greater economic opportunities. In particular, according to Romer, "the feature that will increasingly differentiate one geographic area (city or country) from another will be the quality of public institutions. The most successful areas will be the ones with the most competent and effective mechanisms for supporting collective interests, especially in the production of new ideas."[4]

Even some critics of this endogenous growth explanation concede that institutional and policy failures are an important reason for the inability of poor countries to attain high growth rates. For example, Pack argues that "the potential 'benefit' of backwardness is that, if countries could capitalize on their backwardness, they could enjoy a rapid spurt of catch-up growth." However, he also states that "the benefits from backwardness do not accrue automatically but result from purposive activities on the part of individual firms within a general favorable policy environment. This includes a stable macroeconomic policy and institutions designed to facilitate the identification and absorption of technology."[5] Consequently, the inability of poor countries to "take off" economically "can be attributed to failed policies and weak institutions."

We agree that institutional and policy failures in poor economies are important explanations of their inability to innovate sufficiently to achieve higher long-term growth rates. But this is not the whole story. In this appendix we therefore provide a technical elaboration of the argument introduced in this chapter: in many poor economies the depletion and degradation of natural resources—such as croplands, forests, freshwater and fisheries—contribute to this institutional instability and disruption. Resource scarcities can cause social conflicts that disrupt the institutional and policy environment necessary for producing and using new ideas and for absorbing useful knowledge from the rest of the world. Thus, we argue that in many cases resource scarcities may have their most important effect on developing economies, not by directly constraining economic growth (chap. 5), but by indirectly affecting their potential to innovate.

The Romer-Stiglitz Model

Barbier shows that many low-income and lower-middle-income economies—especially those displaying low or stagnant growth rates—are highly resource-dependent.[6] Not only do these economies rely principally on direct exploitation of their resource bases through primary industries (e.g., agriculture, forestry, fishing, etc.), but over 50 percent or more of their export earnings come from a few primary commodities. These economies tend to be heavily indebted and experiencing dramatic land use changes—especially conversion of forest area to agriculture—as well as problems of low agricultural productivity, land degradation, and demographic stress.

On the whole, endogenous growth theorists have not been concerned with the contribution of natural resources to growth or with innovation's role in overcoming resource scarcities.[7] However, for some years resource economists have explored the effects of resource scarcity on growth.[8] They have usually employed neoclassical growth models that assume exogenous rather than endogenous technological change. In the standard model, the expression for production of aggregate output, Q, can be written as $Q = K^{\alpha 1}L^{\alpha 2}R^{\alpha 3}e^{\tau t}$, where K is the stock of physical capital, L is labor, R the resource input, and τ is the constant rate of technological progress. As shown by Stiglitz, this expression can be rewritten as $Q = K^{\alpha 1}L^{\alpha 2}(Re^{(\tau/\alpha 3)t})^{\alpha 3}$, where τ/α_3 is the (exogenous) rate of resource-augmenting technical progress.[9] The results of this analysis have been generally optimistic: even under conditions with exponential population growth and with exhaustible and limited supplies of natural resources that are essential to production, sustained growth and a long-run steady-state level of positive per capita consumption are attainable.[10]

Barbier extends this analysis to an endogenous growth economy.[11] He combines Stiglitz's exhaustible-resource model and Romer's endogenous-growth model to determine whether natural resource scarcity is necessarily a binding constraint on growth.[12] In this model, the production function becomes

$$Q = \eta^{(\rho-1)}A^{\rho}K^{\alpha 1}L^{\alpha 2}R^{\alpha 3}(H - H_A)^{\alpha 4},$$

where the additional terms include η, which is the amount of foregone capital necessary to create one unit of durable goods; A, the stock of "ideas" or technical designs; H, the total stock of human capital; H_A the amount of human capital allocated to innovation; and the parameter

$$\rho = (1 - \alpha_1) = \alpha_2 + \alpha_3 + \alpha_4.$$

Assuming η is constant, this expression can be rewritten as

$$Q = \eta^{(\rho-1)}(A^{(\rho/\alpha 3)}R)^{\alpha 3}K^{\alpha 1}L^{\alpha 2}(H - H_A)^{\alpha 4},$$

where $A^{(\rho/\alpha 3)}$ represents resource-augmenting endogenous technological progress.

The results of this new analysis are fairly conclusive: although technological change is endogenous, it is still effectively resource-augmenting. Sufficient allocation of human capital to innovation will ensure that in the long run resource exhaustion can be postponed indefinitely, and the possibility exists of a long-run endogenous steady-state growth rate that allows per capita consumption to be sustained, and perhaps even increased, indefinitely.

However, the main body of the present chapter points to another potential relationship between innovation and resource availability. The chapter argues that an economy's supply of ingenuity may itself be constrained by resource scarcities, especially in low-income countries. By this analysis, an increase in the level of technical ingenuity is similar to the technical innovation discussed by endogenous growth theorists. But the supply of this technical ingenuity depends on an adequate supply of social ingenuity at many levels of society, where social ingenuity consists of ideas applied to the creation, reform, and maintenance of institutions. The process of generating and implementing social ingenuity is both separate from and necessary for technical innovation. Therefore, in agreement with the institutional arguments of Romer and Pack above, the present chapter identifies social ingenuity as a precursor to technical ingenuity.

The chapter also describes two key mechanisms by which resource scarcity can limit both the total supply and the rate of supply of ingenuity. First, increased scarcity often provokes competitive action by powerful elite groups and narrow social coalitions to defend their interests or to profit from the scarcity through rent-seeking behavior. This social friction can hinder efforts to create and reform institutions and can generally make it harder to focus and coordinate human activities, talents, and resources in response to scarcity. Second, endogenous-growth theory notes that capital, especially human capital, is essential to the generation of innovation.[13] Yet, resource scarcity may reduce the availability of human and financial capital for the production of ingenuity by shifting investment from long-term adaption to immediate tasks of scarcity management and mitigation.

Figures 6A.1 and 6A.2 illustrate the contrast between the two views of the innovation process proposed by endogenous growth theory and the preceding chapter. According to the former view (fig. 6A.1), market responses to natural resource scarcity automatically induce endogenous technological change, which leads to resource conservation and substitution, and in turn, to the amelioration of scarcity. However, as noted above, this view assumes that stable economic policies and social institutions exist to facilitate endogenous innovation. This assumption may not be valid for many poor economies.

According to an alternative view based on this chapter's analysis (fig. 6A.2), in some poor countries, resource scarcity itself contributes to an unstable social and policy environment at local, regional, and national levels. Scarcity exacerbates social friction and conflict, which results in an undersupply of social ingenuity. Social friction and conflict interfere directly with the smooth functioning of markets, while the reduced supply of social ingenuity perpetuates market, policy, and institutional failures. These failures in turn undermine the innovation process, in particular, by disrupting the ability of poor economies to generate sufficient human capital, to build research and development capacity, to exploit existing technological knowledge available domestically and internationally, and to produce and disseminate new technologies throughout the economy. In short, while resource scarcity often induces mitigating market and endogenous technological responses, it can also disrupt the stable social and policy environment necessary for these responses to occur automatically.

To explore formally the implications of this hypothesis, Barbier modified the basic Romer-Stiglitz model of an endogenous growth economy to allow for the possibility that innovation might be constrained by increased resource scarcity (that is, a faster rate of resource depletion).[14] He considers two scenarios for the model based on different starting assumptions.

First, Barbier assumes that the long-run rate of innovation will exceed any adverse effects of resource scarcity so that net innovation is still positive. The outcome, in this case, is that the economy continues to exhibit long-run en-

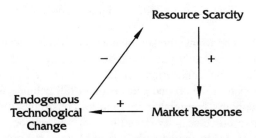

Figure 6A.1. Endogenous Technological Change and Resource Scarcity: Conventional View

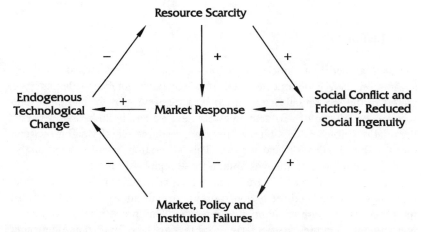

Figure 6A.2. Endogenous Technological Change and Resource Scarcity: Alternative View

dogenous growth, although at a slower rate than predicted by the basic Romer-Stiglitz model. Nevertheless, this scenario implies that sufficient—albeit constrained—endogenous technological change can occur to avert resource exhaustion and to sustain growth in per capita consumption indefinitely. As in the case of the basic Romer-Stiglitz model, therefore, an optimistic outcome is possible.

Second, Barbier assumes that the long-run effects of resource scarcity will just offset additional innovation; that is, increased resource scarcity will so disrupt social and technical innovation that there is no net generation of innovation.[15] However, he then shows that such a constraint on long-run innovation does not necessarily mean that the economy collapses. Sufficient accumulation of technical know-how may occur to avert complete exhaustion of the resource stock in the long run. In this scenario, resource scarcity is still not a binding or absolute constraint: the economy can eventually settle into a long-run steady state in which per capita output and consumption remain constant indefinitely.

This second scenario may be somewhat comforting, because it implies that even low-income economies may avoid dire consequences from resource scarcity. Nonetheless, the implications of Barbier's analysis is that low-income economies trapped in the second scenario will fall behind others. Although a low-income economy facing scarcity-induced constraints on innovation may avoid binding resource-scarcity constraints, it will not be able to match the long-run rates of endogenous technological change and growth displayed by other economies that either face no resource-scarcity constraints or face only limited constraints on innovation.

Conclusion

We have argued that some poor economies may face resource-scarcity constraints on their economic development that have not been adequately explored in the theoretical or empirical literatures on growth, natural resource scarcity, or innovation. To date, analysts have generally addressed separately the relationships between, on the one hand, resource scarcity and growth and, on the other, innovation and growth. This separation has prevented analysts from seeing important linkages among these relationships.

Resource depletion and degradation in poor economies may have their most inimical effect not by directly constraining growth but by indirectly affecting the potential of these economies to innovate. This process may explain why many poor economies, particularly those that are heavily resource-dependent, are failing to achieve high long-run rates of growth and sustained economic development. We have presented preliminary theoretical evidence to support this hypothesis, which merits further empirical research.

7

Violence

IN THE previous three chapters, I have identified key types of environmental scarcity, key negative social effects that result from these scarcities, and several factors that affect whether societies adapt to scarcities. In this chapter I put these pieces together into one encompassing core model of how environmental scarcity and its social effects can cause both rural and urban violence.

Figure 7.1 presents this core model. Supply-induced, demand-induced, and structural scarcities act singly or in interaction to boost local and regional scarcities of cropland, water, forests, and fish. These increased scarcities can reduce or constrain economic productivity (a variable that, within this figure, incorporates scarcity's effects on agricultural production) to the detriment of both local communities and larger regional and national economies. Affected people, who are usually already economically and ecologically marginal, may migrate or be expelled to other rural lands or cities. These migrants often trigger group-identity (usually interethnic) conflicts when they move to new areas, and local decreases in wealth can cause insurgencies and rebellion. Migrations, productivity losses, and the rent-seeking of elites produce social segmentation that deepens group-identity conflict. They also weaken local and national institutions, which decreases central control over ethnic rivalries and increases opportunities for insurgents and elites challenging state authority.

In previous chapters, I have emphasized the critical importance of contextual factors that are often unique to the particular society under study. We can think of figure 7.1 as embedded in a dense fabric of these physical and ideational factors, some of which affect the strength of specific causal links within the figure. Moreover, the arrows across the top of the figure show that there are important feedback loops from the social effects and conflict to the factors that generate scarcity. For example, scarcity-induced conflict might retard the economic development that would reduce high fertility rates. The figure also shows the key points for first-, second-, and third-stage policy interventions (discussed at the start of chapter 6).

The case of Haiti illustrates some of the variables and links in figure 7.1. The irreversible loss of forests and soil in rural areas deepens an economic crisis that spawns internal migration, social strife, and an exodus of boat people. When first colonized by the Spanish in the late fifteenth century and the French in the seventeenth century, Haiti was treasured for its abundant forests. Since then, Haiti has experienced one of the world's most dramatic examples of

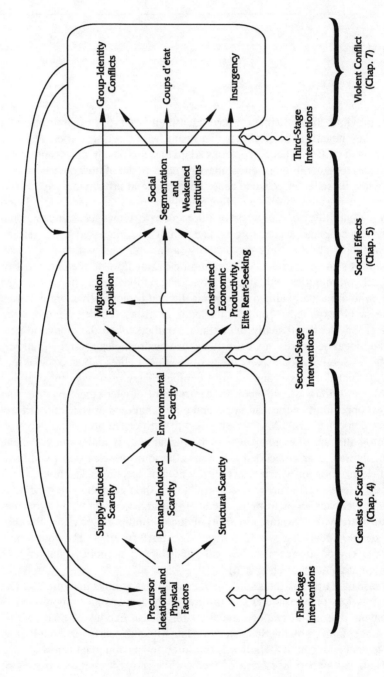

Figure 7.1. The Core Model of the Causal Links between Environmental Scarcity and Violence

environmental despoliation. Less than 2 percent of the country remains forested, and the last timber is being felled at four percent per year.[1] As trees disappear, erosion follows, worsened by the steepness of the land and harsh storms. The United Nations estimates that at least 50 percent of the country is affected by topsoil loss that leaves the land "unreclaimable at the farm level."[2] So much soil washes off the slopes that the streets of the capital, Port-au-Prince, have to be cleared with bulldozers in the rainy season.[3]

Unequal land distribution was not a main cause of this catastrophe. Haiti gained independence in 1804 following a revolt of slaves and ex-slaves against the French colonial regime. Over a period of decades, the old plantation system, associated with slavery, was dismantled and land widely distributed in small parcels.[4] As a result, Haiti's agricultural structure is unique to Latin America, with 73 percent of cropland in private farms of less than four hectares.[5]

Nonetheless, inheritance customs and population growth have combined to produce severe demand-induced scarcity, as in Bangladesh. Land has been subdivided into smaller portions with each generation. Eventually the plots cannot properly support their cultivators, fallow periods are neglected, and greater poverty prevents investment in soil conservation. The poorest leave for steeper hillsides, where they clear the forest and begin farming anew, only to exhaust the land again in a few years.[6] Many peasants try to supplement their falling incomes by scavenging wood for charcoal production, which contributes to further deforestation.

These processes might have been prevented had a stable central government invested in agriculture, industrial development, and reforestation. Instead, since independence, Haiti has endured a ceaseless struggle for power between black and mulatto classes, and the ruling regimes have been solely interested in expropriating any surplus wealth the economy generated. Today, 60 percent of the population is still engaged in agriculture, yet capital is unavailable for agricultural improvement, and the terms of exchange for crop production favor urban regions.[7] The population growth rate has actually increased, from 1.7 percent in the mid-1970s to 1.9 percent today: the UN estimates that the current population of 7.8 million will grow to over 12 million by 2025.[8] As the land erodes and the population grows, incomes shrink: from 1983 to 1993, total agricultural output fell 17 percent, while per capita output plummeted 31 percent.[9]

Analysts agree that rising rural poverty has caused ever-increasing rural-rural and rural-urban migration. In search of work, agricultural workers move from subsistence hillside farms to rice farms in the valleys. From there, they go to cities, especially to Port-au-Prince, which now has a population of over a million. Wealthier farmers and traders, and eventually even those with slimmer resources, try to flee by boat.

In the past, civil strife in Haiti largely occurred within and among elite groups. Now, however, the country's economic and migration stresses—in part generated by environmental crisis—are undoubtedly contributing to broader strife within the population, especially between rich elites and the growing numbers of urban poor. In the aftermath of the collapse of the "Baby Doc" Duvalier regime in 1986, the poor vented their vengeance on those associated with the regime, in particular on Duvalier's informal gangs of enforcers, collectively called *Tontons Macoutes*. During his election campaign and his short first term as President, Jean-Bertrand Aristide reportedly encouraged poor slum-dwellers to attack Haiti's elite. Fearful of uprisings, the subsequent military regime ferociously oppressed the country's poor and peasantry. Even with democracy restored and international sanctions lifted, Haiti will forever bear the burden of its irreversibly damaged environment, which may make it impossible to build a prosperous, just, and peaceful society.

Types of Violent Conflict

In chapters 4 and 5, I addressed the left and central portions of figure 7.1: these represent, respectively, the genesis of scarcity and scarcity's main negative social effects that contribute to violent conflict. But we must still address in detail the right portion of the figure. If agricultural and economic productivity are constrained in some poor societies, if large numbers of people move from their homelands, if societies segment, and if institutions are disrupted, what types of conflict are likely to occur? A number of theories on the nature and sources of social conflict can help us answer this question. Three sets of theories in particular are key: one each at the individual, group, and systemic "levels of analysis."[10]

Frustration-aggression theories use psychological theories of individual behavior to explain civil strife, including revolutions, insurgencies, strikes, riots, and coups. These theories suggest that people become aggressive when they feel frustrated by something or someone they believe is blocking them from fulfilling a strong desire. An important subset of these theories suggests that this frustration and aggression can be caused by *relative deprivation*, which arises when people perceive a widening gap between the level of satisfaction they have achieved (often defined in economic terms) and the level they believe they deserve. Deprivation is therefore *relative to* some subjective standard of equity or fairness, and the size of the perceived gap obviously depends on the beliefs about economic justice held by individuals.[11]

Group-identity theories use social psychological theories of group behavior to explain intergroup conflicts involving nationalism, ethnicity, and religion. These theories aim to explain the way groups reinforce their identities and the "we-they" cleavages that often result. People may have a need for a sense of camaraderie or "we-ness" that can be satisfied in a group when it discriminates against or attacks another group; similarly, a person's sense of self-worth may be strengthened when his or her group's status is enhanced relative to that of other groups. By denigrating outside groups, leaders may try to exploit these needs in order to increase their political power within their own groups, but this behavior makes intergroup divisions deeper and more acrimonious.[12]

Structural theories, which are often grounded in the assumptions of micro-economics and game theory, explain conflicts arising from the rational calculations of actors in the face of perceived external constraints. The structure of an actor's social situation is the perceived set of possible interactions with other actors and the perceived likely outcomes of these interactions. This structure is determined by physical factors such as the number of actors in the system, resource limits, and barriers to movement or communication; by social factors such as shared beliefs and understandings, rules of social interaction, and the set of power relations among actors in the system; and by psychological factors, in particular, the beliefs and preferences of other actors.[13] These structures are assumed to be relatively persistent through time.

Structural theories can be roughly divided into those used to explain conflict in general and those used to explain civil strife. General structural theories, which are often applied to interstate war, suggest that external constraints—such as power imbalances in the international system—can encourage or even compel countries to go to war.[14] Structural theories of civil strife suggest that revolution, insurgency, rioting, and coups d'état are a function of the *opportunity structure* that confronts groups challenging the authority of the state. Serious civil strife is not likely unless the structure of political opportunities facing challenger groups keeps them from expressing their grievances effectively and peacefully, but offers them openings for violence against authority. This opportunity structure depends on the relative power and resources of challenger groups and the state, on the power of groups that might ally themselves with challenger groups or the state, and on the costs and benefits that groups believe they will accrue through different kinds of collective action in support of or in opposition to the state.[15]

Drawing on these theories, we can identify three main kinds of conflict that might arise from environmental scarcity: simple-scarcity conflicts, group-identity conflicts, and insurgencies. These three kinds will rarely, if ever, be found in pure form in the real world, but distinguishing them clearly from each other will aid our understanding of environment-conflict linkages.

Simple-Scarcity Conflicts

Simple-scarcity conflicts are explained and predicted by general structural theories. These are the interstate *resource wars* we intuitively expect when states rationally calculate their interests in a situation where there is a fixed or shrinking pie of natural resources.[16] We have often seen such conflicts in the past: some major wars in this century have undoubtedly been motivated in part by one country's desire to seize another's nonrenewable resources. For instance, prior to and during World War II, Japan sought to secure coal, oil, minerals, and other resources in China and Southeast Asia; Hitler's forces were on their way to seize the Caucasian oil fields when they were stopped at Stalingrad in 1942; and the 1991 Gulf War was at least partly motivated by the desire for oil.[17]

Such conflicts are easily understood within the traditional realist (or balance-of-power) paradigm of international relations theory.[18] Among scholars of international security, it has been conventional wisdom for some time that critical scarcities of natural resources can produce war. During the 1970s, for example, Nazli Chourci and Robert North argued in their book *Nations in Conflict* that countries facing high resource demands and limited resource availability within their territories would seek the needed resources through trade or conquest beyond their boundaries.[19] This *lateral-pressure theory*, they claimed, helped explain some past wars, including World War I.

Four environmental resources in particular would appear likely to spark simple-scarcity conflicts: agriculturally productive land, forests, river water, and fish. Scarcity of these renewables is rising rapidly in some regions; they are often essential for human survival; and they can be physically seized or controlled. But close study of historical and current cases provides little support for this idea. There is, in fact, virtually no evidence that environmental scarcity is a principal cause of major war among modern states.

Arthur Westing has compiled a list of twelve conflicts in the twentieth century involving resources, beginning with World War I and concluding with the Falklands/Malvinas War.[20] Access to oil or minerals was at issue in ten of these conflicts. Just five involved renewable resources, and only two of these—the 1969 Soccer War between El Salvador and Honduras, and the Anglo-Icelandic Cod War of 1972–1973—concerned neither oil nor minerals (cropland was a factor in the former case, and fish in the latter). But, the Soccer War was not a simple-scarcity conflict between states; rather, as explained later in this chapter, it arose from the ecological marginalization of El Salvadoran peasants and their consequent migration into Honduras.[21] And, because the Cod War, despite its name, involved negligible violence, it hardly qualifies as a resource war.

In general, scholars such as Choucri and North have not adequately distinguished between scarcities of renewable and nonrenewable resources as causes of international conflict. They have overlooked two reasons why modern states do not generally fight over renewable resources. First, states cannot easily convert cropland, forests, and fish seized from a neighbor into increased state power; although these resources may eventually generate wealth that can be harnessed by the state for its own ends, this outcome is uncertain and remote in time. In contrast, states can quickly use nonrenewables like oil and iron to build and fuel the military machines of national aggression. (Renewables have not always been less important to state power: in the seventeenth through nineteenth centuries, for example, shortages of timber for naval ships contributed to serious, and sometimes violent, conflict among European powers.[22]) Second, countries with economies highly dependent on renewables tend to be poor, and poor countries cannot easily buy large and sophisticated conventional armies to attack their neighbors. For these reasons, both the incentives and the means to launch resource wars are likely to be lower for renewables than for nonrenewables.

The exception, some might argue, is water, particularly river water: water is a critical resource for personal and national survival, it is essential to the production and use of military power, and rich countries are as dependent on water as poor countries (often, in fact, they are more dependent).[23] Moreover, since river water flows from one area to another, one country's access can be affected by another's actions. About 40 percent of the world's population lives in the 214 river basins shared by more than one country. Thus, at a meeting in Stockholm in August, 1995, Ismail Serageldin, the World Bank's Vice President for Environmentally Sustainable Development, declared that the "wars of the next century will be over water," not oil.[24]

Serageldin is right to focus on the water crisis. As I noted in chapter 5, water scarcity and pollution are already hindering economic growth in some poor regions. With global water use doubling every twenty years, these scarcities—and the subnational social stresses they cause—are going to get much worse. But Serageldin is wrong to declare we are about to witness a surge of water wars.

In reality, wars over river water between upstream and downstream neighbors are likely only in a narrow set of circumstances: the downstream country must be highly dependent on the water for its national well-being; the upstream country must be threatening to restrict substantially the river's flow; there must be a history of antagonism between the two countries; and, most importantly, the downstream country must believe it is militarily stronger than the upstream country. Downstream countries often fear that their upstream neighbors will use water as a means of leverage. This situation is particularly dangerous if the downstream country also believes it has the military power to rectify the situation.

There are, in fact, very few river basins around the world where all these conditions hold now or might hold in the future. The most obvious example is the Nile: Egypt is wholly dependent on the river's water, has historically turbulent relations with its upstream neighbors Sudan and Ethiopia, and is vastly more powerful than either. And, sure enough, Egypt has several times threatened to go to war to guarantee an adequate supply of Nile waters. In 1980, for example, then Egyptian President Anwar el-Sādāt said, "If Ethiopia takes any action to block our right to the Nile waters, there will be no alternative for us but to use force."[25]

Several of the key conditions for simple-scarcity conflict over water also held in the relationship between Lesotho and apartheid South Africa. Facing critical water shortages, South Africa negotiated in vain with Lesotho for thirty years to divert water from the Kingdom's mountains to arid Transvaal. In 1986, South Africa gave decisive support to a successful military coup against Lesotho's tribal government. South Africa stated that it helped the coup because Lesotho had been providing sanctuary to guerrillas of the African National Congress. This was undoubtedly an important motivation, but within months the two governments reached agreement to construct the huge Highlands Water Project to meet South Africa's needs. It seems likely, therefore, that the desire for water was an ulterior motive behind South African support for the coup.[26]

More common than the kind of situation we see in Egypt and South Africa, however, is the situation along the Ganges, where India has constructed a huge dam—the Farakka Barrage—with harsh results for downstream cropland, fisheries, and villages in Bangladesh. Bangladesh is so weak that the most it can do is plead with India to release more water.[27] There is little chance of a water war here between upstream and downstream countries (although the barrage's effects have contributed to the huge migrations out of Bangladesh into India).[28] The same holds true for other river basins where alarmists speak of impending wars, including the Mekong, Indus, Paraná, and Euphrates.

The case of the Euphrates shows how a weak and antagonistic downstream country might respond to upstream diversions. The Euphrates originates in Turkey, and by early in the next century Turkey plans to build a huge complex of twenty dams and irrigation systems along the upper reaches of the river.[29] This $21 billion Great Anatolia Project, if fully funded and built, will reduce the annual average flow of the Euphrates within Syria from 32 billion cubic meters to 20 billion.[30] The water that passes through Turkey's irrigation systems and on to Syria will be laden with fertilizers, pesticides, and salts. Syria is already seriously short of water, with an annual water availability of not much more than a thousand cubic meters per capita.[31] Between 80 and 85 percent of the water for its towns, industries, and farms comes from the Euphrates, and the country has been chronically vulnerable to drought. Furthermore, Syria's population growth rate—at 3.3 percent per year in 1995—is one of the highest in the world, and this adds further impetus to the country's demand for water.

Turkey and Syria have exchanged angry threats over this situation, yet Syria is too weak, relative to Turkey, to rectify the situation directly. Instead, Syria has given sanctuary to guerrillas of the Kurdish Workers Party (the PKK), which has long been waging an insurgency against the Turkish government in eastern Anatolia. Turkey suspects that Syria might be using these separatists to gain leverage in bargaining over Euphrates water. In October 1989, then Prime Minister Turgut Ozal suggested that Turkey might impound the river's water if Syria did not restrain the PKK. Although he later retracted the threat, the tensions have not been resolved, and as of early 1996 there had been no progress on the matter since 1993.[32]

In general, the historical and contemporary evidence shows that violent conflict related to river water is almost always internal rather than international. A careful study of 412 international crises between 1918 and 1994 shows that only 7 involved water issues, and none of those involved significant violence. The author concludes that "as near as we can find, there has never been a single war fought over water," although there is a great deal of evidence of subnational water-related violence.[33]

The huge dams that countries frequently build to deal with water scarcity are especially disruptive. Relocating large numbers of upstream people generates turmoil among the relocatees and clashes with local groups in areas where the relocatees are resettled. The people affected are often members of ethnic or minority groups outside the power hierarchy of their society, and the result is often rebellion by these groups and repression by the state. Moreover, water developments also induce conflict among downstream users over water and irrigable land, as we saw in the Senegal River basin in chapter 5.[34]

Group-Identity Conflicts

Group-identity conflicts are explained and predicted by group-identity theories. In chapter 5, I argued that severe scarcities of land, fuelwood, and water in South Africa's former homelands encouraged large numbers of blacks to move into the country's urban areas, which boosted scarcities of urban environmental resources. These urban scarcities, in turn, increased social segmentation and deepened "we-they" cleavages in townships and squatter settlements, further inflaming struggles over remaining environmental resources in those communities. In general, group-identity conflicts often arise from the large-scale movements of populations that can be caused, in part, by environmental scarcity. As different ethnic and cultural groups are propelled together under stressful circumstances, we often see intergroup hostility with a strong identity dynamic.

The situation in the Bangladesh-Assam region is a good example.[35] The enormous flux of migrants from Bangladesh into Assam and Tripura over the last forty years (chap. 5) has produced pervasive social changes in the receiving regions. It has altered land distribution, economic relations, and the balance of political power between religious and ethnic groups, and it has triggered serious intergroup conflict.[36] Members of the Lalung tribe in Assam, for instance, have long resented Bengali Muslim migrants: they accuse them of stealing the area's richest farmland. In early 1983, during a bitterly contested election for federal offices in the state, violence finally erupted. In the village of Nellie, Lalung tribespeople massacred nearly seventeen hundred Bengalis in one five-hour rampage.[37]

Various contextual factors can exacerbate or dampen the volatility of such situations. For example, during the colonial period, the British used Hindus from Calcutta to administer Assam, and Bengali became the official language. As a result, the Assamese are particularly sensitive to their loss of political and cultural control in the state. On the other hand, as Astri Suhrke points out, migrants are often weak and marginal in their home society and, depending on context, they may remain weak in the receiving society. This weakness limits their ability to organize and to make demands. States play a critical role here: migrants often need the backing of a state (either of the receiving society or an external one) before they have sufficient power to cause conflict, and this backing depends on the region's politics. Without it, migration is less likely to produce violence than silent misery and death, which is rarely destabilizing.[38]

We must remember too that migration is often beneficial. It can act as a safety valve by reducing conflict in the sending area, and migrant remittances can be a huge boon to the sending area's economy. Depending on the economic context, migration can ease labor shortages in the receiving society, as it sometimes has, for instance, in Malaysia. Both Thailand and Malawi in the 1980s and early 1990s showed that developing countries often have an astonishing capacity to absorb migrants without major turmoil.[39]

Environmentally induced migration is not a phenomenon only within and among developing countries, however. As the perceived gap between the quality of life in the North and the South widens, we are seeing greater immigration to the developed world.[40] The people able to move such long distances tend to be relatively wealthy; usually, therefore, they have not been directly affected by environmental scarcity. Nonetheless, scarcity is undoubtedly behind the migration of many poor people from Mexico and Central America to the United States, and from North Africa and the Middle East to Europe. Moreover, to the extent that scarcity constrains economic development in some developing countries or contributes to turmoil (as it has in Haiti), it increases the incentives for the wealthy to move. This migration is shifting the ethnic balance in many cities and regions of developed countries, and their governments are struggling to contain a xenophobic backlash. Such racial strife will undoubtedly become worse.

Insurgencies

Violent challenges to the state—challenges that range from rebellion to guerrilla war and that I collectively call "insurgency"—are explained and predicted by a combination of relative-deprivation theories and structural theories of civil strife. Taken together, these two theoretical perspectives suggest that insurgency is a function of both the level of *grievance* motivating challenger groups and the *opportunities* available to these groups to act violently on their grievances.[41] If a group's sense of relative deprivation rises, then its level of grievance will rise; if the group perceives that the structure of power relations surrounding it has changed in its favor, then it will perceive greater opportunities to address its grievances.

The likelihood of insurgency is greatest when multiple pressures at different levels in society interact to boost grievance and opportunity simultaneously. Environmental scarcity can change both variables by contributing to economic hardship and dislocation, by increasing intergroup segmentation, and by weakening institutions such as the state. Figure 7.1 reflects this insight: it shows that these factors combine to cause insurgency.

With regard to grievances, as environmental scarcities hinder wealth production, relative-deprivation theory says that some groups will become increasingly frustrated and aggrieved by the widening gap between their actual level of economic achievement and the level they feel they deserve. The rate of change is key: the faster the growth of the gap, the greater the grievance. Lower-status groups will be more discontented than others because elites (see chap. 5) will often use their power to profit from scarcity, thus maintaining or increasing their standard of living while others experience hardship. At some point, the strength of grievances of disadvantaged groups may cross a critical threshold, and they will act violently against those groups perceived to be the agents of their economic misery or those thought to be benefiting from a grossly unfair distribution of economic goods in the society.

Although this kind of reasoning is intuitively plausible, once again contextual factors are key to any full understanding of specific cases. Contrary to common intuition, for example, there is no clear correlation between economic hardship and violence.[42] Whether or not people become aggrieved and violent when they confront economic difficulty depends, in part, on their notion of economic justice. People belonging to a culture that inculcates acceptance of deprivation and unequal distribution of wealth—as has been the case among lower castes in India—will not be as prone to violence as people believing they have a right to economic well-being and an egalitarian distribution of wealth. Relative-deprivation theory explicitly incorporates this contextual factor, because deprivation is understood to be relative to an individual or group's subjective notion of economic justice. Because grievance is influenced by such ideational factors, it is quite possible that the people who are most aggrieved by environmental scarcity's effects are not those suffering most severely or directly—in objective terms—from the scarcity. Frequently, for example, it is not the poorest groups that initiate challenges against the state, but middle-income or even elite groups with higher expectations and at least the modest resources necessary to give them the freedom to think about broader issues of economic or social justice.

Unfortunately, even with this added sophistication, research once again shows little correlation between measures of relative deprivation and civil conflict.[43] Part of the problem is that analysts have commonly used societywide averages (such as GDP/capita and average educational levels) to measure deprivation; yet such averages do not tell us anything about which groups within a society are affected particularly harshly by economic difficulties. Moreover, people's subjective ideas of economic justice, which as noted are key to predicting their level of grievance, are notoriously hard to measure. In addition, a sense of injustice and deprivation felt at the level of the individual person does not necessarily express itself as action by a group of people; although individual-level grievance may be a necessary condition for insurgency by a group of people, other conditions must also hold. In particular, conditions must be in place that overcome the tendency of aggrieved individuals to "free ride," which is their tendency to let others undertake the high-risk option of violent action and then to reap the benefits if, and when, things change for the better.[44]

Perhaps most importantly, however, research has shown that to cause civil conflict economic crisis must be severe, persistent, and pervasive enough to erode the legitimacy—that is, the perceived fairness and reasonableness—of the dominant social order and system of government. System legitimacy is therefore a critical intervening variable between economic hardship and insurgency: hardship must first lead to a crisis of legitimacy before widespread insurgency can occur.[45] Legitimacy is influenced by people's subjective *blame system*, which consists of their beliefs about who or what is responsible for their plight.[46] If people come to believe that the state is responsible for their hardship, its legitimacy will be reduced, and the likelihood that they will engage in violence against the state will increase.

In sum, the extent and degree of grievance caused by environmental scarcity is a function of relative deprivation, but this relative deprivation must be measured at the level of specific subgroups within a society, and it is powerfully influenced by local contextual factors, such as the groups' blame systems and conceptions of economic justice. The cases of banditry in rural Sind in Pakistan, the guerrilla war waged by the Sendero Luminoso in Peru, and the New People's Army (NPA) insurgency in the Philippines—all discussed below—are good illustrations of the links between environmental scarcity, grievances, and violence.

Not only can environmental scarcities influence grievances, but, by disrupting institutions and increasing social segmentation, scarcities can also open up structural opportunities for aggrieved groups to challenge the state. The balance of coercive power among social actors affects the probability of success and, as a result, the expected costs and benefits of different actions by challenger groups, the state, and its supporters. A state debilitated by powerful rent-seekers profiting from resource scarcity, by falling revenues and rising demand for services, or by factional conflicts among elites (chap. 5) will be

more vulnerable to seizure or violent challenges by political and military opponents; also vital to state strength is the cohesiveness of the armed forces and
its loyalty to civil leadership.[47] As McAdam says, "*any* event or broad social
process that serves to undermine the calculations and assumptions on which
the political establishment is structured occasions a shift in political opportunities. Among the events and processes likely to prove disruptive of the political
status quo are wars, industrialization, international political realignments, prolonged unemployment, and widespread demographic changes."[48]

Challengers will have greater relative power if their grievances are articulated and actions coordinated through well-organized, well-financed, and autonomous opposition groups. Because grievances felt by individuals are not
automatically expressed by groups, the probability of civil violence is higher
if the society already includes groups that are organized around clear social
cleavages, such as ethnicity, religion, or class. Strong identity groups can help
overcome the free-rider problem mentioned above: it is harder to sit back and
let other people do the dirty work when one feels a strong sense of camaraderie
with the risk-takers. Strong identity groups also act as nuclei around which
highly mobilized and angry elements of the population, such as unemployed
and urbanized young men, coalesce.

Some contextual factors influence both grievance and opportunity. These
factors include the leadership and ideology of challenger groups, rapid urbanization (which I will discuss in detail shortly), and international shocks and
pressures, such as changes in trade and debt relations and in costs of imported
factors of production like energy.[49]

For example in Chiapas, Mexico, in the early 1990s, the weakening of the
PRI regime by economic reform opened up political opportunities for challenger groups, especially land-poor peasants, whose grievances had been
boosted by both scarcity and economic reform itself.[50] Following a debt crisis
in 1982, and under pressure from international financial institutions, Mexico
introduced a sweeping liberalization of its economy. Reductions in market
controls, subsidies, and public credits eroded the regime's ability to bribe and
co-opt challengers. The national and state PRI governments had less money to
spend on maintaining political consensus, and in the absence of political consensus, groups hurt by economic reform and scarcity found it easier to organize ever more vociferous and violent opposition.

In the past in Chiapas, the PRI used co-optive methods, and sometimes
outright coercion, to secure voter support: *caciques* (political bosses) established political ties with influential landowners, business people, and union
heads who guaranteed votes from the people they oversaw; commercial and
transportation licenses were granted and removed according to political allegiance; and even access to basic judicial procedures, such as divorce, was used
to isolate community members who supported opposition parties.[51] But economic reforms weakened this structure of co-option and coercion, and there

are indications that the regime had to rely more and more on outright electoral fraud to maintain its political control of the state.[52]

In Chiapas and elsewhere, leaders play a crucial role by helping members of a challenger group come to believe that their situation should and can be changed.[53] McAdam calls this process a group's *cognitive liberation*. Leaders define the categories through which challenger groups see their situations and themselves.[54] By developing and exploiting a particular view of economic justice, leaders can cause members of a challenger group to view their situation as illegitimate and intolerable, thus increasing their sense of relative deprivation. Leaders can also influence the members' blame system in order to focus their grievances on the state or another social group.[55] Finally, leaders can alter the perceived opportunity structure by altering group members' self-perceptions, their understandings of the nature of power, and their assumptions about the best means to achieve political change (especially their assumptions about the efficacy of violence).

In Chiapas, the Catholic and Protestant Churches have powerfully influenced peasants' understandings of their situation. Relations between the Catholic Church and the Mexican state have been strained since before the Mexican Revolution, because the state expropriated church lands and enforced a separation of responsibilities in such areas as education. However, the Catholic Church remains a tremendously powerful social institution for many rural communities. The Diocese of San Cristobal has drawn heavily on liberation theology to inspire the faith of the region's peasants. Liberation theology emphasizes the basic needs of the poor, including adequate food and shelter; it argues that peasants must be free from exploitation. The Protestant evangelicalism that has taken root in some communities in the state's Eastern Lowlands has similar principles. The effect of the activities of both the Protestant and Catholic Churches has been to create networks of lay preachers and catechists with parishes that cooperate remarkably well across denominations.

Protestantism and liberation theology have encouraged the state's indigenous peoples and campesinos to set up non-PRI social organizations, including peasant cooperatives, agricultural federations, and unions. These groups work for land reform, labor rights, and fair credit programs. Such grassroots organizations experiment with community development, create networks among different ethnic groups, and foster regional and class identities.[56] Since the mid-1970s, these groups have become increasingly radical.[57]

The intellectual leadership provided by such figures as Subcommandante Marcos (the Zapatista leader) gave the peasants an insurgent consciousness. They acquired an interpretation of the economic, social, and ecological forces that entrapped them. Many peasants who supported the Zapatistas had intimate ties to local environmental resources and had long lived with inadequate, marginal lands. Their awareness of the effect of environmental scarcity was shown by their repeated demands for healthy land and their refusal to accept land titles in state bioreserves. Zapatista leaders built on this ecological awareness by explaining to the peasants not only why the best land in the state had gone to elites, but also how the economic reforms had damaged the ecological bases of peasant culture.[58]

To conclude this section, when taken together the relative-deprivation and domestic-structural perspectives tell us that serious insurgency is likely when: (1) there are clearly defined, organized, and well-led groups in a society; (2) some of these groups regard their level of economic achievement, and in turn the broader political and economic system, as wholly unfair; (3) these same groups have identified certain other groups or the state as the cause or beneficiaries of this unfair situation; and (4) these groups believe that all peaceful opportunities to effect change are blocked, yet regard the balance of power within the society as unstable; that is, they believe there are structural opportunities for violently challenging the state or the groups that they blame for their situation.[59]

Other Forms of Violent Conflict

I have argued that scarcities of renewable resource are unlikely to cause simple-scarcity conflicts—that is, resource wars among countries. On the other hand, I have also argued that environmental scarcities can spur group-identity conflicts by contributing to large migrations and by increasing intergroup segmentation. And I have shown how modern conflict theories allow us to understand better the influence of environmental scarcities on grievances and opportunity and, in turn, on the probability of insurgency.

Group-identity conflicts and insurgency are, I believe, the most important types of conflict likely to arise from severe environmental scarcity; they are important both in terms of their probable frequency in the future (which will rise, I suggest, as scarcities worsen in some parts of the world) and their policy implications. But environmental scarcity also contributes to several other types of conflict. Under certain circumstances, for instance, scarcity can stimulate coups d'état as aggrieved and conflicting elites take advantage of a weakened state (see fig. 7.1). For example, drought and a severe food shortfall in Ethiopia opened up structural opportunities for the 1974 coup against Emperor Haile Selassie.[60] The motivation to launch a coup can be powerful: in many developing societies, control of the state is a principal route to wealth, status, and power for ambitious individuals and groups.

Environmental scarcity sometimes stimulates a form of insurgency that combines both group-identity and relative deprivation motivations. If the historical identity of a clearly defined social group is strongly linked to a particular set of natural resources or a particular pattern of resource use, degradation or depletion of that resource can accentuate a feeling of relative deprivation.

Members of the group can come to feel that they are being denied their rightful access to resources that are key to their self-definition as a group. This relative deprivation boosts grievances that may eventually be expressed through aggressive assertion of group identity. Good recent examples are the sporadic violence in southeastern Nigeria in 1994 and 1995, when the Ogoni people protested pollution of the Niger Delta by multinational oil companies, and the secessionist rebellion on the island of Bougainville in Papua New Guinea from the late 1980s to mid-1990s, which was partly motivated by anger against a foreign-owned copper mine that had severely damaged the island's environment.[61]

Finally, environmental scarcity also sometime causes a rise in rural banditry and gang violence. The bandits (or *dacoits*) of rural Sind in Pakistan are a good example.[62] Although banditry has a long history in Pakistan, the 1980s witnessed a sharp increase in its frequency and scope.[63] It is now no longer the vocation of a few isolated individuals but involves organized gangs that are increasingly able to elude punishment by local authorities. The bandits are mostly migrants from the barren northern regions of Sind: many were once sharecroppers, but they lost their livelihoods because of multiple economic and environmental problems.

According to Christina Lamb, members of one group of bandits, operating in and around the forest of Dadu, describe their actions as driven by "a combination of the feudal system, unemployment, and the difficulty of eking a living from the unforgiving land through which salinity is creeping like a white plague, rendering thousands more acres uncultivable each year."[64] The bandits place their criminal activities in a context of revolt against a landed elite whose control over resources has combined with severe resource degradation to threaten the livelihood of rural laborers. In other words, supply-induced and structural scarcities have combined to increase grievances and violence in these rural areas of Pakistan.

Four Further Cases

The core model presented in this chapter can be thought of as a set of hypotheses about possible links between environmental scarcity and violence. Various means can be used to test these hypotheses, including large-scale statistical analysis, controlled case comparisons, and process tracing of causal pathways within single cases. The appendix to this chapter describes these methods and addresses the contentious issue of how researchers can best select cases for testing purposes. I argue that in the early stages of research on the behavior of complex ecological-political systems, researchers should use process tracing of single cases that show a prima facie link between the variables of interest (in this case, the variables environmental scarcity and violence). Nonetheless, at best such an approach demonstrates only the plausibility of the hypothesized causal linkages. As process tracing of single cases was the principal method used in the research discussed in this book, the findings presented here can be regarded as no more than preliminary.

More careful case-study research is needed. This research should focus mainly on contemporary cases. While often of great interest, historical cases are, I believe, of limited value for testing purposes. Economic optimists rightly argue that modern societies have endowments of institutions, human capital, and knowledge—including, most importantly, modern markets and science— that permit unprecedented adaptability to scarcity. Without these endowments, past societies were inevitably far more vulnerable to scarcity's dislocations. Nevertheless, as I showed in the previous chapter, even modern societies do not always generate the ingenuity they need to adapt. Close study of contemporary cases helps determine the conditions under which adaptation fails and violence occurs.

We should not ignore historical cases entirely, however. They often provide key insights into contextual variables that influence the strength of the links between environmental scarcity and violence. Below, as further illustrations of the core model presented in this chapter, I discuss one historical case, that of food riots in medieval Castile, and three contemporary cases: the "Soccer War" between El Salvador and Honduras, the rise of the Sendero Luminoso in Peru, and the NPA insurgency in the Philippines.

Medieval Castile

Angus MacKay examines the relationship between climate change and civil violence in the kingdom of Castile (much of modern-day Spain).[65] His analysis shows how environmental stress can interact with people's blame systems to cause strife.

During the fifteenth century, there were numerous well-documented episodes of popular unrest in Castile, and some seem to have been produced by climate-induced food shortages. In March of 1462, for instance, rioters rampaged through Seville after floods forced the price of bread beyond the means of the poor. Usually, however, the causal connections were more complex. Demographic changes and the monarchy's debasement of the currency sometimes accentuated food scarcity caused by environmental stress. Other important contextual factors, according to MacKay, were the religious and social beliefs promoted by preachers, especially those beliefs attributing weather fluctuations to the sin of someone in the midst of the community. Anger over food scarcity was sometimes turned against Jews and *conversos* (Jews who had converted to Christianity after Iberian pogroms in the late fourteenth century), and sometimes against small shopkeepers who were accused of the sins of creating shortages and overpricing food.

MacKay thus rightly argues against a simplistic "stimulus-response" model of environment-conflict linkages but instead for one that allows for "culturally mediated" behavior. He notes: "The fact that people believed that sins explained the occurrence of a natural disaster is of crucial significance, and it follows that the reactions of contemporaries to disaster can only be properly explained within this context."[66]

The Soccer War

Addressing a modern conflict, William Durham has analyzed the demographic and environmental pressures behind the 1969 "Soccer War" between El Salvador and Honduras.[67] In July 1969, the two countries fought a brief but very violent war immediately after a series of bitterly contested semifinal matches in the World Cup competition (hence the popular name for the war). Durham notes that analysts commonly adduce three underlying causes of this conflict: the differential economic impact on the two countries of a 1960 Common Market agreement to which they were both parties; a long-standing border dispute; and the presence in Honduras of three hundred thousand immigrants from El Salvador (about 12 percent of Honduras' total population). A month before the war, Honduras had begun forcibly removing these immigrants from their rural plots. El Salvador promptly closed its borders in an effort to change the Honduran policy and to prevent an influx of returning peasants. When Honduras continued its expulsions, El Salvador launched the Soccer War.

Because of the prominence in this conflict of previous migration from El Salvador to Honduras, and because of the striking evidence of population growth and land stress in the two countries (most notably in El Salvador), a number of analysts have asserted that the Soccer War is a first-class example of an ecologically driven conflict.[68] A simple Malthusian interpretation does seem to have credibility when one looks at the aggregate data. El Salvador was the most densely populated country in the western hemisphere (190 people per square kilometer in 1976 compared to 186 for India), with a population growth rate of 3.5 percent per year (representing a doubling time of about twenty years).[69] Most of the country had lost its virgin forest, land erosion and nutrient depletion were severe; and total food production fell behind consumption in the mid-1950s. Per capita farmland used for basic food crops fell from 0.15 hectares in 1953 to 0.11 hectares in 1971. These statistics would appear to explain Salvadorean migration to Honduras.

But when the evidence is examined more closely, the Malthusian model does not tell the full story. The Soccer War is, in fact, a classic example of a conflict arising from ecological marginalization. Durham shows that changes in agricultural practice and land distribution—to the detriment of poor farmers—combined with population growth to induce migration from El Salvador to Honduras. In El Salvador, while food production for domestic consumption may have lagged, total agricultural production increased geometrically, indicating that "large increases in export production were realized in the face of growing food shortages."[70] Cotton and coffee supplanted maize, corn, rice, and beans. Land scarcity developed not because there was too little to go around, but because of "a process of competitive exclusion by which the small farmers [were] increasingly squeezed off the land—a process due as much to the dynamics of land concentration as to population pressure."[71] The consequences for the peasants were often disastrous: access to land strongly influenced malnutrition, illness, and death rates, especially among children; and many people were forced to move to find farming land in Honduras.

Durham thus correctly notes that ecologists cannot directly apply to human societies the simple, density-dependent models of resource competition commonly used in studies of asocial animals: as we have seen in the previous chapters, a distributional component must be added, because human behavior is powerfully influenced by social structure and the resource access it entails.

Peru

The rise of the Sendero Luminoso in Peru can be attributed to a subsistence crisis caused, in part, by a similar process of ecological marginalization.[72] The country's mountainous southern highlands are not suitable for farming. The hills are steep, and the soil is thin and dry. Nonetheless, during the colonial period, Indian peoples in the region were displaced onto hillsides when Spanish settlers seized richer valley lands. In the 1970s, the Velasco government undertook a sweeping land-redistribution program. But people in the highlands benefited little, because the government was reluctant to break up large agricultural enterprises that generated much of the country's export earnings.

Natural population growth and an inability to find good land or jobs elsewhere boosted population densities in the southern highlands. The department of Ayacucho saw density increase from 8.1 people per square kilometer in 1940 to 12.1 in 1980. Cropland availability dropped below 0.2 hectares per capita.[73] These densities exceeded sustainable limits, given the inherent fragility of the region's land and prevailing agricultural practices. Cropland was therefore badly degraded by erosion and nutrient depletion.

Cynthia McClintock notes that "if population increases while the soil deteriorates, food production per capita can be expected to decline."[74] Wealth in the region was almost entirely derived from subsistence agriculture. Family incomes—already among the lowest in Peru—dropped sharply in real terms in the 1970s and 1980s; in 1980, per capita income in the Peruvian highlands was 82 percent of the 1972 level. This poverty translated directly into declining caloric intake; in 1980, people in the southern highlands had less than 70 percent of the FAO daily requirement. In 1983, a drought made the subsistence crisis even worse, and production of the staple crop of potatoes fell by 40 to 50 percent.

Although government policies were partly responsible for the long-term income decline in the Peruvian highlands, the particularly harsh drop in the southern region was a result of population pressures, poor land, and the lack of alternative sources of income. The peasants' sense of deprivation was increased by the land reform in the 1970s, which raised their expectations in vain. There was thus a strong correlation between areas suffering severe poverty and Sendero Luminoso strongholds in the first stages of the insurgency: "The sinequa non element" of these strongholds was "the subsistence crisis in the country's southern highlands during the early 1980s."[75]

In terms of contextual factors, Ayacucho offered special opportunities to insurgents. It was physically remote, which reduced the government's control, and it had a major university that served as an organizational base for radicals that became the core of Sendero. The university's remoteness also meant that students were disproportionately from the peasantry and could therefore return to their communities with ease; moreover, they were less likely to find professional jobs on graduation. The relative power of the government was also weakened, ironically, by the land reform, which caused large landowners to leave the region. The Velasco regime did not fill the vacuum with new political and security institutions, in part because an economic downturn later in the decade reduced the government's resources for the task.

McClintock is not hopeful about the future. She believes the poverty of these regions condemns the country to chronic, long-term turmoil. The government may be civilian, but is unlikely to be very democratic, and will confront "virtually constant revolutionary and criminal violence."

The Philippines

The Philippines has also exhibited clear links between ecological marginalization and conflict. In the early 1990s, Daniel Lascon, the governor of the province of Negros Occidental under President Aquino, identified two sources of poverty and injustice behind the country's chronic insurgency: the accumulation of land in the hands of a few who failed to deal with the problems of the poor, and land degradation that affected small farmers and was not alleviated by government action.[76]

The Philippines has suffered from serious strife for many decades, usually motivated by economic hardship.[77] But cropland and forest degradation have sharply worsened this hardship in the central hilly regions of the archipelago's islands. The country's upland insurgency—which peaked in the 1980s and still included regular guerrilla attacks and assaults on military stations in the mid-1990s—was motivated by the relative deprivation of landless agricultural laborers and poor farmers displaced into the remote hills, where they tried to eke a living from the failing land; and it exploited the structural opportunities provided by the central government's weakness in the country's hinterland (see fig. 7.2).[78] During the 1970s and 1980s, the communist New People's Army (NPA) and the National Democratic Front (NDF) found upland peasants receptive to revolutionary ideology, especially where coercive landlords and local governments left them little choice but to rebel or starve.

To understand this case fully, we must pay close attention to contextual factors. For instance, property rights governing upland areas in the Philippines are, for the most part, either nonexistent or very unclear. Legally these areas are a public resource, and their open-access character encourages in-migration. Yet, upon arrival, many upland peasants find themselves under the authority of concessionaires and absentee landlords who have claimed the land. Neither peasants, nor concessionaires, nor landlords, though, have secure enough title to have incentive to protect the land from degradation.

The country's external debt encouraged the Marcos government, under pressure from international financial agencies, to adopt Draconian stabilization and structural adjustment policies. These policies caused an economic crisis in the first half of the 1980s, which boosted agricultural unemployment, reduced opportunities for alternative employment in urban and rural industries, and gave a further push to migration into the uplands.[79]

Finally, in the 1970s and 1980s, the creative leadership of the cadres of the NPA and the NDF facilitated the insurgency. In a clear example of cognitive liberation, these leaders built on indigenous beliefs and social structures to help shape peasants' understandings of their situation, focus their discontent, and assist them in extracting concessions from landlords. Gary Hawes points out that the rationality of Filipino peasants must be understood within their own world of meaning, which includes a strong commitment to family and community. The NDF used this world of meaning to create "a national community linked not by kinship, but by something analogous, a commitment to a vision of a better future for all those who are exploited."[80] He writes:

> According to the farmers, they did not think about struggling to change their situation before the comrades came. They felt it was enough just to work and eat. Although they believed they had a right to own land, the legal concept of private property had penetrated deeply; it was, to them, a right to *buy* the land. The cadres taught them how to struggle, how to petition for changes, and how to confront the landlord. Now they feel they have a right to land even if they cannot afford to buy it. Their vision of acceptable patterns of landholding has changed, as has the ability to implement their vision.[81]

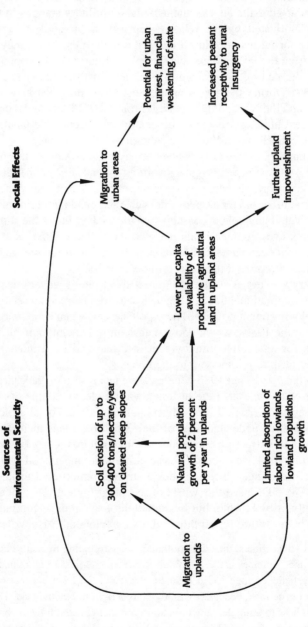

Figure 7.2. Environmental Scarcity and Insurgency in the Philippines

Richard Kessler offers a similar analysis. The most successful rebellions in Filipino history, he says, have drawn on peasants' millenarian vision—rooted in their Catholicism—of "an idealized pre-Spanish condition of wholeness."[82] The 1980s insurgency was particularly potent because it mingled "the spiritual search for liberation and the political search for independence, into the over-arching quest for Filipino identity." The new identity provided peasants with an alternative moral system to the traditional patron-client relationship be-tween peasants and landowners. These latter, feudal norms had imposed obli-gations on landowners, which had given peasants rudimentary economic secu-rity. But the system disintegrated with the commercialization of agriculture and the urbanization of elites in the early and mid-twentieth century.[83]

The NPA insurgency waned significantly with the fall of President Marcos and the adroit peace overtures of President Ramos. There were a number of reasons for this change: the democratically elected central government was more legitimate; an expanding economy generated alternative job opportuni-ties for people affected by environmental scarcity (although the economic boom has had, to date, only limited effect in interior hills); and the insurgent leadership became ideologically rigid.

Nonetheless, causal processes like those in the Filipino case can be seen around the planet. Population growth and unequal access to good land force huge numbers of rural people onto marginal lands. There, they cause environ-mental damage and become chronically poor. Eventually they may be the source of persistent upheaval, or they may migrate yet again, helping to stimu-late ethnic conflicts or urban unrest elsewhere.

Urban Growth and Violence

To this point in this book, we have focused mainly on links between environ-mental scarcity and rural violence. Yet we have also seen—in countries like China, India, and South Africa—that rural scarcity often contributes to the rapid growth of urban populations. Many commentators argue that the explod-ing megacities of the South are potential hotbeds of violence and civil strife. But past research has shown surprisingly little correlation between urban growth and strife, and the megacities in developing countries have been re-markably quiet in recent decades. This situation may be changing: as noted in chapter 2, India has lately witnessed ferocious urban violence, often in the poorest slums, and sometimes directed at new migrants from the countryside. Fundamentalist opposition to the Egyptian government is also located in poor sectors of Cairo and other cities like Asyût. Moreover, heavy subsidization of urban food, transport, and other amenities in developing countries shows that their governments believe the threat of urban unrest is very real. The presiden-tial palace is often a short walk from the slums.

Past research neglected a number of factors that might interact with urban growth to cause violence. These factors include economic crisis, weakening of the state, ethnic or communal segmentation that erodes social capital, rising demands for democratization, and the existence of strong criminal groups with ready access to light weapons. By itself, rapid urban growth is probably quite benign; but in interaction with these other factors, it appears much more likely to contribute to violence.[84]

Rates and Causes of Urban Growth

Between 1950 and 1990, there was a fivefold increase—to 1.5 billion—in the number of urban residents in developing countries; about 37 percent of the population of the developing world now lives in cities. By 2025, the United Nations projects a further tripling of the total to 4.4 billion, at which point nearly two-thirds of the citizens of the developing world will live in cities.[85]

Although urban growth rates in much of the developing world have declined slightly from the very high rates that prevailed in the 1960s and 1970s (see table 7.1), in aggregate the developing world's cities are still expanding by about 160,000 persons a day. Mexico City, which had a population of 3.1 million in 1950, is projected to reach over 25 million by the end of the 1990s; estimates for São Paulo suggest a population of 22 million by year 2000, almost ten times the 1950 total. While it took New York City almost 150 years to grow by 8 million people, Mexico City and São Paulo will add this number in less than fifteen years. In 1970 there were only three megacities in Asia with more than 8 million inhabitants, by the year 2000 there will be seventeen. The number of cities with at least 1 million inhabitants has gone from 31 in 1950 to 180 in the early 1990s and is expected to rise to more than 300 by the end of the century.

Three major factors account for urban population growth: natural growth, net migration, and reclassification. (Reclassification occurs as a result of changes in government definitions of what constitutes an urban area.) Of these, the first two contribute the most. Natural growth results from an excess of births over deaths within a city; this is growth caused by the natural reproduction of the city's residents. Net migration produces urban growth when migration into the city exceeds migration out of the city. In the developing world, these urban migrants usually come from rural areas. As indicated in chapter 5, the key factor driving this migration is the gap between the standard of living available in rural areas and the perceived standard of living in the city. Dire rural conditions often arise from an interaction of fast population growth, environmental degradation, and skewed distribution of environmental resources that drives down wage levels, marginalizes weaker groups, and contributes to further environmental degradation. In contrast, cities are perceived to provide

TABLE 7.1
Annual Urban Growth Rate by Region

	1965–80	1980–90
Sub-Saharan Africa	5.8	5.9
East Asia	4.3	3.3
China	2.3	13.5
South Asia	3.9	3.9
Middle East/North Africa	4.6	4.4
Latin America	3.9	3.0

Source: Alan Gilbert, "Third World Cities: Changing Development System," Urban Studies 30, nos. 4–5 (1993): 722.

better job opportunities. They are major engines of wealth generation, providing dense and synergistic concentrations of capital, talent, and entrepreneurial opportunity.

In recent years, scholars have recognized that much rural-urban migration in developing countries is *circular*. Some migrants move to the city for relatively short periods of time and then return to the country. The changing availability of seasonal employment in the countryside and the city often prompts this migration; migrants also want to remain in contact with their home communities. Circular migration makes it hard to estimate the relative contribution of movement from rural to urban areas. Such migration by a single member of a rural family is often the first step in the movement of the family and, eventually, of whole communities into the city.[86]

The contribution of permanent migration to urban growth varies in the developing world (see table 7.2). Although the contribution is now below 50 percent for most large cities, it is still a large share. Migration generally contributes more than natural growth at early stages of economic development, with natural growth predominating at intermediate stages.[87] During later stages, rates of natural growth tend to drop and net migration is once again dominant.[88] Because many developing countries are still in an intermediate stage of development, we can expect higher relative contributions from migration in the future.[89]

Rural-urban migrants tend to be relatively young, which accentuates the youth bulge in urban populations in poor countries (see table 7.3). This age distribution contributes to natural population growth in cities, because a younger population has more children and fewer deaths compared to an older population, even though individual mothers in urban areas usually have lower fertility rates than their rural counterparts.[90] Young urban populations, especially unemployed young men, are easier to mobilize for radical political ends; and young populations generate enormous demands for the provision of social resources like education and jobs.

TABLE 7.2
Net Migration Contribution to Urban Growth, Selected Countries, 1975–1990

	Migrant Share of Urban Growth (Percent)		Migrant Share of Urban Growth (Percent)
Africa		Latin America	
Kenya	64.17	Brazil	59.35
Senegal	75.16	Colombia	21.35
Tanzania	84.96	Costa Rica	52.59
Tunisia	76.84	Cuba	89.50
		Ecuador	49.91
Asia		Guatemala	34.34
Bangladesh	77.77	Honduras	50.33
Fiji	37.97	Panama	30.73
Indonesia	61.61	Peru	61.82
Iran	47.84	Puerto Rico (US)	61.04
Iraq	38.62	Uruguay	23.17
Philippines	49.68		
South Korea	72.77		
Sri Lanka	−7.37		
Thailand	69.43		

Source: Sally E. Findley, "The Third World City: Development Policy and Issues," in *Third World Cities: Problems, Policies and Prospects*, ed. John D. Kasarda and Allan M. Parnell (London: Sage, 1993), 15.

TABLE 7.3
Proportion of Population in 0–19 Age Cohort, Selected Cities

Developed Countries	Year	Percent	Developing Countries	Year	Percent
Amsterdam	1980	22.1	Bangkok	1981	44.1
Birmingham	1980	29.9	Bombay	1981	41.5
Frankfurt	1981	24.8	Cairo	1986	44.4
London	1981	27.6	Delhi	1980	48.9
Los Angeles	1980	28.8	Jakarta	1981	52.9
Madrid	1980	33.5	Lagos	1985	45.7
Montreal	1980	23.3	Mexico City	1985	47.0
New York	1980	28.1	Rio de Janeiro	1980	36.5
Paris	1982	18.7	Sao Paulo	1980	40.0
Rome	1981	29.6	Seoul	1980	42.5
Tokyo	1981	28.2	Shanghai	1988	24.3

Source: A. S. Oberai, *Population Growth, Employment and Poverty in Third-World Mega-Cities* (New York: St. Martin's Press, 1993), 28.

Types of Urban Violence

We can distinguish among three broad types of urban violence: *political violence*, including both violence directed against the state and collective violence by the state against challengers; *communal and ethnic violence*; and *criminal/anomic violence*. (In terms of the types of conflict already discussed in this chapter, these correspond roughly to insurgency, group-identity conflict, and banditry, respectively.) Researchers have mainly focused on the first type, and they have usually studied violence directed against the state. However, the second type appears to be evermore conspicuous in today's cities. Here, the protagonists are generally private parties, yet the issues in contention and the violence itself may have great political consequences for the state and society in general.[91] Ethnic and communal rivalries often involve perceived disparities in access to political and economic opportunities. Racial, ethnic, religious, or other group identities serve as rallying points for political mobilization to address these disparities.

Wanton acts of destruction, armed robbery, assault, murder, and racketeering by individuals and groups fall into the category of criminal and anomic violence. This activity is not necessarily devoid of political significance. Theorists from Emile Durkheim to Chalmers Johnson have argued that an erosion of society's moral unity is a key precursor to anomic violence.[92] To the extent that such violence reflects alienation from society, or a calculation that the potential gains of ignoring society's rules exceed the costs of doing so, it indicates a breakdown in the moral and coercive authority of society as a whole.

The developing world offers many examples of these three types of urban violence. In the mid-1970s, for instance, austerity measures adopted by debt-ridden countries sparked a worldwide wave of urban protest and violence against the state.[93] Ethnic and communal strife is also widespread in cities. Communal issues vent the pent up anger and frustration produced by the high tension of urban life. Since the 1950s, there has been a steady rise in India in the frequency of communal incidents and in the number of persons killed and injured as a result.[94] Although the frequency has increased rapidly in rural areas, most incidents remain urban.[95] Moreover, the rate of increase has been faster than either rural or urban population growth, which means that the per capita incidence of communal violence has sharply increased.

Criminal and anomic violence often accompanies such intergroup strife. During the late 1980s and early 1990s, criminals exploited interethnic violence among rival black groups in the urban settlements of South Africa.[96] The expansion of immense, peri-urban squatter settlements and slums in Africa, Asia, and Latin America is closely associated with surging crime. For example, in the early 1990s, Rio de Janeiro led Brazil in negative urban indicators: the largest concentration of slum dwellers (1 million), the highest murder rate (one of seven hundred residents per year), and the highest kidnapping rate (four per week).[97] The city's homicide rate was three times higher than New York's, and the rate of urban violence continued to rise. Almost one-quarter of all homicides occurred among people between the ages of ten and nineteen. In such circumstances, organized crime gains an easy foothold. Drug lords establish retail centers in the city's shantytowns (*favelas*), while children serve as sentries and distributors of the illegal product. Male teenagers and young adults are recruited into death squads in the war against rivals and authorities.[98]

Links between Urban Growth and Violence

Beginning in the 1960s, some scholars suggested that rural-to-urban migration in the developing world would cause an increase in urban violence. According to Wayne Cornelius, there were three key hypotheses in this literature.[99] First, some scholars said migration would breed economic frustration. The public and private sectors would be unable to accommodate the rapid influx, and migrants' expectations of improved lives would not be fulfilled. Moreover, the nearby conspicuous consumption of elites would raise migrants' awareness of their marginal status. As a result, they would experience rising relative deprivation, and they would become increasingly involved in radical political activity.[100]

Second, other analysts suggested that migrants would have problems adjusting socially and psychologically to the urban environment. Culture conflicts and the disruption of past living habits and customs would cause personal identity crises, increasing the chances of primary group breakdown and weakening traditional social controls on deviant behavior. And, as migrants sought entry into new protective groups, they would be easily recruited into extremist political movements.[101] Third, some experts said that rural-to-urban migration, increased political awareness, and mobilization of radical opposition would go hand-in-hand. The urban environment would allow high levels of social communication and would produce intense competition among various interest groups. Organized political activity would be conspicuous, which would politicize migrants and encourage mass involvement in political action.[102]

The above three processes could presumably occur simultaneously—with the first and second boosting certain types of grievance among migrants (for example, deprivation, feelings of alienation, anomie, and rootlessness), and the third expanding opportunities for those grievances to be articulated and acted upon (by facilitating social communication and comparisons with others, and by altering the balance of power in society as challenger groups become stronger relative to the state).

Scholars disputed whether violence would follow quickly on the heels of migration or erupt some years after migrants had been absorbed into the urban environment.[103] Early arguments merely warned of "disruptive migrants," torn from rural roots, isolated in the city and prone to violence and extremism as a result of increasing disillusionment with urban life. Later arguments suggested that violence was most likely after migrants had become more firmly established. Only after they shed their rural outlook and sense of strangeness and diffidence would their inability to find decent jobs and housing translate into the strong sense of deprivation and frustration needed to prompt violent political action. In short, a socialization period was important for transforming migrants into "radicalized marginals."

Early research on links between urban growth and violence yielded little empirical support for any these hypotheses. For instance, fluctuations of collective political violence in the United States, Britain, France, and Mexico did not correspond to the pace of urbanization.[104] In the United States, a 1967 Presidential Commission on Civil Disorders found that migrants were less involved in violence than people raised in cities. Nor was there much evidence of a positive relationship between urban growth and crime. A correlation between population growth and property crime was found in some cases, yet it was not strong and may have been better associated with city size.[105]

There are a number of explanations of these findings. Migrants from rural areas might be ignorant of structural obstacles to their mobility in cities and therefore might not develop strong feelings of deprivation and injustice. Urban governments can prevent uprisings by addressing grievances, co-opting dissent with patronage, and using repression against challengers. The conservatism and acquiescence common among migrants could stem from rural values that promote deference and political passivity. Certain cultures might also resist the corrosive effects of urban life on family and kinship ties. Recent migrants also tend to be preoccupied with acquiring the basic necessities of life, which generally means that they must work through existing institutions rather than challenge them.[106] And the nature of social organization in urban slums might create feelings of distrust among subgroups within migrant communities. The communities are usually organized around clearly defined urban territories and neigborhoods; this very localized and insular culture does not lend itself to mobilization based on broader groupings and more universal ideas.[107] Divisions along ethnic, religious, or caste lines often prevent the emergence of effective mass movements by obscuring economic stratification and defusing class conflict.

Most importantly, early research showed that many migrants did not feel deprived; rather, they were satisfied with urban life in comparison to the rural existence they had left. Many in fact viewed conditions in the city as much better than in the country. Migrants seemed to find jobs quickly, often securing employment before their arrival. Data indicated relative improvements in migrant family income levels.[108] And, migrant occupation patterns were found to differ little from those of the urban born.[109] Tested less was the hypothesis that a period of socialization was required before migrant radicalization could occur; it was difficult to get data tracking migrants over time.

Overall, the early research clearly showed that simple, bivariate arguments about the links between rural-urban migration and violence were misguided. These arguments took little account of the many ways differing political systems, societies, and cultures could cope with migration. They also usually focused on mass political violence to the exclusion of other forms of urban strife. Moreover, they said virtually nothing about the international and domestic contexts in which states and their urban centres were embedded.

Most early research studied rural-to-urban migration during periods of relative political and economic stability (if not growth) in the societies affected. Consequently, states and institutions might have responded more effectively to migrant demands, and these demands might have been lower, than would have been the case in more difficult economic times. In fact, after noting a weak relationship between rural-urban migration and violence, early researchers often argued that continued stability depended on sustained economic expansion, upward movement in real incomes, strengthening of government capabilities, and a sustained ability of government to coopt leaders from newly urbanized populations. Without success in these areas, some researchers suggested, the potential for political strife would be far higher.[110]

Later studies touched upon the relationship between urban growth and violence during periods of economic stress and offered hints that a causal link might in fact exist. For instance, an examination of Mexican squatter settlements during the 1980s showed that squatters in shanty-towns were especially prone to random violence in economically hard times.[111] Compared to residents of inner-city slums, squatters were far from major commercial markets and were therefore disadvantaged in economic competition in the informal sector. Unable to afford income-producing land plots, and lacking basic social and urban services given the reduced outlays of financially strapped governments, these settlements became "settlements of despair," with crime and violence an increasing part of day-to-day life.[112]

Several studies of the widespread protest in cities in the developing world during the debt crisis of the late 1970s and early 1980s also stressed the importance of general economic context. These studies attributed the protest to austerity measures adopted under pressure from international financial institutions. The austerity measures eliminated mechanisms for distributing wealth set up by governments during years of heavy borrowing in the 1960s and 1970s, and they imposed severe hardships on the urban poor and working classes. The measures were often perceived as a violation of certain tacit norms of justice and fairness—of a "moral economy" between elites and the poor—

that had emerged under previous economic arrangements.[113] The dismantling of these arrangements provoked a wave of strikes, riots, and demonstrations throughout the developing world. The timing and intensity of these protests correlated strongly with rural-to-urban migration.[114]

In recent years, there has been little critical analysis of the links between migration, urban growth, and violence. Yet it is clear that researchers need to examine the possibility that the links are strengthened when large migrations interact with other factors. A protracted economic crisis, for instance, squeezes tax revenues and weakens all state institutions, including the bureaucracy, judiciary, police, and military; meanwhile, cutbacks and lower salaries encourage corruption within the civil service. The state becomes more unable to meet the demands of competing elites or the grievances of a rapidly growing population; and it cannot confront potential challenger groups with sufficient coercive force. Opportunities for popular protest and rebellion therefore increase.

Whether or not economic crisis produces institutional breakdown and violence depends on the character of civil society, particularly on the society's stock of social capital. Social capital provides a degree of cooperation and social solidarity that can buffer people from the harshest effects of economic and state crisis. Unfortunately, as we have seen in South Africa in chapter 5, in many cities in the developing world, deep-seated rivalries among communal and ethnic groups—rivalries often aggravated by huge migrations into cities—segment communities and shred networks of trust and reciprocity.

Economic crisis and decaying state capacity usually boost pressure for democratization, since effective solutions to these problems often entail sacrifices from citizens, and citizens see an expansion of political participation as a reasonable quid pro quo.[115] All too often, though, the initial response by the state to calls for more democracy is repression. If peaceful channels of political expression are foreclosed, protest can be increasingly violent.

The growing strength and reach of organized crime in the developing world also compounds the stresses of migration and rapid urban growth. In many poor societies, the balance of power seems to be shifting from the state and its coercive institutions toward gangs and organized crime. A vigorous global trade in light weapons and plastic explosives means that criminals have easy access to the means of violence. With the end of the cold war, some regions are awash in small arms, and many former communist states are eager suppliers of weapons for hard currency. As a result, criminals are frequently better armed and organized than financially strapped and technologically backward police forces. Moreover, organized crime often penetrates into the heart of the state through blackmail, bribery, and threats of violence. Today, criminal organizations are so well entrenched in some Latin American and South Asian cities that their power clearly exceeds that of local authorities; the central government has often had to use the army to reassert control.

Karachi: An Example of Interaction

Events in the early to mid-1990s in Karachi, Pakistan's largest city and premier industrial port, are a good example of how the multiple forces described above can interact to produce explosive results.

Successive waves of migration to Karachi have produced a city of considerable ethnic diversity. After the division of the subcontinent in 1947, the city's indigenous Sindhi population was overtaken by Urdu-speaking refugees (Muhajirs). In the 1960s, the national government's green-revolution and industrialization policies caused a wave of Pushto speakers (Pathan) to move in from Pakistan's northern provinces. These changes have marginalized Karachi's Sindhi population both linguistically and culturally, yet the new migrant groups are under-represented within the provincial bureaucracy.[116]

Today, Urdu is the lingua franca of Karachi, and Muhajirs run much of the city's business and industry. The Pathan make up the majority of the working class and have gained a virtual monopoly over Karachi's transport sector. Retaining deeply rooted tribal traditions and support systems, they are in effect a separate state within the city. Meanwhile, the Sindhi minority dominates government and educational institutions through a system of quotas.[117] Rivalries among these groups are common and flow largely from the positions in society that the groups occupy. The presence of contending religious sects worsens the conflict: Shia-Sunni confrontations occur with almost ritualized regularity.

The Pakistani state at the national, provincial, and local levels lacks the capacity and basic institutions needed to accommodate the needs of the city's diverse and quarreling population. Pakistan's overdeveloped military-bureaucratic oligarchy is rife with corruption and patronage; truly independent and representative political institutions have never been developed at any level of governance; and few public institutions are available to ease the transition of migrants to urban life. Local government is characterized by murky lines of authority, few taxing powers, and little accountability.

Karachi grows by about 400,000 people per year. Many of these new residents are migrants from rural areas, and a large proportion are escaping environmental scarcity in the countryside. The rising population intensifies popular demands, underlines state impotence, and further polarizes society. As Karachi's population rises at around 5 percent per annum (far above the national rate of 2.7 percent), urban services expand by only 1.2 percent.[118] Government and development authorities cannot provide residents with basic services; the city's aging infrastructure is overtaxed and does not properly service new communities. Housing is in critically short supply: the government is able to meet only about one-eighth of total annual demand.[119] Meanwhile, an informal system of illegal occupation and subdividing of state land for sale to low-income families has developed. Managed by middlemen and corrupt government officials, this system of blatant rent-seeking defies state regulations.

Acute shortages of electricity and water are pervasive. Powerful communities in the city are able to insure better service through political pressure and bribes and by building private wells and electrical generators, but those in less fortunate areas are ignored. High demand for water along with rampant corruption and mismanagement in the Karachi Water and Sewage Board has created a *tanker Mafia*. Tankers obtain water from illegal hydrants or from poorer districts in the city and then sell it for profit.[120] The customers are often the inhabitants of the very districts from which the water was taken, and exorbitant prices force many to buy the water on credit.[121] The results are increasing profits for entrepreneurs and local authorities and growing impoverishment for low-income urban dwellers.

Karachi's transportation system, which is largely made up of privately owned minibuses, also stands in disarray. Operators work long hours to repay loans taken for bus purchase. Traffic laws and established transport routes are routinely violated, passengers are mistreated, and accidents are common. The result is acute public resentment, both of the government for its inaction and of an overwhelmingly Pathan core of operators.[122]

Adding to the problems is the ever-present influence of organized crime. Trafficking in narcotics and arms has gained a foothold in many parts of the city, because Karachi is an exit point for the narcotics trade to the rest of the world. Working with Afghan refugees and corrupt government and police officials, Mafia-type syndicates prey on the city's weaknesses and are adept at exploiting ethnic rivalries to block state challenges to their power.[123] All the while, the accessibility of inexpensive armaments has risen, especially following the Afghan war, which magnifies the potential for violence among rival groups.

A general climate of insecurity pervades the city. The population is increasingly divided by ethnic and class affiliation. Meanwhile, much needed investment is driven elsewhere, further eroding the city's economic base. The climate of insecurity has also crippled Karachi's educational system. Some colleges have been forced to close, and others now serve as armed strongholds for warring factions; education has become privatized and increasingly segregated along class lines.

With institutionalized channels of protest and action on grievances unavailable, state legitimacy suffers. The people's loyalties and allegiances remain local, and efforts to redress grievances often take the form of ethnic and class-based violence. Frustration stemming from the lack of urban services has prompted attacks on the offices of the Karachi Electricity Supply Corporation and the Karachi Water and Sewage Board.[124] Minibus accidents spark ethnic riots, and fights between Karachi residents and an underfunded police force are common. The fact that the police are heavily drawn from the Northern provinces heightens ethnic tension.[125]

Overall, therefore, violence in Karachi stems from a variety of factors that interact to magnify the impacts each might produce separately. The inability of state institutions to address diverse demands accentuates latent ethnic and class tensions. In-migration and high urban population growth further boost grievances, highlight the impotence of the state, and reduce state legitimacy. Criminal elements exploit state weakness and social conflicts, and they import small arms that make it easier for all contending parties to use violence. All the while, the social fabric and the economy continue to erode.

The Future

Huge migrations from rural to urban areas will continue, in many cases propelled by rising environmental scarcity in the countryside. These migrations will often magnify the social and economic problems of cities. Nonetheless, it seems likely that most participants in urban violence in the future will be urban-born. As societies become increasingly urbanized and rural ways of life decline, there may be ever fewer opportunities to draw favourable comparisons between urban and rural lifestyles. In fact, a very large majority of people will be born in cities and will have had no rural experience. In the context of economic stagnation or recession, relative differences between rich and poor in the city and between different ethnic groups and classes will become evermore salient in people's minds. In these circumstances, feelings of relative deprivation are likely to rise.

For example, the street crime in many Latin American cities suggests a growing tendency toward violence among better educated, urban-born males with few avenues for economic advancement.[126] Expectations outstrip opportunities. In these cases, urban growth plays a role, not by creating angry communities of recent migrants from rural areas, but by creating a glut of young, urban-born job and status seekers who cannot be satisfied without fast economic expansion.

Criminal violence, however, does not necessarily translate into the organized political violence that students of urban conflict emphasize. But it bears repeating that more frequent acts of individual or gang violence indicate a general breakdown of societal norms and state legitimacy that could eventually translate into broadly based movements against the state.

Implications for International Security

In this and preceding chapters, we have seen that under certain circumstances environmental scarcity contributes to violent conflict. This violence is generally diffuse, persistent, and internal to countries—that is, subnational. It can occur in urban areas, but it is generally rural, because environmental scarcity has its most profound effects on people's lives in rural areas. This violence will probably increase in frequency and extent as these scarcities worsen in some poor societies.

This subnational violence is not as conspicuous or dramatic as interstate resource wars, but nonetheless it has serious implications for the security interests of both the developed and developing worlds. It can overwhelm the management capacity of institutions in developing countries, contributing to praetorianism or even widespread social disintegration, as we have seen in Haiti.[127] Countries under high internal stress can fragment as their states become enfeebled and peripheral regions are seized by renegade authorities and warlords. Governments of countries as different as the Philippines and Peru have, at times, lost control over outer territories; although both these cases are complicated, environmental stress has certainly contributed to this weakening of control.

Fragmentation of any sizeable country—such as Pakistan or India—would produce outflows of migrants; it would prevent the country from effectively negotiating and implementing international agreements on collective security, global environmental protection, and other matters of critical concern to the international community; and it would also disrupt trade ties with the rest of the world.

Internal conflicts can generate complex humanitarian emergencies that embroil outside countries in expensive peacemaking and peacekeeping operations. (In general, conventional militaries are badly equipped and designed for such operations.) Moreover, states confronting internal turmoil often become extremist, authoritarian, militarized, and abusive of human rights.[128] Such hard regimes frequently adopt more belligerent foreign policies to divert attention from internal grievances. Research shows that the strength of the links between civil strife and a regime's foreign conflict behavior depends on the regime's nature and on the kind of internal strife it faces. For example, highly centralized dictatorships threatened by revolutionary actions, purges, and strikes are especially prone to engage in external war and belligerence. Less centralized dictatorships are prone to these behaviors when threatened by guerrilla action and assassinations.[129] Regimes borne of revolution are particularly good at mobilizing their citizens and resources for military preparation and war.[130] If a number of developing countries evolve in the direction of hard regimes, especially if they are pivotal countries (chap. 2), the military and economic interests of rich countries would be directly threatened.

The probability that a state will become a hard regime in the response to environmentally induced turmoil depends, I believe, on three factors. First, it must have sufficient remaining capacity—despite the effects of scarcity—to mobilize or seize resources for its own ends. Second, the state must have a history of authoritarianism. And third, the country's ecological-economic system must still generate enough surplus wealth to allow the state, once it seizes this wealth, to pursue its authoritarian course. Consequently, the countries with the highest probability of becoming hard regimes, and potential military threats to their neighbors, are large, relatively wealthy developing countries that are dependent on a declining environmental base but that retain considerable state capacity and have a history of authoritarianism. Candidates include Indonesia, Pakistan, and Nigeria.[131]

In this chapter, I have introduced and discussed a detailed model of the links between environmental scarcity and violent conflict. I reviewed several theories of conflict that help us understand what types of conflict this scarcity is most likely to cause, and I illustrated these types using examples drawn from a number of case studies of rural conflict. I also surveyed the literature on the relationship between rapid urban growth and violence, and I identified several variables that can interact with this growth to boost the probability of violence. Finally, I considered the implications of environmentally induced violence for international security.

In the next chapter, I summarize this book's key findings and respond to common criticisms of these findings. I also offer some ideas for future research.

Appendix

Hypothesis Testing and Case Selection

The research findings discussed in preceding chapters were derived from careful study of a large number of cases of specific regions and countries. Political scientists debate the best procedures for selecting cases for such research. In this appendix I argue that some commonly advocated principles of case selection are inappropriate for the preliminary study of highly interactive and complex ecological-political systems, such as those considered in this book.

North American political scientists often advocate a quasi-experimental method of hypothesis testing and causal inference modeled after the natural sciences. By this method, researchers ideally use broad theories of political behavior (such as the theories of conflict discussed early in this chapter) to generate hypotheses about causal relations between variables that interest them. These should be key or critical hypotheses that are both testable and linked directly to core concepts and laws within the more general theories. The researchers then test the hypotheses, and, in turn, the more general theory, against empirical data.[1] Of key importance, according to this method, is the choice of data. Data should provide for variation of both the hypothesized independent and dependent variables while allowing for control of all other potentially confounding variables.

The problem of data choice is particularly acute in the field of comparative politics. Researchers must often rely on selected case studies—of specific countries, for example—to test their hypotheses. Recently, some commentators have focused criticism on the procedure of selecting "on the dependent variable," in which cases are chosen that exhibit a particular value, or range of values, of the dependent variable. It is generally thought that this procedure gives biased estimates of the effect of the independent variable and cannot therefore be used to draw causal inferences or test hypotheses.[2]

However, analysts have shown that selection of the cases on the dependent variable is the best testing procedure when the independent variable is hypothesized to be a *necessary* cause of the dependent variable.[3] I will show here that there are additional circumstances where selection on *both* the dependent and independent variables is warranted. Specifically, in its early stages, research on the links between environmental scarcity and conflict is often aided by explicit selection of cases in which environmental scarcity and conflict both occur. This is so because the subject matter is extraordinarily complex: the systems under study are characterized by an immense number of unknown variables and unknown causal connections among these variables, by interactions, feed-backs, and nonlinear relationships, and by high sensitivity to small perturba-tions. Such complexities and uncertainties make it extremely difficult to choose cases that control for potentially confounding variables.

Hypothesis Testing

All empirical research must begin with hypotheses. These often take the form of "if-then" statements about causal relations, or, at least, about correlations between types of event.[4] "If" in the if-then statement identifies the independent variable, and "then" identifies the dependent variable. "If" also states any "scope conditions," which are additional circumstances that must be true if the whole "if-then" statement is to be valid.[5]

Development of hypotheses is not a simple process. Researchers usually start with very simple causal or correlational hypotheses, perhaps—but not necessarily—derived from a general theory. They use each hypothesis to inter-rogate available evidence by asking the question: what does the evidence say about the hypothesized correlation or causal process? Evidence that flatly con-tradicts the hypothesis—often called a *null* finding—is valuable, but other kinds of evidence are also valuable, including evidence that supports the hy-pothesis and evidence that is equivocal but suggests alteration of category boundaries, introduction of scope conditions, or addition of new causal link-ages. On the basis of all this evidence, not just of null findings, researchers refine their hypotheses as their work progresses.

Over time the boundaries of the independent and dependent variables are more precisely defined (which often involves generating additional categories of these variables), and the understanding of the scope conditions becomes more textured. This process is neither purely deductive (from hypotheses to evidence) nor inductive (from evidence to hypotheses), but rather an iterative cycle between increasingly sophisticated hypotheses and an increasingly com-prehended empirical world.[6] If, eventually, the hypotheses become sufficiently refined, and if they are linked by a definable set of binding assumptions or concepts, then we can reasonably speak of a theory that explains the set of events under study.

In environment-conflict research, a number of methods are available to test hypotheses against empirical evidence. Three deserve close attention, of which the first two are conventional, quasi-experimental methods in political science. First, researchers can undertake a *correlational analysis* of large amounts of quantitative data on the relative frequencies of environmental scarcity and con-flict across many societies and over time. Such an approach involves statistical estimation of the probability of obtaining a given correlation observed in the data if, in actuality, there is no correlation in the real world between the variables in question.[7] Second, researchers can undertake a *controlled case comparison* in which cases are selected that vary on the independent variable, environmental scarcity, but that are essentially the same for all other variables that might affect the incidence of the dependent variable, conflict. Researchers aim to select cases that control for all variables except environmental scarcity so that scarcity's effect on conflict can be isolated.[8] If sufficiently similar cases are not available, researchers can instead undertake thought experiments using counterfactual analysis in which researchers ask, "What would have happened if the independent variable changed its value but all other factors remained constant?"[9]

Finally, researchers can undertake *process tracing* of the causal processes in a selection of cases where environmental scarcity apparently contributes to conflict. Here, in violation of the strict canons of conventional political science, cases are selected explicitly on both the independent and dependent variables. The aim is to determine if the independent and dependent variables are actually causally linked, and, if they are, to induce from a close study of many such cases the common patterns of causality and the key intermediate variables that characterize these links.[10] Process tracing often involves dropping down one or more levels of analysis to develop a more finely textured and detailed understanding of the causal steps between the independent and dependent variables.[11] In process tracing, George and McKeown write:

> The process of constructing and explanation is much like the construction of a web or network. The researcher assembles bits and pieces of evidence into a pattern; whether a piece is to be changed or added depends on whether the change fits with what already has been constructed, and whether it strengthens the web's structure. Does the modification of the explanation create internal inconsistencies in the theory? Does the modification of the explanation create more new puzzles than it solves? If yes is the answer to these questions, the modification is rejected. Modifications that are consistent and produce smaller, more localized, and less frequent research puzzles are to be valued. The growth of the web orients the search for new pieces, just as the growth of a jig-saw puzzle guides the search for pieces that will fit together with what is already assembled.[12]

A central claim of this appendix is that the stage of research strongly influences the method of hypothesis testing a researcher can use to best advantage. During early research in a new field, especially if the subject matter is highly complex, hypotheses are liable to be too crude to support testing that involves quantitative analysis of large numbers of cases. Similarly, it may be inefficient for a researcher to spend a great deal of time examining cases in which the cause of interest does not occur, as would be required by a methodology of controlled comparison. Initially, at least, the researcher can often use research resources to best advantage by examining cases that appear, prima facie, to demonstrate the causal relations hypothesized—that is, by selecting on the independent and dependent variables. This narrow focus will allow the researcher to efficiently identify conceptual errors and basic empirical weaknesses in the early hypotheses. Later, as the hypotheses become more refined and understanding of scope conditions more textured, the hypotheses can be subjected to much more rigorous analysis.

Case Selection

The issue of selecting on the independent and dependent variables is contentious within environment-conflict research. Much of the research discussed in this book, for example, focused explicitly and intentionally on cases in which the hypothesized causal link between environmental scarcity and conflict appeared to exist. Given prevailing methodological thought within political science, it could be claimed that this approach biased the work's results in favor of positive findings.

The criticism would take the following form. If environmental scarcity is the independent variable and violent conflict the dependent variable, and if each variable, crudely, has two possible values, then we have four possible outcomes, as illustrated in the matrix in figure 7A.1. All cases (say, countries) will be located in one of the four quadrants of the matrix. If environmental scarcity is a *necessary* cause of conflict, there will be no cases in quadrant 1, but there may be cases in any of the other three. If scarcity is a *sufficient* cause of conflict, there will be no cases in quadrant 4, but, again, there may be cases in the others. If scarcity is both necessary and sufficient, there will be cases only in quadrants 2 and 3.

A correlational analysis will attempt to determine if the distribution of cases across the four quadrants is significantly different from a distribution that could be expected by chance alone. A distribution that is significantly different provides evidence that environmental scarcity and conflict are correlated. A controlled case comparison will vary cases on the independent variable, environmental scarcity, without regard to values of the dependent variable; of particular interest are any null cases in quadrant 4 in which all the preconditions of the hypotheses connecting environmental scarcity with conflict hold, yet conflict does not occur. Finally, process tracing will focus mainly on cases selected from quadrant 2. This is the method used in much environment-conflict research to date.

Critics might contend that process tracing of a relatively small number of cases that fall in quadrant 2 somehow avoids a fair test of hypotheses. However, in the early stages of research, such a procedure is often the best, and sometimes the only, way to begin. It can show, for particular cases, whether or not the proposed independent variable is a cause of the dependent variable. It answers the important first questions identified in chapter 1 of this book: Are

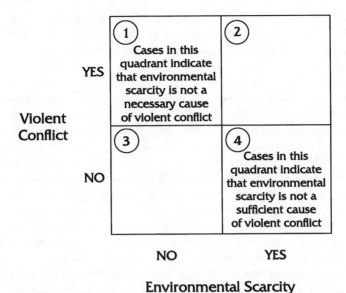

Violent Conflict

YES

1 — Cases in this quadrant indicate that environmental scarcity is not a necessary cause of violent conflict

2

NO

3

4 — Cases in this quadrant indicate that environmental scarcity is not a sufficient cause of violent conflict

NO   YES

Environmental Scarcity

Figure 7A.1. Matrix of Case Distribution on Values of the Independent and Dependent Variables

there any cases in which the independent variable is causally linked, in a significant and important way, to the dependent variable? If so, how does this causation work?

More importantly, in highly complex systems such as ecological-political systems, it is likely that the proposed independent variable will not be a sufficient cause of the dependent variable. Rather, as I noted in the appendix to chapter 5, multiple factors, including the hypothesized independent variable, will interact to produce the effect in question. If a hypothesis is to be valid for such a system, therefore, it will have to be more than a simple statement of "X causes Y" or "X is correlated with Y." The hypothesis will require, in addition, numerous and detailed scope conditions; it will take the form, for example, of "X causes Y, when A, B, and C are true."[13] Adding the right scope conditions should increase the causal strength of the whole set of independent variables and scope conditions taken together. As the causal strength of the whole set increases, and if the whole set together is taken as the independent variable, cases in quadrant 4 should move to quadrant 3. If enough conditions are specified, it might be possible to identify a set that is a *jointly sufficient* cause of Y. In this case, quadrant 4 should be empty.

Without including adequate scope conditions, a statistical analysis of the distribution of cases across the quadrants in figure 7A.1 will probably reveal little correlation, even though there might be important and interesting causal links between environmental scarcity and conflict. Yet careful process tracing, involving close examination of the causal process operating in the cases in quadrant 2, will help identify the relevant scope conditions.

Highly complex systems also present problems for controlled case comparisons. Such an approach, which, ideally, varies cases on the independent variable, is appropriate only if researchers can be sure to control *all* other variables that might significantly affect the incidence of the dependent variable. Unfortunately, however, with ecological-political systems researchers can never be sure that everything relevant is controlled. These systems are so complex that analysts may not even be aware of the existence of key variables and causal linkages. Moreover, as discussed in chapter 3, the relationships among these systems' variables are often nonlinear, reciprocal, and interactive, which makes them highly sensitive to small perturbations by what might seem peripheral variables. It is therefore often impossible to identify cases similar enough that the independent variables of interest can be isolated. Unknown and ill-understood differences among cases selected to vary only on a specific independent variable may have a great influence on the occurrence of conflict. Consequently, a comparison of the incidence of conflict in cases that do exhibit severe environmental scarcity with the incidence in cases that do not may reveal nothing about whether and how environmental scarcity contributes to conflict.[14]

One possible response to this problem of lack of adequate control is to carefully compare positive cases in quadrant 2 with any null cases that appear in quadrant 4.[15] Such a comparison might help identify hidden factors and processes that influence links between environmental scarcity and conflict. However, once again, the high uncertainty about the character of the systems under investigation means that it is not sensible for researchers to conduct such a comparison before they have a good idea of how environment-conflict linkages might work. Early in a research program, a focus on cases in quadrant 2 using process tracing is an efficient use of resources. If, instead, researchers spend much of their time examining null cases in quadrant 4, they will probably waste resources following red herrings and bad leads.

Close study of quadrant 2 cases using process tracing allows researchers to determine key scope conditions and intermediate processes and variables. Eventually, on examining cases in quadrant 4, researchers can ask whether these scope conditions and intermediate variables were present, and, if not, why not. If these factors were present, researchers could then determine what other factors prevented environmental scarcity from causing conflict. This staged approach permits progressive refinement of hypotheses and their scope conditions.

In sum, when researchers investigate highly complex causal systems, such as ecological-political systems, the choice of methodology to test hypotheses should be partly determined by the stage of research. In early stages, more attention should be given to the process tracing of causal links in cases where the hypothesized causal links appear to exist. As hypotheses are refined, an expanded range of methodologies can be used, including correlational analysis and controlled case comparison. Truly robust hypotheses—that is, hypotheses that reflect the complexity of the system under examination and that have a high probability of validity—are necessarily a product of later stages of research. They are the product of an iterative process of engagement with empirical data using a range of quantitative and case-based tests.

Conclusions

Experts on methodology in political science often advocate a rigidly orthodox approach to hypothesis testing and causal inference that is modeled after the natural sciences. Certain principles reside at the core of this orthodoxy: researchers should strive for parsimony, avoid selection on the dependent variable, seek to find necessary and/or sufficient causes of variation in the dependent variable, and focus—at least at first—on bivariate causal relations. This orthodoxy consequently stresses quasi-experimental research designs—including large-scale statistical analysis and controlled case comparisons—that supposedly permit control of confounding variables, allow for variance on selected dependent and independent variables, and permit the disaggregation of the relative causal weight of different independent variables. The study of ecological-political systems highlights some weaknesses of this approach.

First, as we saw in the appendix to chapter 5, political scientists, and social scientists in general, tend to use "folk" concepts of causation. Often, these concepts get in the way of a good understanding of complex systems. Researchers need a more precise and differentiated grasp of the possible causal roles of environmental scarcity as a contributor to conflict (along the lines of the schema offered in chapter 5's appendix) to guide their methodological decisions about how to test hypotheses. They need to recognize that, because ecological-political systems are multivariate and highly interactive, it is usually impossible to identify a single, sufficient cause of variation in a given dependent variable. Instead, researchers need multivariate and complex theories and hypotheses to explain system behavior. Moreover, it is often pointless to ask questions about the relative weight or power of causal factors in specific cases.

Second, as discussed in this appendix, ecological-political systems are very "opaque" to researchers. They are extremely complex, ill-understood, and sensitive to small perturbations—characteristics that can together overwhelm both statistical and controlled-comparison methods. Consequently, in early stages of research involving such systems, process tracing is the best method to develop, refine, and test hypotheses. As research progresses and hypotheses become more sophisticated, researchers can fruitfully use a broader range of methodologies.

8

Conclusions

In the preceding chapters, I developed a theory of the causal links between severe environmental scarcity and violence. I illustrated this theory with evidence drawn from numerous case studies. I also reviewed the long debate between optimists and pessimists on the ability of societies to adapt to natural resource scarcity, and I identified reasons why some poor societies may not be able to adapt to severe scarcity in the future. In this concluding chapter, I summarize the book's main findings, respond to some common skeptical arguments, and offer suggestions for future research.

My key finding is straightforward: preliminary research indicates that scarcity of renewable resources—or what I call *environmental scarcity*—can contribute to civil violence, including insurgencies and ethnic clashes. Although environmental scarcity has often spurred violence in the past, in coming decades the incidence of such violence will probably increase as scarcities of cropland, freshwater, and forests worsen in many parts of the developing world. Scarcity's role in such violence, however, is often obscure and indirect. It interacts with political, economic, and other factors to generate harsh social effects that in turn help produce violence. Analysts often interpret these social effects as the conflict's principal causes, thus overlooking scarcity's influence as an underlying stress.

Environmental scarcity is caused by the degradation and depletion of renewable resources, the increased demand for these resources, and/or their unequal distribution. These three sources of scarcity often interact and reinforce one another. Two kinds of interaction are particularly important: *resource capture* and *ecological marginalization*.

Resource capture occurs when the degradation and depletion of a renewable resource interacts with population growth to encourage powerful groups within a society to shift resource distribution in their favor. These groups tighten their grip on the increasingly scarce resource and use this control to boost their wealth and power. Resource capture intensifies scarcity for poorer and weaker groups in society. Ecological marginalization occurs when unequal resource access combines with population growth to cause long-term migrations of people dependent on renewable resources for their livelihood. They move to ecologically fragile regions such as steep upland slopes, areas at risk of desertification, tropical rain forests, and low-quality public lands within urban areas. High population densities in these regions, combined with a lack of knowledge and capital to protect the local ecosystem, cause severe resource degradation.

Developing economies tend to rely on environmental resources for a large part of their economic production and employment. Environmental scarcities, reinforced by resource capture and ecological marginalization, constrain local agricultural and economic production, affect the overall health of the economy, and cause economic hardship for marginal groups. To escape this hardship and improve their lives, people often migrate in large numbers. Environmental scarcities also strengthen group identities based on ethnic, class, or religious affiliations, a process called *social segmentation*; strengthened identities intensify competition among groups, reducing social trust and useful intergroup interaction. Finally, in some poor countries, the multiple effects of environmental scarcity increase demands on the state, stimulate predatory elite behavior, and depress state tax revenues. Such processes, in turn, widen wealth and power differentials among groups and weaken the administrative capacity and legitimacy of the state.

These harmful social effects of environmental scarcity—constrained agricultural and economic productivity, migrations, social segmentation, and state weakening—can cause insurgencies, ethnic clashes, and coups d'état. Declining or stagnant economic production sometimes generates deprivation conflicts, such as rural insurgencies and urban riots. Migrating groups can trigger ethnic conflicts when they move to new areas. State weakening shifts the social balance of power in favor of challenger groups (whose identities have often been strengthened by social segmentation) and increases opportunities for violent collective action by these groups against the state.

Some skeptics claim, however, that environmental scarcity is never a powerful cause of violent conflict. At most, it is an aggravating cause in a highly complex, multicausal system. Political, economic, and social factors—including failed institutions and policies—are much more important contributors to violence.[1] In fact, skeptics continue, these political, economic, and social factors are actually the ultimate causes of environmental scarcity. Environmental scarcity is therefore subordinate to these factors; it never plays an independent causal role. Consequently, it is of little fundamental interest to policymakers concerned about the causes of violence in our world.

It is true that environmental scarcity produces its effects within extremely complex ecological-political systems. Furthermore, environmental scarcity is not sufficient, by itself, to cause violence; when it does contribute to violence, research shows, it always interacts with other political, economic, and social factors. Environmental scarcity's causal role can never be separated from these contextual factors, which are often unique to the society in question. The preliminary analysis in this book identifies some that are particularly important. In chapter 6, for example, I highlighted the character of markets, the autonomy of the state, and the strength of norms of trust, reciprocity, and responsibility to the commonweal; in chapter 7, I discussed the nature of society's pre-existing ethnic and class divisions, the conception of justice held by challenger groups, the level of resources and organizational coherence of these groups, and the capabilities of leaders in challenger groups, elites, and the state. I have shown how such contextual factors can combine with severe environmental scarcity to produce the harmful social effects mentioned above and to influence the degree of instability and violence in a society.

Because the relationship between environmental scarcity and contextual factors is interactive, it is often impossible to determine the relative weight or power of environmental scarcity as a cause of violence in specific cases. But this does not mean that environmental scarcity is always an unimportant cause. A large proportion of the world's population is almost completely reliant on local cropland, water, and forest supplies for its daily existence. Skeptics usually underestimate the extent to which much of humankind still depends on its natural environment and therefore underestimate the social stress that environmental scarcity can cause.

In addition, environmental scarcity's role as a cause of violence should not always be subordinated to that of political, economic, and social factors. First, environmental scarcity often reciprocally influences the political and economic character of social systems—as, for example, when it stimulates resource capture by powerful elites or competition among narrow social coalitions that impedes institutional and policy reform. Second, environmental scarcity is partly a function of the character of a society's physical environment—whether, for instance, that environment is robust or fragile. And third, if severe environmental damage becomes irreversible, it can become a permanent source of social stress; even if the political and economic factors that originally produced the damage are fixed, it remains an independent burden on the society.

In this book, we have seen that environmental scarcity contributes to diffuse, persistent, subnational violence, such as ethnic clashes and insurgencies. It rarely, if ever, contributes directly to conflict among states, that is, to *resource wars*. During the twentieth century there have been a number of interstate wars over, in part, access to nonrenewables like oil and minerals. But there are few modern examples of interstate war over renewables such as cropland, forests, fresh water, and fish. There are two explanations for this difference. First, in general, states cannot easily or quickly convert renewable resources into assets that significantly augment their power. Second, the very countries that are most dependent on renewable resources, and that are therefore most motivated to seize resources from their neighbors, also tend to be poor, which lessens their capability for aggression.

The renewable resource most likely to stimulate interstate war is river water. However, wars over river water between upstream and downstream neighbors are likely only in a narrow set of circumstances: the downstream country must be highly dependent on the water for its national well-being, the upstream country must be threatening to restrict substantially the river's flow, there must be a history of antagonism between the two countries, and, most importantly, the downstream country must be militarily stronger than the upstream country. Research shows that conflict and turmoil related to river water is more often internal than international; this conflict results from dams and other major water projects that relocate large numbers of people.

If environmental scarcity contributes mainly to civil not interstate violence, why should policymakers in developed countries be concerned? Some skeptics argue that such conflict will occur only in regions of marginal importance to the national security interests of rich countries.[2] The countries most prone to instability will be the poorest, and they will not have the resources to cause serious security problems for other countries.

Yet conflicts generated partly by environmental scarcity, although perhaps not as conspicuous or dramatic as interstate wars, can nonetheless have serious indirect effects on the international community. The changing nature of the international system—heightened economic interdependence, easier long-distance travel, and increased access to arms—makes previously insignificant regions of interest to policymakers. Crises in small countries, such as Haiti, often create serious foreign policy difficulties for developed countries, and large and significant countries—including Pakistan, China, India, and Indonesia—are not immune to the severe stresses environmental scarcity generates. Major civil violence within states can affect external trade relations, cause refugee flows, and produce humanitarian disasters that call upon the military and financial resources of developed countries and international organizations. Moreover, countries destabilized by civil violence may fragment as they become enfeebled and as peripheral regions are seized by renegade authorities and warlords. Their regimes might avoid fragmentation by becoming more authoritarian, intolerant of opposition, and militarized; they might also try to divert attention from domestic grievances by threatening neighboring states.

Skeptics often claim, finally, that environmental scarcity will rarely contribute to conflict, because human societies show great capacity to adapt to resource scarcity, especially through market mechanisms. When a resource becomes scarce, its price increases, which encourages conservation, substitution, and technological innovation. Scarcity also encourages institutional adaptations, such as changes in property rights, that raise incentives to conserve and innovate and that reduce the hardship scarcity produces.[3]

It is true that scarcity often stimulates useful technological and social changes. Yet a society's ability to adapt to rising scarcity depends on the relationship between its requirement for ingenuity to respond to scarcity and its supply of ingenuity, which includes the implementation of this ingenuity. (As I define it, *ingenuity* consists of ideas for new technologies and new and reformed institutions.) Societies in which requirement outstrips supply face an *ingenuity gap*; they will be unable to adapt adequately to environmental scarcity and will, consequently, be vulnerable to scarcity's harsh social effects, including economic dislocation, migrations, social segmentations, and state weakening.

In the next decades, population growth, rising average resource demand, and persistent inequalities in resource access ensure that scarcities will affect many environmentally sensitive regions with unprecedented severity, speed, and scale. Ingenuity requirements will therefore rise rapidly. But this situation need not lead to crisis, since, by changing prices and incentives, scarcity often does stimulate a flow of ingenuity sufficient to meet the rising need.

Nevertheless, there are several reasons why this beneficial response may not occur in some poor societies. The prerequisites for effective adaptation to scarcity often do not exist: states are weak, bureaucracies incompetent, judicial systems corrupt, research centers underfunded, and property rights unclear. Markets often do not work well: prices in most developing countries—especially for water, forests, and other common resources—do not adjust to reflect accurately rising scarcity, and therefore incentives for entrepreneurs are inadequate. Low levels of education, technological capacity, and financial capital also depress the supply of ingenuity. Finally, environmental scarcity can actually undermine the ability of developing societies to generate and implement social and technical solutions to scarcity. Under certain circumstances, scarcity mobilizes narrow coalitions and powerful elites to block the institutional reforms that could reduce scarcity's broader social impact.

Positive economic, social, and technological responses to environmental scarcity are therefore not guaranteed. Some societies will adapt well, others will not. In coming decades, worsening environmental scarcities in many regions will further exaggerate the world's already gaping differentials between rich and poor societies and between the powerful and weak people within those societies. The world's wealthy regions should not assume that they will be able to wall themselves off from turmoil in societies that do not adapt well to scarcity. We are living cheek by jowl on this planet now. We are all next-door neighbors.

The analysis in the foregoing chapters shows that many things can be done to prevent such turmoil. Although this book has not offered policy prescriptions, it has identified a range of social, economic, and political variables open to policy manipulation. The situation in some parts of the planet may be grave, but the story presented here is decidedly not a deterministic or apocalyptic one.

Policy interventions will, of course, be aided by a better understanding of the physical and social processes that link environmental scarcity and violence. We therefore need more and better research into these processes. The study of the environmental causes of violence began in earnest only about a decade ago, and the work discussed in this book represents only some of the first, very preliminary forays into this new field.

Where might future research go? Any list of new directions cannot possibly be exhaustive, but a few seem especially promising. Particular deserving of study is democracy's effect on the connections between environmental scarcity and violence. Although recent decades have seen a surge of democratization around the world, the term *democracy* is used too loosely by lay commentators and experts alike. It commonly encompasses an extraordinarily variegated set of social phenomena and institutions that have complicated and multiple effects on the incidence of social turmoil and violence.

Research addressing how democracy, environmental scarcity, and violence are related is only just beginning.[4] Depending on its form, democracy can help people mobilize to reduce environmental degradation and to change skewed distributions of resources. Democracy can also increase state legitimacy and offer challenger groups nonviolent opportunities to act on their grievances. All of these processes reduce the probability that environmental scarcity will cause civil strife. On the other hand, in societies that are already highly segmented, certain kinds of democratic institutions can further aggravate cleavages and weaken the state.

Closer study is also needed of factors (other than democracy) that affect adaptation to scarcity, especially the obstructionist behaviors of narrow coalitions and rent-seeking elites. Moreover, we need to understand better not only the factors that affect a society's aggregate supply of social and technical ingenuity in response to scarcity, but also those that affect the quality of ingenuity produced, its distribution with the society, how it is used, and for what ends it is used.

Finally, to date, most environment-conflict researchers have used a process tracing methodology. In the early stages of this research program, such an approach was justified. Process tracing helped researchers identify key contextual factors and scope conditions pertinent to their hypotheses. But researchers can now derive from the preliminary findings of this work more sophisticated hypotheses, and these hypotheses should be tested using a broader range of methodologies, including cross-national statistical analysis, counterfactual analysis, and carefully controlled comparisons of cases varied on both the dependent and independent variable. Of particular interest are cases that exhibit all the precursor conditions hypothesized to produce violence (including environmental scarcity) but that do not exhibit violence. Such cases, if found, will further our understanding of the many contextual factors that can influence the strength of the relationship between environmental scarcity and violence.

Notes

Chapter 1
Introduction

1. See "General Readings on Environmental Security" at the end of this book.

2. Readers interested in a careful argument for an expanded notion of security (that includes nonmilitary threats to national well-being) should see Richard Ullman, "Redefining Security," *International Security* 8, no. 1 (1983): 133, 143. He proposes the following definition: "A threat to national security is an action or sequence of events that (1) threatens drastically and over a relatively brief span of time to degrade the quality of life for the inhabitants of a state, or (2) threatens significantly to narrow the range of policy choices available to the government of a state or to private, nongovernmental entities (persons, groups, corporations) within the state." By this definition, environmental degradation and population growth in the developing world are threats to security, because they are "bound to degrade the quality of life, and diminish the range of options available, to governments and persons in the rich countries."

3. For example, see David Wirth, "Climate Chaos," *Foreign Policy*, no. 74 (spring 1989): 10. Numerous scholars of international relations, especially those of the realist school, claim that shifting power relations can prompt war. See Robert Gilpin, *War and Change in World Politics* (Cambridge: Cambridge University Press, 1981), 94, 191; A. F. K. Organski and Jacek Kugler, *The War Ledger* (Chicago: University of Chicago Press, 1980); and Jack Levy, "Research Note: Declining Power and the Preventive Motivation for War," *World Politics* 40, no. 1 (1987): 82–107.

4. Robert Heilbroner, *An Inquiry into the Human Prospect* (New York: W. W. Norton, 1980), 39, 95; William Ophuls, *Ecology and the Politics of Scarcity: A Prologue to a Political Theory of the Steady State* (San Francisco: Freeman, 1977), 214–17.

5. Fen Hampson, "The Climate for War," *Peace and Security* 3, no. 3 (1988): 9; Ian Cowan, "Security Implications of Global Climatic Changes," *Canadian Defence Quarterly* (October 1989): 47.

6. Jodi Jacobson, *Environmental Refugees: A Yardstick of Habitability*, Worldwatch Paper 86 (Washington, D.C.: Worldwatch Institute, 1988). Paul Ehrlich, Anne Ehrlich, and John Holdren, *Ecoscience: Population, Resources and Environment* (San Francisco: Freeman, 1977).

7. Peter Gleick, "Climate Change and International Politics: Problems Facing Developing Countries," *Ambio* 18, no. 6 (1989): 336; Malin Falkenmark, "Fresh Waters as a Factor in Strategic Policy and Action," in *Global Resources and International Conflict: Environmental Factors in Strategic Policy and Action*, ed. Arthur Westing (New York: Oxford University Press, 1986), 85–113.

8. Peter Wallensteen, "Food Crops as a Factor in Strategic Policy and Action," in *Global Resources and International Conflict*, ed. Westing, 151–55.

9. Ibid., 146–51.

10. Ted Gurr, "On the Political Consequences of Scarcity and Economic Decline,"

International Studies Quarterly 29, no. 1 (1985): 51–75; and Jessica Tuchman Mathews, "Redefining Security," *Foreign Affairs* 68, no. 2 (1989): 162–77.

11. Ophuls writes: "The disappearance of ecological abundance seems bound to make international politics even more tension ridden and potentially violent than it already is. Indeed, the pressures of ecological scarcity may embroil the world in hopeless strife, so that long before ecological collapse occurs by virtue of the physical limitations of the earth, the current world order will have been destroyed by turmoil and war" Ophuls, *Ecology and the Politics of Scarcity*, 214.

12. The writings of Norman Myers, in particular, are marked by an almost complete absence of empirical rigor and theoretical structure. See especially Norman Myers, *Ultimate Security: The Environmental Basis of Political Stability* (New York: W. W. Norton, 1993).

13. The cases were Mauritania-Senegal, Rwanda, South Africa, Bangladesh-Assam, Bihar, Pakistan, Indonesia, Philippines, China, Haiti, Chiapas, Nicaragua, Peru, Gaza, the Jordan River basin, and the Nile basin. Many of these case studies can be found at www.library.utoronto.ca/www/pcs/eps.htm and www.library.utoronto.ca/www/pcs/state.htm. See also Thomas Homer-Dixon and Jessica Blitt, eds., *Ecoviolence: Links among Environment, Population, and Security* (Boulder, Colo.: Rowman & Littlefield, 1998).

14. The Environment and Conflicts Project (ENCOP) was a collaborative effort of the Centre for Security Studies and Conflict Research at the Swiss Federal Institute of Technology, Zurich, and the Swiss Peace Foundation, Berne. It examined the causal relationships between environmental degradation and both international and internal violent conflicts. For a list of some of ENCOP's publications, see "ENCOP Materials" at the end of this book.

The International Peace Research Institute (PRIO) in Oslo, Norway, is an independent international institution conducting research on three broad themes: conditions of war and peace; ethnic and nationalist conflicts; and foreign and security policies. For a list of some of PRIO's publications, see "PRIO Materials" at the end of this book.

15. I wish to thank Jack Goldstone who proposed an early version of this list. I have omitted a number of less plausible types of environmentally induced conflict. Declining biodiversity might contribute to conflict (by, for example, weakening agricultural productivity over the long term and thereby worsening poverty), but only in a highly indirect manner. Increased dumping of toxic wastes in the South, and accidents in the South involving subsidiaries of Northern companies (such as the Bhopal tragedy in India), will probably only strain economic and diplomatic relations, although such incidents could lead to sporadic, localized violence. Perceptions of environmental damage or potential damage (whether or not the perceptions are justified) might also induce tensions; for instance, the proposed siting of a nuclear plant close to an international border could lead to protests in neighboring countries. However, it seems unlikely that such perceptions by themselves could cause widespread violent conflict.

16. For example, environmental problems such as transboundary pollution or depletion of stratospheric ozone can encourage collaboration of scientific and technical communities that cut across national boundaries. This collaboration in turn encourages international cooperation at the policymaking level. See Peter Haas, *Saving the Mediterranean* (New York: Columbia University Press, 1990).

17. David Dessler similarly distinguishes between a focus on outcomes and a focus on causal factors. "The analyst interested in some phenomenon might treat it as an outcome or feature of some process or structure and search for conditions associated with its appearance. Alternatively, the researcher might choose a factor known or thought to play a role in causing the phenomenon and analyze the tendencies of this factor in isolation. Both categories of analysis link factors to outcomes, but convey different information about this link. While the first category (focus on *outcome*) tells us what configuration of conditions lead to some specified observed outcome in the world, the second one (focus on *factor*) tells us what outcomes tend to be brought about by the workings of a specified factor, whether or not these outcomes are actually produced." See David Dessler, "The Architecture of Causal Analysis" (paper prepared for the Seminar for Philosophy and Methodology of the Social Sciences, Center for International Affairs, Harvard University, April 1992), 8. Dessler derives his distinction from John Stuart Mill's book *System of Logic: Ratiocinative and Inductive* (New York: Harper, 1859).

18. In cases where the value of the hypothesized independent variable has changed little or only slowly in the past, standard statistical procedures will reveal little relationship between this variable and other variables. If researchers are interested in the potential causal role of the independent variable, they will need to study past cases selected specifically to accentuate its variance.

19. The meaning of "important" is, of course, open to various interpretations. For example, an important cause could be one that is a necessary or sufficient condition for a given effect, that has a high probability of producing a given effect, or that explains a significant proportion of the variance of a dependent variable.

20. This figure was provided to the author by Barbara Boyle Torrey, Director of the Commission on Behavioral and Social Science Education of the National Research Council. It is based on a 1990 estimate by the Center for International Research of the U.S. Census Bureau.

Chapter 2
Overview

1. B. L. Turner II et al., eds., *The Earth as Transformed by Human Action* (Cambridge: Cambridge University Press, 1990), 13.

2. For example, climate change may interact with long-term soil degradation that produces a loss of rooting depth and increased susceptibility of crops to drought. Together, these changes could cause much greater declines in agricultural yields than either would produce by itself.

3. "From Rwanda to Cairo," *Washington Post*, 25 August 1994, p. A18.

4. Thomas Homer-Dixon and Valerie Percival, "Environmental Scarcity and Violent Conflict: The Case of Rwanda," *Journal of Environment and Development* 5, no. 3 (1996): 270–91.

5. For an argument that stresses the importance of such factors, see Ronnie Lipschutz, "Environmental Conflict and Environmental Determinism: The Relative Importance of Social and Natural Factors," in *Conflict and the Environment*, ed. Nils Petter Gleditsch (Dordrecht, The Netherlands: Kluer, 1997), 35–50; see also Wenche Hauge

and Tanja Ellingsen, "Beyond Environmental Scarcity: The Casual Pathways to Conflict," *Journal of Peace Research* 35, no. 3 (1998): 299–317.

6. Hauge and Ellingsen, "Beyond Environmental Scarcity."

7. For a definition, see Robert Chase, Emily Hill, and Paul Kennedy, "Pivotal States and U.S. Strategy," *Foreign Affairs* 75, no. 1 (1996): 33–51.

8. Robert Repetto, *The "Second India" Revisited: Population, Poverty, and Environmental Stress over Two Decades* (Washington, D.C.: World Resources Institute, 1994), 5.

9. United Nations Population Division, *World Population Prospects: The 1996 Revision, Demographic Indicators 1950–2050*, Diskettes 1–4 (New York: United Nations, 1996); see also Leela Visaria and Pravin Visaria, *Prospective Population Growth and Policy Options for India, 1991–2101* (New York: Population Council, 1996), 6.

10. Repetto, *The "Second India" Revisited*, 6.

11. Jack Goldstone analyzes the effects of population growth on competition for social resources, such as job and status opportunities. See Jack Goldstone, *Revolution and Rebellion in the Early Modern World* (Berkeley: University of California Press, 1991); and Jack Goldstone, "Saving the Environment (and Political Stability too): Institutional Responses for Developing Nations," *Environmental Change and Security Project Report*, Issue 2 (Washington, D.C.: Woodrow Wilson Centre, 1996), 33–34.

12. Sanjoy Hazarika, "Week of Rioting Leaves Streets of Bombay Empty," *New York Times*, 12 January 1993, p. A3, national edition.

13. Raj Chengappa and Ramesh Menon, "The New Battlefields," *India Today* 18, no. 2 (31 January 1993): 28.

14. See, for example, Barber Conable and David Lampton, "China: The Coming Power," *Foreign Affairs* 72, no. 5 (92/93): 133–49. In their assessment of the pressures on contemporary China, the authors devote one-half sentence to these stresses. Even commentators who are skeptical about China's rise neglect ecological issues. See Robert Dujarric, "No Solid Foundations: China's Prospects of Becoming a Great Power," *Internationale Politik und Gesellschaft*, 3 (1997): 276–90.

15. Griffith Feeney et al., "Recent Fertility Dynamics in China: Results from the 1987 One Percent Population Survey," *Population and Development Review* 15, no. 2 (1989): 297–321; Shanti Conly and Sharon Camp, *China's Family Planning Program: Challenging the Myths*, Country Study Series, No. 1 (Washington, D.C.: Population Crisis Committee, 1992).

16. Nicholas Kristof, "China's Crackdown on Births: A Stunning, and Harsh, Success," *New York Times*, 25 April 1993, p. A1, national edition.

17. Elizabeth Economy, *Reforms and Resources: The Implications for State Capacity in the People's Republic of China*, Occasional Paper of the Project on Environmental Scarcities, State Capacity and Civil Violence (Cambridge, Mass.: American Academy of Arts and Sciences and the University of Toronto, 1997).

18. Patrick Tyler, Huge Water Project Would Supply Beijing by 800-Mile Aqueduct," *New York Times*, 19 July 1994, p. A8, national edition.

19. The author obtained much of the data and material in the following pages during a research trip to China, and to Shanxi province specifically, in 1995.

20. Vaclav Smil, *China's Environmental Crisis: An Inquiry into the Limits of National Development* (Armonk, N.Y.: M. E. Sharpe, 1993).

21. "Beijing Faces Cash Troubles," *South China Morning Post*, 9 June 1995, p. 10.

Chapter 3
Two Centuries of Debate

1. Various authors propose divisions of the debate analogous to that offered in this chapter. See, for example Edward Barbier, *Economics, Natural-Resource Scarcity and Development: Conventional and Alternative Views* (London: Earthscan, 1989); and Julie Matthaei, "Rethinking Scarcity: Neoclassicism, NeoMalthusianism, and Neo-Marxism," *Review of Radical Political Economics* 16, no. 2/3 (1984): 81–94. Warrick and Riebsame similarly describe and contrast four important theoretical perspectives on social vulnerability to environmental stress: the perceptual, environmental/ecological, economic, and social-structural perspectives. The second and third roughly correspond to the neo-Malthusian and economic optimism views discussed here, and the fourth represents the distributional perspective. See Richard Warrick and William Riebsame, "Societal Response to CO_2-Induced Climate Change: Opportunities for Research," *Climatic Change* 3, no. 4 (1981): 398–401.

2. Perhaps the most famous modern statement of the Malthusian thesis is the computerized model described in Donella Meadows et al., *The Limits to Growth: A Report for the Club of Rome's Project on the Predicament of Mankind* (New York: Signet, 1972). The Meadows team has recently revised their model in Donella Meadows, Dennis Meadows, and Jorgen Randers, *Beyond the Limits: Confronting Global Collapse, Envisioning a Sustainable Future* (Post Mills, Vt.: Chelsea Green, 1992). Similar neo-Malthusian perspectives are offered in John Gever et al., *Beyond Oil: The Threat to Food and Fuel in the Coming Decades* (Cambridge, Mass.: Ballinger, 1986); Paul Ehrlich and Anne Ehrlich, *The Population Explosion* (New York: Touchstone, 1991); W. E. Rees and M. Wackernagel, "Ecological Footprints and Appropriated Carrying Capacity: Measuring the Natural Capital Requirements of the Human Economy," in *Investing in Natural Capital: The Ecological Economics Approach to Sustainability*, ed. A. Jannson et al. (Washington, D.C.: Island Press, 1994); and L. R. Brown and H. Kane, *Full House: Reassessing the Earth's Population Carrying Capacity* (New York: W. W. Norton, 1994). A response to the Meadows work is H. S. D. Cole et al., *Models of Doom: A Critique of the Limits to Growth* (New York: Universe Books, 1973).

3. Neoclassical economics is a body of theory grounded in nineteenth-century marginal economics, which emphasizes the relationship between factor prices and scarcity, the rational maximizing behavior of individuals in markets, the idea of a perfectly competitive economy in equilibrium, and the market's natural tendency toward full employment.

4. An exemplary statement of the neoclassical position is Harold Barnett and Chandler Morse, *Scarcity and Growth: The Economics of Natural Resource Availability* (Baltimore: Johns Hopkins Press for Resources for the Future, 1963). For a more contemporary treatment, see V. Kerry Smith, ed., *Scarcity and Growth Reconsidered* (Baltimore: Johns Hopkins Press for Resources for the Future, 1979), especially chapter 2, J. E. Stiglitz, "A Neoclassical Analysis of the Economics of Natural Resources," 36–66. A less technical discussion of resource and environmental issues, one that generally reflects economic optimism, is Jesse H. Ausubel et al., "The Liberation of the Environment," *Dædalus* 125, no. 3 (1996). Policy implications are discussed in Terry Anderson and Donald Leal, *Free Market Environmentalism* (Pacific Research Institute for Public

Policy: San Francisco, 1990); see also R. N. Cooper, *Environment and Resource Policies for the World Economy* (Washington, D.C.: Brookings Institution, 1994).

5. See, for example, Frances Moore Lappe, *Food First* (London: Souvenir Press, 1980); Pier Blaikie, *The Political Economy of Soil Erosion* (London: Longman, 1985); James Boyce, *Agrarian Impasse in Bengal: Institutional Constraints to Technological Change* (Oxford: Oxford University Press, 1987); and Amartya Sen, *Poverty and Famines: An Essay on Entitlement and Deprivation* (Oxford: Clarendon Press, 1981).

6. Julian Simon, *The Ultimate Resource* (Princeton, N.J.: Princeton University Press, 1981); Julian Simon, *The Ultimate Resource 2* (Princeton, N.J.: Princeton University Press, 1996); Julian Simon and Herman Kahn, eds., *The Resourceful Earth: A Response to Global 2000* (Oxford: Basil Blackwell, 1984); and Ehrlich and Ehrlich, *The Population Explosion*. See also, Norman Myers and Julian Simon, *Scarcity or Abundance? A Debate on the Environment* (New York: W. W. Norton, 1994).

7. Examples are World Bank, *World Development Report 1992: Development and the Environment* (New York: Oxford University Press, 1992); "Summers on Sustainable Growth," *Economist* 323, no. 7761 (29 May 1992): 65; "Senator Malthus," *Wall Street Journal*, 3 August 1992, p. A18; and Ronald Bailey, *Eco-Scam: The False Prophets of Ecological Apocalypse* (New York: St. Martin's Press, 1993).

8. K. J. Holsti, "The Horsemen of the Apocalypse: At the Gate, Detoured, or Retreating?" *International Studies Quarterly* 30, no. 4 (1986): 356.

9. The following is a representative and chronological sample of some of the best literature on this issue: Robert Repetto, ed., *The Global Possible* (London: Yale University Press, 1985); D. Coleman and R. Schofield, eds., *The State of Population Theory: Forward from Malthus* (New York: Basil Blackwell, 1986); Robert Repetto, "Population, Resources, Environment: An Uncertain Future," *Population Bulletin* 42, no. 2 (1987): 1–43; Barbier, *Economics, Natural-Resource Scarcity and Development*; Michael Teitelbaum and Jay Winter, eds., *Population and Resources in Western Intellectual Traditions*, a project of the American Association for the Advancement of Science Committee on Population, Resources, and the Environment, supplement to *Population and Development Review* 14 (New York: The Population Council, 1989); Kingsley Davis and Mikhail S. Bernstam, eds., *Resources, Environment, and Population: Present Knowledge, Future Options* (New York: Oxford University Press, 1991); Nathan Keyfitz, "Are There Ecological Limits to Population?" *Proceedings of the National Academy of Sciences USA* 90, no. 15 (1993): 6895–99; Geoffrey McNicoll, *Malthusian Scenarios and Demographic Catastrophism*, Working Paper No. 49 (New York: The Population Council, 1993); A. Jannson et al., eds., *Investing in Natural Capital: The Ecological Economics Approach to Sustainability* (Washington, D.C.: Island Press, 1994); K. Lindahl-Kiessling and H. Landberg, eds., *Population, Economic Development, and the Environment* (Oxford: Oxford University Press, 1994); World Bank, *Population and Development: Implications for the World Bank* (Washington, D.C.: World Bank, 1994); J. E. Cohen, *How Many People Can the Earth Support?* (New York: W. W. Norton, 1995); P. S. Dasgupta, "Population, Poverty and the Local Environment," *Scientific American* 272, no. 2 (February 1995): 40–45; Kenneth Arrow et al., "Forum on Economic Growth, Carrying Capacity, and the Environment," *Ecological Economics* 15, no. 2 (1995); Ester Boserup, "Development Theory: An Analytical Framework and Selected Applications," *Population and Development Review* 22, no. 3 (1996): 505–15; Ausubel et al., "Liberation of the Environment."

10. Thomas Malthus, *An Essay on the Principle of Population* (1798; reprint, with an introduction by Anthony Flew, New York: Penguin, 1970), 70–71; see also William Peterson, *Malthus* (Cambridge, Mass.: Harvard University Press, 1979).

11. Malthus allowed for the expansion of cropland area but believed that this expansion could not completely compensate for population growth. David Ricardo, while largely in agreement with Malthus's grim predictions, introduced the variable of resource quality: he argued that the price mechanism would encourage people to use the highest-quality cropland first, followed by land of progressively lower quality. See Barnett and Morse, *Scarcity and Growth*, 59–64.

12. A. J. Coale and E. M. Hoover, *Population Growth and Economic Development in Low-income Countries: A Case Study of India's Prospects* (Princeton, N.J.: Princeton University Press, 1959).

13. Kingsley Davis, *The Population of India and Pakistan* (Princeton, N.J.: Princeton University Press, 1951), 203–12.

14. Marquis de Condorcet, *Sketch for a Historical Picture of the Progress of the Human Mind* (1795), cited in Robert Repetto, "Population, Resources, Environment," 5.

15. Sherry Olson, *The Depletion Myth: A History of Railroad Use of Timber* (Cambridge, Mass.: Harvard University Press, 1971).

16. David Pimentel et al., "Food Production and the Energy Crisis," *Science* 182, no. 4111 (2 November 1973): 443–49.

17. Ester Boserup, *The Conditions of Agricultural Growth: The Economics of Agrarian Change under Population Pressure* (Chicago: Aldine, 1965); Ester Boserup, *Economic and Demographic Relationships in Development*, essays selected and introduced by T. Paul Schultz (Baltimore: Johns Hopkins University Press, 1990). For similar findings, see also Mary Tiffen, Michael Mortimore, and Francis Gichuki, *More People, Less Erosion: Environmental Recovery in Kenya* (Chichester, U.K.: John Wiley, 1994); and B. L. Turner, Goran Hyden, and Robert Kates, *Population Growth and Agricultural Change in Africa* (Gainesville: University Press of Florida, 1993).

18. Jacob Schmookler, *Invention and Economic Growth* (Cambridge, Mass.: Harvard University Press, 1966), 199.

19. Gene Grossman and Elhanan Helpman, *Innovation and Growth in the Global Economy* (Cambridge, Mass.: MIT Press, 1991), 335. The hypothesis that large, monopolistic firms will achieve higher rates of technological innovation was first elaborated by Joseph Schumpeter in *Capitalism, Socialism and Democracy* (New York: Harper & Row, 1942).

20. J. R. Hicks, *The Theory of Wages* (London: Macmillan, 1932).

21. Yujiro Hayami and Vernon Ruttan, *Agricultural Development: An International Perspective* (Baltimore: Johns Hopkins University Press, 1971, 1985). For a survey of induced innovation theory, see Hans Binswanger, "Induced Technical Change: Evolution of Thought," in *Induced Innovation: Technology, Institutions, and Development*, ed. Hans Binswanger and Vernon Ruttan (Baltimore: Johns Hopkins University Press, 1978).

22. Vernon Ruttan and Yujiro Hayami, "Toward a Theory of Induced Institutional Innovation," *Journal of Development Studies* 20, no. 4 (1984): 203–23; Vernon Ruttan, "Institutional Innovation and Agricultural Development," *World Development* 17, no. 9 (1989): 1375–87.

23. A variable is fully endogenous if it is fully internal to a causal system—if, in other words, other variables in the system determine changes in its value. See the discussion of endogeneity and exogeneity in the appendix to chapter 5.

24. H. E. Goeller and A. M. Weinberg, "The Age of Substitutability," *Science* 191, no. 4228 (20 February 1976): 683–89.

25. Barnett and Morse, *Scarcity and Growth*, 10.

26. Ibid., 11.

27. New archaeological evidence suggests that overpopulation and land degradation helped topple Sumerian, Mayan, and Easter Island civilizations; and recent historical sociology shows that population growth was a major force behind civil strife in early-modern Eurasian societies. See Daniel Hillel, *Out of the Earth: Civilization and the Life of the Soil* (New York: Free Press, 1991); Clive Pointing, *A Green History of the World: The Environment and the Collapse of Great Civilizations* (New York: Penguin, 1991); J. M. Diamond, "Ecological Collapses of Ancient Civilizations: The Golden Age That Never Was," *Bulletin*, The American Academy of Arts and Sciences, 47, no. 5 (1994): 37–59; and Jack Goldstone, *Revolution and Rebellion in the Early Modern World* (Berkeley: University of California Press, 1991).

28. Theodore Panayotou, "Roundtable Discussion: Is Economic Growth Sustainable?" *Proceedings of the World Bank Annual Conference on Development Economics 1991* (Washington, D.C.: World Bank, 1992), 357.

29. Repetto, "Population, Resources, Environment," 24.

30. World Bank, *World Development Report 1992*, 9.

31. See John Tierney, "Betting the Planet," *New York Times Magazine*, 2 December 1990, 52–81. It is not clear, however, that a steady downward movement in resource prices can be counted as evidence in support of neoclassical economists' standard arguments about resource scarcity. Neoclassical theory implies that resource prices must increase, at least some of the time, to provide incentives for exploration, conservation, and substitution.

32. Margaret Slade, "Trends in Natural Resource Commodity Prices: An Analysis of the Time Domain," *Journal of Environmental Economics and Management* 9, no. 2 (1982): 122–37; and B. Moazzami and F. Anderson, "Modelling Natural Resource Scarcity Using the 'Error-Correction' Approach," *Canadian Journal of Economics* 27, no. 4 (1994): 801–12.

33. Robert Gordon et al., *Toward a New Iron Age? Quantitative Modelling of Resource Exhaustion* (Cambridge, Mass.: Harvard University Press, 1987), 63, 155.

34. Uma Lele and Steven Stone, *Population Pressure, the Environment and Agricultural Intensification: Variations on the Boserup Hypothesis*, MADIA Discussion Paper 4 (Washington, D.C.: World Bank, 1989).

35. Repetto, "Population, Resources, Environment," 35–36. In the 1980s, population growth outpaced food production in two-thirds of developing countries and in more than 80 percent of African countries. Per Pinstrup-Anderson, "Global Perspectives for Food Production and Consumption," *Tidsskrift for Land Okonomi* 4, no. 179 (1992): 167.

36. Alan Olmstead and Paul Rhode, "Induced Innovation in American Agriculture: A Reconsideration," *Journal of Political Economy* 101, no. 1 (1993): 105, 110. For criticism of the application of induced-innovation theory to developing economies, see Richard Grabowski, "The Theory of Induced Institutional Innovation: A Critique," *World Development* 16, no. 3 (1988): 385–94.

37. James Boyce, *Agrarian Impasse in Bengal: Institutional Constraints to Technological Change* (Oxford: Oxford University Press, 1987).

38. The relationship between flooding and soil fertility is not well understood. See James Boyce, "Birth of a Megaproject: Political Economy of Flood Control in Bangladesh," *Environmental Management* 14, no. 4 (1990): 419–28, especially 424.

39. Controversy surrounds the question of whether Himalayan deforestation contributes to flooding; see Lester Brown and John Young, "Feeding the World in the Nineties," in *State of the World: 1990* (Washington, D.C.: W. W. Norton, 1990), 61; and Centre for Science and Environment, *Floods, Flood Plains, and Environmental Myths* (New Delhi: CSE, 1991), especially 68–69.

40. On the Farakka Barrage, Ashok Swain writes: "It has disrupted fishing and navigation [in Bangladesh], brought unwanted salt deposits into rich farming soil, affected agricultural and industrial production, changed the hydraulic character of the rivers and caused changes in the ecology of the Delta." See Ashok Swain, "Environmental Destruction and Acute Social Conflict: A Case Study of the Ganges Water Dispute," Department of Peace and Conflict Research, Uppsala University, Uppsala, Sweden, November 1992, 24; Ashok Swain, "Conflicts Over Water: The Ganges Water Dispute," *Security Dialogue* 24, no. 4 (1993): 429–39; and Ashok Swain, "Displacing the Conflict: Environmental Destruction in Bangladesh and Ethnic Conflict in India," *Journal of Peace Research* 33, no. 2 (1996): 189–204.

41. United Nations Population Division, *World Population Prospects: The 1996 Revision, Demographic Indicators 1950–2050*, Diskettes 1–4 (New York: United Nations, 1996).

42. Boyce, *Agrarian Impasse*, 252.

43. Ibid., 255.

44. Francesco Goletti, *The Changing Public Role in a Rice Economy Approaching Self-Sufficiency: The Case of Bangladesh*, IFPRI Research Report 98 (Washington, D.C.: International Food Policy Research Institute, 1994). It should be noted, however, that much well-water in Bangladesh is contaminated with arsenic. The increased reliance on this well-water for irrigation and personal consumption has afflicted tens of millions of people with arsenic poisoning. See Suzanne Goldenberg, "Death by a Thousand Drops of Water," *Manchester Guardian Weekly*, 27 July 1997, p. 10.

45. John F. Burns, "Economic Surge in Bangladesh Undercut by Political Turmoil," *New York Times*, 27 January 1996, p. A1, national edition.

46. Some people might argue that environmental thresholds, interdependence, and interactivity can boost the supply of environmental resources: for example, climate change that causes a sharp and unanticipated increase in precipitation in a drought-prone region could reduce local water scarcity. I agree that such effects might sometimes be positive, but I argue in chapter 6 that on balance they restrict resource availability. Among other things, it is often hard for human societies to adjust their institutions and technologies rapidly enough to prevent sudden changes in environmental systems' behavior from producing a grave impact on human well-being.

47. See William Clark, *On the Practical Implications of the Carbon Dioxide Question* (Laxenburg, Austria: International Institute of Applied Systems Analysis, 1985), 41.

48. Chaos should not be confused with randomness: deterministic causal processes still operate at the microlevel and, although the system's state may not be precisely predictable for a given point in the future, the boundaries within which its variables

must operate are often identifiable. See James Crutchfield, J. Doyne Farmer, and Norman Packard, "Chaos," *Scientific American* 255, no. 6 (December 1986): 46–57. A popularized account is James Gleick, *Chaos: Making of a New Science* (New York: Viking, 1987).

49. Wallace Broecker, "Unpleasant Surprises in the Greenhouse?" *Nature* 328, no. 6126 (9 July 1987): 123–26.

50. Wallace Broecker and George Denton, "What Drives Glacial Cycles?" *Scientific American* 262, no. 1 (January 1990): 48–56; and Andrew Weaver and Tertia Hughes, "Rapid Interglacial Climate Fluctuations Driven by North Atlantic Ocean Circulation," *Nature* 367, no. 6462 (3 February 1994): 447–50.

51. Broecker, "Unpleasant Surprises," 123. A recent sudden change in deep water currents in the Mediterranean provides evidence for the possibility that larger currents, such as the Gulf Stream, could "flip" to a new equilibrium. See Debora MacKenzie, "Ocean Flip Puts Modellers on Med Alert," *New Scientist* 147, no. 1993 (2 September 1995): 8.

52. J. C. Farman, B. G. Gardiner, and J. D. Shanklin, "Large Losses of Total Ozone in Antarctica Reveal Seasonal ClO_x/NO_x Interaction," *Nature* 315, no. 6016 (16 May 1985): 207–10.

53. See Schneider, *Global Warming: Are We Entering the Greenhouse Century?* (San Francisco: Sierra Club Books, 1989), 226.

54. See Owen Toon and Richard Turco, "Polar Stratospheric Clouds and Ozone Depletion," *Scientific American* 264, no. 6 (June 1991): 68–77; and Richard Stolarski, "The Antarctic Ozone Hole," *Scientific American* 258, no. 1 (January 1988): 30–8.

55. S. Edouard et al., "The Effect of Small-scale Inhomogeneities on Ozone Depletion in the Arctic," *Nature* 384, no. 6608 (28 November 1996): 444–47.

56. The collapse of the Peruvian fishery probably resulted from an interaction of multiple factors, including overharvesting and changes in Pacific currents due to El Niño. On the nonlinear response of fisheries and other natural systems see Donald Ludwig, Ray Hilborn, and Carl Walters, "Uncertainty, Resource Exploitation, and Conservation: Lessons from History," *Science* 260, no. 5104 (2 April 1993): 17, 36; see also Nathan Keyfitz, "Population Growth Can Prevent the Development That Would Slow Population Growth," in *Preserving the Global Environment: The Challenge of Shared Leadership*, ed. Jessica Tuchman Mathews (New York: W. W. Norton, 1991), 42–46.

57. William Stevens, "New Eye on Nature: The Real Constant Is Eternal Turmoil," *New York Times*, 31 July 1990, p. B5, national edition.

58. David Tilman and David Wedin, "Oscillations and Chaos in the Dynamics of Perennial Grass," *Nature* 353, no. 6345 (17 October 1991): 653–55; and Alan Hastings and Kevin Higgins, "Persistence in Spatially Structured Ecological Models," *Science* 263, no. 5150 (25 February 1994): 1133–36.

59. Commenting on the mathematical models of crab populations, population ecologist William Murdoch says that "if this is what real populations are like, it presents a big difficulty in analyzing and predicting how they're going to behave. It makes things even harder than they were before." Carol Kaesuk Yoon, "Boom and Bust May Be the Norm in Nature, Study Suggests," *New York Times*, 15 March 1994, p. B7, national edition.

60. C. S. Holling, "An Ecologist View of the Malthusian Conflict," in *Population, Economic Development, and the Environment*, ed. Kerstin Lindahl Kiessling and Hans Landberg (Oxford: Oxford University Press, 1994), 88.

61. T. M. L. Wigley, "Impact of Extreme Events," *Nature* 316, no. 6024 (11 July 1985): 106–7.

62. M. L. Parry, *Climate Change, Agriculture and Settlement* (Folkstone, U.K.: Dawson, 1978); see also Clark, *On the Practical Implications*, 40–41.

63. In contrast, the loss of a body of a nonrenewable resource like iron ore has no ramifications within the ecological system. The ore's increased scarcity will not affect surrounding renewable and non–renewable resources, because a body of ore is ecologically inactive. Of course, the extraction process—which may involve heavy equipment, explosives, and chemicals—can damage renewable resources like local rivers and forests.

64. Economists have traditionally overlooked the impact of such ramifying scarcities on wealth production. Robert Gottfried develops a methodology to take account of these multiple effects in Gottfried, "The Value of a Watershed as a Series of Linked Multiproduct Assets," *Ecological Economics* 5, no. 2 (1992): 145–61. He writes: "Increased use of one ecosystem good or service (function) often affects the supplies of other ecosystem functions. The relationships between these functions can be modeled in terms of key variables related to ecosystem management."

65. Robert Chen and Myron Fiering, *Climate Change in the Context of Multiple Environmental Threats*, Research Report RR-89–1, World Hunger Program (Providence, R.I.: Brown University, 1989).

66. D. W. Schindler et al., "Consequences of Climate Warming and Lake Acidification for UV-B Penetration in North American Boreal Lakes," *Nature* 379, no. 6567 (22 February 1996): 705–8.

67. The recently defined field of ecological economics has generated some of the most innovative ideas; see, for example, the journal *Ecological Economics*. Groundbreaking political and social analyses can often be found in the new journal *Environment and Development*. Three recent, particularly synthetic books are Barbier, *Economics, Natural-Resource Scarcity and Development*; Cohen, *How Many People can the Earth Support?*; and Partha Dasgupta, *An Inquiry into Well-Being and Destitution* (Oxford: Oxford University Press, 1993).

68. Daniel Deudney, "Bringing Nature Back In" in *Contested Grounds: Security and Conflict in the New Environmental Politics*, ed. Daniel Deudney and Richard Matthew. (Albany: State University of New York, 1999).

69. See the appendix to chapter 5 for a related discussion of the endogeneity/exogeneity of environmental scarcity as a cause of social stress and conflict.

Chapter 4
Environmental Scarcity

1. Several similar definitions are offered in David Pearce and Kerry Turner, *Economics of Natural Resources and the Environment* (Baltimore: Johns Hopkins University Press, 1990), 52–53. Although the distinction between renewables and nonrenewables is generally useful, it blurs at the edges: certain "renewables," such as biodiversity and fossil aquifers, are not really renewable during a time span relevant to our species. And some "nonrenewables," including oil and coal, are actually regenerated over long periods of time by natural processes. Moreover, some nonrenewables, like iron and aluminum, are apparently available in such vast quantities that their supply is limitless for all practical purposes.

2. For comparison, the United States Soil Conservation Service estimates that eleven metric tons per hectare per year is the maximum soil loss consistent with long-term maintenance of soil productivity. Some experts believe that the rate for thinner and more fragile tropical soils is considerably lower.

3. Of course, the economic optimists discussed in the last chapter have a much more flexible conception of ecological capital than neo-Malthusians. They do not worry much about protecting the stock of any single resource, because they believe that market-driven human ingenuity can always be tapped to allow the substitution of more abundant resources to produce the same end-use services.

4. Economists define a pure public good, such as national defense, as one that is both nonrival and nonexcludable.

5. For further details on the distinctions in this and the previous paragraph, see Richard Cornes and Todd Sandler, *The Theory of Externalities, Public Goods, and Club Goods* (Cambridge: Cambridge University Press, 1986).

6. In 1971, Paul Ehrlich and John Holdren introduced a similar product formula, in which the human impact on the environment is a product of population size and per capita impact (which increases with per capita resource consumption if technology is held constant). See Paul Ehrlich and John Holdren, "Impact of Population Growth," *Science* 171, no. 3977 (26 March 1971): 1212–17. After subsequent revisions by Paul and Anne Ehrlich, the formula became known as the I=PAT (usually pronounced "eye-pat") model. In this revised version, human impact on the environment (I) is equal to population size (P) times per capita resource consumption or "affluence" (A) times the environmental impact of technology used by that population (T). See Paul Ehrlich and Anne Ehrlich, *The Population Explosion* (New York: Touchstone, 1990), 58–59.

The I=PAT formula is now widely cited in technical and policy discussions of global environmental change. In particular, it is used to illustrate the interactive relationship between population size and consumption per capita, and to support the claim that both population size in developing countries and consumption rates in rich countries contribute to global change. Although this general argument is valid, the I=PAT formula is misleading in several ways that Figure 4.1 is not.

First, the "I" in the formula refers mainly to the waste output of the human economy (for example, carbon dioxide emissions) or to the quantity of a particular resource consumed (for instance, trees cut in logging). It does not refer to a drop in the total availability of a particular resource, which is a better measure of the ecosystem impact of human resource consumption. If a drop in availability is of interest, then the formula should include a variable indicating the total availability of the resource prior to consumption, as does Figure 4.1. In general, a given amount of consumption of a resource will have a greater ecological impact if it represents a large share of the total amount of the resource available than if it represents a small share.

Second, the "A" in the formula is a function of various institutions, social relations, and cultural factors. An understanding of these factors is key to understanding affluence (or per capita resource consumption), yet they are nowhere included in the formula (in contrast, such ideational factors are explicitly incorporated in Figure 4.1). Moreover, the "A" is intended as a measure of wealth, but wealth is a distraction in this context: humans affect the environment by using particular technologies in particular ways, not by being wealthy per se. Wealth is, in part, a function of preferences; it is partly determined by what we value. If we come to prefer things and services that are not materially intensive, we can be wealthier without consuming more ecological resources.

Third, the "T" does not adequately represent the interactive nature of impacts of human activity on the environment. As Figure 4.1 shows, the impact of a given technology on the environment is a function, not just of the character and rate of use of the technology, but also of the character of the environmental resources being affected by the technology. Some resources are particularly sensitive to overexploitation and may respond with sharp nonlinear changes to human-induced perturbations, whereas others are remarkably robust. The I=PAT formula makes no allowance for these critical differences, because the character of the resource that is damaged is included nowhere in the formula.

7. Numerous writers, especially those considering the social impact of climate change, have generated similar diagrams. See in particular the excellent survey article by Richard Warrick and William Riebsame entitled "Societal Response to CO_2-Induced Climate Change: Opportunities for Research," *Climatic Change* 3, no. 4 (1981): 387–428. Three points should be noted about figure 4.1: First, there are many ways it could be made more accurate, but at the cost of greater complexity; it highlights the variables and causal linkages most important to our discussion. The figure leaves out, in particular, a number of factors that influence the use and types of technology in an economy, including the costs and quality of labor and capital. Second, each variable in figure 4.1 aggregates many subvariables. For instance, "use per capita of technology" encompasses subvariables ranging from the extent of cattle ranching to the rate of automobile use. As a result, an arrow in figure 4.1 may represent either a positive or a negative correlation, depending on the specific subvariables considered.

Third, analysts who wish to apply the model in figure 4.1 to a specific society or ecosystem should be aware that the model averages out the contributions of various social groups to environmental damage, and thereby distributes responsibility for the damage evenly across society. The formula emphasizes the contribution of total population to supply-induced scarcity, despite the fact that the principal contributors may be relatively small groups, perhaps high-consumption elites, within that population. Analysts can overcome this problem, however, by disaggregating the total population into the relevant social groups (including elites), applying the model in Figure 4.1 within each group, and then summing the total effects of the groups.

8. In many cases, if researchers want to gauge the impact of ideational factors on resource-use behavior (and social behavior more generally), they will have to use assessment techniques very different from those conventionally used to measure the physical variables in Figure 4.1 (such as population size, use per capita of technologies, and physical availability of natural resources). Researchers will need to use techniques drawn from anthropology, ethnomethodology, and interpretivism to develop a detailed "internal" understanding of the societies they are studying. For an exposition of these techniques, see Clifford Geertz, *The Interpretation of Cultures* (New York: Basic Books, 1973). The appendix to chapter 5 briefly considers the ontological issue of combining social and physical variables within causal hypotheses or generalizations.

9. Social vulnerability and adaptability have been the focus of much research and thought (adaptability to environmental scarcity is addressed in chapter 6 of this book). For a survey, see Warrick and Riebsame, "Societal Response." According to these authors, there has been a good deal of research on social adaptation to extreme events

in nature such as storms and droughts, but "much less attention has been directed toward learning about adaptation to slow environmental change." They also suggest there has been little consideration of social costs associated with various adjustment mechanisms. On the conditions and variables that determine vulnerability, see Diana Liverman, "Vulnerability to Global Environmental Change," in *Understanding Global Environmental Change: The Contributions of Risk Analysis and Management*, ed. Roger Kasperson et al., Report of an international workshop, Clark University, 11–13 October 1989 (Worcester, Mass.: Clark University, 1989), 32–33.

10. Robert Kates has made an important distinction between "impact" and "interaction" models of the relationship between environmental change and society. An impact model ignores—often to simplify the research problem—the contribution of ideational factors. An interaction model, however, takes account of these factors. See Robert Kates, Jesse Ausubel, and Mimi Berberian, eds., *Climate Impact Assessment: Studies of the Interaction of Climate and Society*, Scientific Committee on Problems of the Environment (SCOPE), No. 27 (New York: John Wiley & Sons, 1985), 5–6.

11. Environmental determinism holds that external environmental conditions—such as climate, natural resource availability, and geographic position—largely determine the nature of society's institutions and behavior. Up to the early twentieth century, much literature on the relationship between environment and society adopted this perspective. See, for instance, Ellsworth Huntington, *Civilization and Climate* (New Haven: Yale University Press, 1915). The view has seen something of a resurgence in recent decades in the work of, for example, M. Biswas and A. Biswas, eds., *Food, Climate and Man* (New York: Wiley, 1979). Perhaps the most extreme example of environmental determinism in the contemporary environmental-security literature is Neville Brown, "Climate, Ecology and International Security," *Survival* 31, no. 6 (1989): 523–24. Brown implies that climate change was an important and relatively proximate cause of social upheaval in Europe in the 1840s, the imperial expansion between 1850 and 1940, the Cold War, and the 1974 Ethiopian coup.

Much of the best modern literature on human-environment interactions (literature that in general does not adopt an environmentally deterministic perspective) concerns the social impact of climate change. See, for example, Kates, Ausubel, and Berberian, eds., *Climate Impact*; T. M. Wigley, M. J. Ingram, and G. Farmer, *Climate and History: Studies in Past Climates and Their Impact on Man* (Cambridge: Cambridge University Press, 1981), 356–76; and Hubert Lamb, *Weather, Climate and Human Affairs* (London: Routledge, 1988). An excellent survey is William Clark, "The Human Dimensions of Global Change," in *Toward an Understanding of Global Change: Initial Priorities for U.S. Contributions to the International Geosphere-Biosphere Program*, by Committee on Global Change (U.S. National Committee for the IGBP) (Washington, D.C.: National Academy Press, 1988), 134–213.

12. Bernard Nietschmann, "Environmental Conflicts and Indigenous Nations in Central America," paper prepared for the project on Environmental Change and Acute Conflict, Peace and Conflict Studies Programme, University of Toronto, May 1991; and accompanying "Comments on Nietschmann's Paper," by Sergio Diaz-Briquets.

13. This latter process is represented in Figure 4.1 by the feedback link between the use of technology and the ideational factors.

14. This selection of trends is illustrative and therefore somewhat arbitrary. These trends are the ones most often encountered in current discussions of global environ-

mental change. I do not discuss here other environmental issues, such as dispersal of toxic wastes and acid deposition, because they are less prominent in the environmental literature or because their effects are generally less pronounced or widespread. Readers interested in technical background on all these issues should consult World Resources Institute (WRI), *World Resources 1996–97* (New York: Oxford University Press, 1996). This publication, produced biennially by the World Resources Institute (WRI) is widely regarded as the most accessible, accurate, and comprehensive source for information on global change. The more popular *State of the World* report published annually by the Worldwatch Institute is useful but sometimes selective and tendentious.

15. However, as noted in chapter 3, nonlinear or threshold effects in the atmospheric system could produce a sudden shift of the *climate* to a new equilibrium by altering, for example, the direction of major ocean currents such as the Gulf Stream. Wallace Broecker, "Unpleasant Surprises in the Greenhouse?" *Nature* 328, no. 6126 (9 July 1987): 124; and Wallace Broecker and George H. Denton, "What Drives Glacial Cycles?" *Scientific American* 262, no. 1 (January 1990): 49–56.

16. For a review of scale issues in environmental-social research, see Clark, "Human Dimensions," 142–43, and William Clark, *On the Practical Implications of the Carbon Dioxide Question* (Laxenburg, Austria: International Institute of Applied Systems Analysis, 1985), 25–36. He notes that global change research generally involves "coupling observations and explanations across multiple scales" in both space and time, which can impede research and collaboration.

17. World Resources Institute (WRI), *World Resources 1990–91* (New York: Oxford University Press, 1990), 111.

18. The basic method used by today's demographers to project future population growth was developed by Frank Notestein, who published the first modern world population projections in 1945. Notestein's model was used by the U.N. in 1957 to make its first projection extended to the year 2000; now it appears that the medium projection of 5.9 billion will be remarkably close to the actual world population in 2000. For an excellent discussion of the methodology of population projections, see W. Lutz, ed. *The Future Population of the World: What Can We Assume Today?*, prepared under the auspices of the International Institute for Applied Systems Analysis (London: Earthscan, 1994).

19. Once again, understanding the interactions of population growth with other factors is key to understanding its impacts on the environment. Debates on these matters are complex and largely unresolved, although there appears to be an emerging consensus that rapid population growth is correlated with at least higher rates of deforestation in tropical countries. See Richard Bilsborrow and H. W. O. Okoth Ogendo, "Population-Driven Changes in Land Use in Developing Countries," *Ambio* 21, no. 1 (1992): 37–45; and Tom Rudel and Jill Roper, "Regional Patterns and Historical Trends in Tropical Deforestation, 1976–1990: A Qualitative Comparative Analysis," *Ambio* 25, no. 3 (1996): 160–66.

20. Paul Ehrlich, *The Population Bomb* (New York: Ballantine Books, 1968).

21. Simon Szreter, "The Idea of Demographic Transition and the Study of Fertility Change: A Critical Intellectual History," *Population and Development Review* 19, no. 4 (1993): 659–701.

22. For detailed discussions of the determinants of fertility transitions, see Geoffrey McNicoll and Mead Cain, eds., *Rural Development and Population: Institutions and*

Policy, based on the Expert Consultation on Population and Agricultural and Rural Development convened by the Food and Agriculture Organization, Rome, a supplement to *Population and Development Review* 15 (New York: Oxford University Press and The Population Council, 1990); Ester Boserup, "Shifts in the Determinants of Fertility in the Developing World: Environmental, Technical, Economic and Cultural Factors," in *The State of Population Theory: Forward from Malthus* (Oxford: Basil Blackwell, 1986), 239–55; and R. W. Fogel, *Economic Growth, Population Theory, and Physiology: The Bearing of Long-Term Processes on the Making of Economic Policy* (Cambridge, Mass.: National Bureau of Economic Research, 1994).

23. Bryant Robey, Shea Rutstein, and Leo Morris, "The Fertility Decline in Developing Countries," *Scientific American* 269, no. 6 (December 1993): 60–67.

24. United Nations Population Division, *World Population Prospects: The 1996 Revision, Demographic Indicators 1950–2050*, Diskettes 1–4 (New York: United Nations, 1996).

25. John Bongaarts, "Population Policy Options in the Developing World," *Science* 263, no. 5148 (11 February 1994): 771–76.

26. On the disparity in population growth between the North and the South, see Nathan Keyfitz's review of Alfred Sauvy, *L'Europe submergée: Sud → Nord dans 30 ans* (Paris: Dunod, 1987), in *Population and Development Review* 15, no. 2 (1989): 359–62.

27. United Nations Population Division, *World Population Prospects*.

28. Steven Holmes, "Global Crisis in Population Still Serious, Group Warns," *New York Times*, 31 December 1997, p. A7, national edition.

29. See, for example, Ben Wattenberg, "The Population Explosion Is Over," *New York Times Magazine*, 23 November 1997, pp. 60–63; Barbara Crossette, "How to Fix a Crowded World: Add People," *Sunday New York Times*, Week in Review, 2 November 1997, p. 1; Nicholas Eberstadt, "The Population Implosion," *Wall Street Journal*, 16 October 1997, p. A22; and Eberstadt, "World Population Implosion?" *Public Interest*, no. 129 (fall 1997): 3–22.

30. Holmes, "Global Crisis."

31. Ibid.

32. Jane Willms carried out much of the research and wrote portions of the text for this subsection.

33. Primary energy is "the energy directly recovered from the Earth—coal, crude oil, natural gas, collected biomass, hydraulic power, heat produced in a nuclear reactor from processed natural uranium. . . . Primary energy is generally not used directly." Primary energy is converted in refineries and power plants into secondary energy (such as fuels and electricity); secondary energy, in turn, is delivered to consumers as final energy for use in appliances and machines. Commercial energy is bought and sold in a market; this category generally excludes traditional fuels such as straw, fuelwood, and cow dung. See World Energy Council, *Energy for Tomorrow's World: The Realities, the Real Options, and the Agenda for Achievement* (New York: St. Martin's Press, 1993), 111; and World Energy Council and International Institute for Applied Systems Analysis, *Global Energy Perspectives to 2050 and Beyond* (London: World Energy Council, 1995), 45.

34. Thomas Lee, "Advanced Fossil Fuel Systems and Beyond," in *Technology and Environment*, ed. Jesse Ausubel and Hedy Sladovich (Washington, D.C.: National Academy Press, 1989), 114–36.

35. In 1983, the FAO estimated that up to 2.5 billion people in the developing world would face acute fuelwood shortages by the year 2000. M. R. de Montalembert and J. Clément, *Fuelwood Supplies in the Developing Countries*, FAO Forestry Paper 42 (Rome: Food and Agriculture Organization of the United Nations (FAO), 1983). For general information on the fuelwood crisis in developing countries, see Dan M. Kammen, "Cookstoves for the Developing World," *Scientific American* 273, no. 1 (July 1995): 72–75; U.S. Congress, Office of Technology Assessment, *Fueling Development: Energy Technologies for Developing Countries*, OTA-E-516 (Washington, D.C.: U.S. Government Printing Office, 1992); U.S. Congress, Office of Technology Assessment, *Energy in Developing Countries*, OTA-E-486 (Washington, D.C.: U.S. Government Printing Office, 1991), especially chapter 4, "Energy Supplies in the Developing World"; P. A. Dewees, "The Woodfuel Crisis reconsidered: Observations on the Dynamics of Abundance and Scarcity," *World Development* 17, no. 8 (1989): 1159–1172; and Timothy S. Wood and Sam Baldwin, "Fuelwood and Charcoal Use in Developing Countries," *Annual Review of Energy* 10 (1985): 407–29.

36. The figures in the previous two sentences are estimates based on the summary material provided in Bill Keepin, "Review of Global Energy and Carbon Dioxide Projections," *Annual Review of Energy* 11 (1986): 357–92.

37. World Energy Council, *Energy for Tomorrow's World*.

38. S. W. Gouse, et al. (MITRE Corporation), "Potential World Development Through 2100: The Impacts of Energy Demand, Resources and the Environment," in *World Energy Council Journal*, by World Energy Council (London: World Energy Council, 1992), 18–32.

39. World Energy Council and International Institute for Applied Systems Analysis, *Global Energy Perspectives to 2050 and Beyond*.

40. A. A. Churchill, "Energy Demand and Supply in the Developing World, 1990–2020: Three Decades of Explosive Growth," in *Proceedings of the World Bank Annual Conference on Development Economics, 1993*, ed. M. Bruno and B. Pleskovic (Washington, D.C.: World Bank, 1994), 441–61.

41. Global mean temperature is also affected, of course, by changes in the amount of radiation released by the sun, in Earth's orbital parameters, and in global volcanic activity.

42. The consensus on the likely magnitude, rate, and timing of human-induced greenhouse warming is summarized in the contributions of Working Groups I and II to the Second Assessment Report of the Intergovernmental Panel on Climate Change. See J. T. Houghton et al., eds, *Climate Change 1995—The Science of Climate Change*, contribution of Working Group I to the Second Assessment Report of the Intergovernmental Panel on Climate Change (IPCC) (Cambridge: Cambridge University Press, 1996); and Robert T. Watson, Marufu C. Zinyowera, and Richard H. Moss, eds., *Climate Change 1995—Impacts, Adaptions and Mitigation of Climate Change: Scientific-Technical Analyses*, contribution of Working Group II to the Second Assessment Report of the Intergovernmental Panel on Climate Change (IPCC) (Cambridge: Cambridge University Press, 1996).

43. Houghton et al., eds., *Climate Change 1995—Science of Climate Change*, 6.

44. William Stevens, "Global Climate Stayed Warm in 1996, with Wet, Cold Regional Surprises," *New York Times*, 14 January 1997, p. B9, national edition.

45. Houghton et al., eds., *Climate Change 1995—Science of Climate Change*, 4.

46. Houghton et al., eds., *Climate Change 1995—Science of Climate Change*, 6–7.

47. World Meteorological Organization, *Scientific Assessment of Ozone Depletion: 1994*, Global Ozone Research and Monitoring Project, Report No. 37 (Geneva: World Meteorological Organization, National Oceanic and Atmospheric Administration, National Aeronautics and Space Administration, and United Nations Environment Programme, 1995).

48. Optimism about the success of the various treaties to protect the ozone layer may be premature. Widespread smuggling and illegal manufacture of CFCs has been reported in industrialized countries, while many eastern European and developing countries are seeking to circumvent the accords. See "The Treaty that Worked—Almost: Will the Black Market for CFCs Short-Circuit the Montreal Protocol?" *Scientific American* 273, no. 3 (September 1995): 18–20.

49. World Meteorological Organization, *Scientific Assessment of Ozone Depletion*, xiv.

50. Ibid., xxxiv.

51. Ibid., xvi.

52. Ibid., xxxiii.

53. "Ultraviolet Radiation on the Rise," *Scientific American* 275, no. 4 (October 1996): 28.

54. Gert Kelfkens, Frank de Gruijl, and Jan van der Leun, "Ozone Depletion and Increase in Annual Carcinogenic Ultraviolet Dose," *Photochemistry and Photobiology* 52, no. 4 (1990): 819–23.

55. For a survey of the impacts of increased UV radiation, see "Environmental Effects of Ozone Depletion: 1994 Assessment," special issue of *Ambio* 24, no. 3 (1995). See especially J. D. Longstreth et al., "Changes in Ultraviolet Radiation Reaching the Earth's Surface," 153–65; M. M. Caldwell et al., "Effects of Increased Solar Ultraviolet Radiation on Terrestrial Plants," 166–73; and D.-P. Häder et al., "Effects of Increased Solar Ultraviolet Radiation on Aquatic Ecosystems," 174–80. On the impact of increased UV radiation on amphibians, see Andrew Blaustein et al., "UV Repair and Resistance to Solar UV-B in Amphibian Eggs: A Link to Population Declines?" *Proceedings of the National Academy of Sciences, USA* 91, no. 5 (1994): 1791–95. Further information on UV's effects on aquatic ecosystems can be found in A. McMinn, H. Heijnis, and D. Hodgson, "Minimal Effects of UVB Radiation on Antarctic Diatoms over the past 20 years," *Nature* 370, no. 6490 (18 August 1994): 547–49; M. Bothwell, D. Karentz, and E. Carpenter, "No UVB Effect?" *Nature* 374, no. 6523 (13 April 1995): 601; and Kirk Malloy et al., "Solar UVB-induced DNA Damage and Photoenzymatic DNA Repair in Antarctic Zooplankton," *Proceedings of the National Academy of Sciences, USA* 94, no. 4 (1997): 1258–63.

56. WRI, *World Resources 1990–91*, 5.

57. Nafis Sadik, *The State of the World Population 1990* (New York: United Nations Population Fund, 1990), 8.

58. In the late 1980s, Jeffrey Leonard estimated that "935 million rural people live in households that have too little land to meet the minimum subsistence requirements for food and fuel. These data exclude China, which could add as many as 100–200 million more people to the category." See Jeffrey Leonard, "Overview," in *Environment and the Poor: Development Strategies for a Common Agenda* (New Brunswick, N.J.: Transaction, 1989), 13.

59. For an overview of research and data on land degradation, including a survey of

regional "hot spots" and "bright spots," see Sara Scherr and Satya Yadav, *Land Degradation in the Developing World: Implications for Food, Agriculture, and the Environment to 2020*, IFPRI Food, Agriculture, and the Environment Discussion Paper 14 (Washington, D.C.: International Food Policy Research Institute, 1996).

60. Experts give "desertification" a variety of meanings. In general, it implies a complex syndrome of very low soil productivity, poor rain-use efficiency by vegetation, and consequent adverse changes in the hydrological cycle. See Michel Verstraete, "Defining Desertification: A Review," *Climatic Change* 9, no. 1/2 (1986): 5–18.

61. See Vaclav Smil, *Energy, Food, Environment: Realities, Myths, Options* (Oxford: Oxford University Press, 1987), 223, 230.

62. Richard Louis Edmonds, *Patterns of China's Lost Harmony: A Survey of the Country's Environmental Degradation and Protection* (London: Routledge, 1994), 7; Gerhard Heilig, "Anthropogenic Factors in Land-Use Change in China," *Population and Development Review* 23, no. 1 (1997): 139–68, especially 143–45.

63. Global Assessment of Soil Degradation, *World Map on Status of Human-Induced Soil Degradation* (Nairobi, Kenya/Wageningen, The Netherlands: United Nations Environment Programme/International Soil Reference Centre, 1990); and L. R. Oldeman, R. T. A. Hakkeling, and W. G. Sombroek, *World Map of the Status of Human-Induced Soil Degradation: An Explanatory Note*, 2d ed. (Nairobi, Kenya/Wageningen, The Netherlands: United Nations Environment Programme/International Soil Reference Centre, 1991). To obtain copies of the maps, contact the International Soil Reference Centre (ISRC), P.O. Box 353, 6700 AJ Wageningen, The Netherlands.

64. For a critique, see Pierre Crosson and Jock Anderson, *Resources and Global Food Prospects: Supply and Demand for Cereals to 2030*, World Bank Technical Paper Number 184 (Washington, D.C.: World Bank, 1992), 33–35.

65. WRI, *World Resources 1996–97*, 203.

66. Smil, *Energy, Food, Environment*, 231–37.

67. World Resources Institute (WRI), *World Resources 1992–93* (New York: Oxford University Press, 1992), 118.

68. World Resources Institute (WRI), *World Resources 1994–95* (New York: Oxford University Press, 1994), 130–35; this publication provides a detailed breakdown of the FAO statistics by forest ecological zone.

69. WRI, *World Resources 1996–97*, 205.

70. WRI, *World Resources, 1994–95*, 129.

71. Diana Jean Schemo, "Burning of Amazon Picks up Pace, with Vast Areas Lost," *New York Times*, 12 September 1996, p. A3, national edition; and Schemo, "Brazil Says Amazon Burning Tripled in Recent Years," *New York Times*, 27 January 1998, p. A3, national edition.

72. Gareth Porter and Delfin Ganapin, Jr., *Resources, Population, and the Philippines' Future: A Case Study*, WRI Paper No. 4. (Washington, D.C.: World Resources Institute, 1988), 24. These authors call this "perhaps the most rapid destruction of forest reserves in the world." The figures cited refer to adequately stocked forested land and are approximate. For a more complete account of Filipino deforestation, see David Kummer, *Deforestation in Postwar Philippines* (Manila: Ateneo de Manila University Press, 1992).

73. The standard reference on fresh water supply and demand is Peter Gleick, ed., *Water in Crisis: A Guide to the World's Fresh Water Resources* (New York: Oxford

University Press, 1993). A useful survey is Robert Engelman and Pamela LeRoy, *Sustaining Water: Population and the Future of Renewable Water Supplies* (Washington, D.C.: Population Action International, 1993).

74. Linda Nash, "Water Quality and Health," in *Water in Crisis: A Guide to the World's Fresh Water Resources*, ed. Peter Gleick (New York: Oxford University Press, 1993), 26. See also Nicholas Kristof, "For Third World, Water is Still a Deadly Drink," *New York Times*, 9 January 1997, p. A1, national edition.

75. Figures calculated from those in WRI, *World Resources 1990–91*, 170–71, assuming annual increase in global water consumption of 2.5 percent.

76. Peter Gleick, "Water in the 21st Century," in *Water in Crisis*, ed. Gleick, 105. The introduction of the 1000 cubic meter benchmark is usually attributed to the Swedish hydrologist, Malin Falkenmark; see Malin Falkenmark, "Fresh Water: Time for a Modified Approach," *Ambio* 15, no. 4 (1986): 192–200.

77. Malin Falkenmark, "The Massive Water Scarcity Now Threatening Africa— Why Isn't It Being Addressed," *Ambio* 18, no. 2 (1989): 112–18.

78. Tom Gardner-Outlaw and Robert Engleman, *Sustaining Water, Easing Scarcity: A Second Update* (Washington, D.C.: Population Action International, 1997); and Malin Falkenmark and Asit Biswas, "Synopsis—Further Momentum to Water Issues: Comprehensive Water Problem Assessment in Being," *Ambio* 24, no. 6 (1995): 380–82.

79. John K. Cooley, "The War Over Water," *Foreign Policy*, no. 53 (winter 1983– 84): 3–26.

80. Food and Agriculture Organization (FAO), *The State of World Fisheries and Aquaculture* (Rome: FAO, 1995), 47.

81. Ibid., 2.

82. Food and Agriculture Organization (FAO), *World Fisheries Situation and Outlook* (Rome: FAO, 1987), 6.

83. FAO, *The State of World Fisheries and Aquaculture*, 6.

84. Ibid., 5.

85. D. Hawksworth and M. Kalin-Arroyo, "Magnitude and Distribution of Biodiversity," section 3 in *Global Biodiversity Assessment*, ed. V. H. Heywood and R. T. Watson (Cambridge: Cambridge University Press, 1995), 111. The *Assessment* is the state-of-the-art account of scientific understanding of biodiversity.

86. Ibid.

87. S. Naeem et al., "Declining Biodiversity Can Alter the Performance of Ecosystems," *Nature* 368, no. 6473 (21 April 1994): 734–37; D. Tilman, et al., "Productivity and Sustainability Influenced by Biodiversity in Grassland Ecosystems," *Nature* 379, no. 6567 (22 February 1996): 718–20.

88. Edward O. Wilson, "Threats to Biodiversity," *Scientific American* 261, no. 3 (September 1989): 111.

89. Ibid., 112.

90. The *Assessment* notes that this figure "should be interpreted as the fraction of species eventually going extinct according to the species-area relationship." R. Barbault and S. Sastrapradja, "Generation, Maintenance and Loss of Biodiversity," section 4 in *Global Biodiversity Assessment*, ed. Heywood and Watson, 198.

91. Ibid.

92. Ibid.

93. R. Doyle, "Threatened Mammals," *Scientific American* 276, no. 1 (January 1997): 32.

94. V. Heywood and I. Baste, "Introduction," section 1 in *Global Biodiversity Assessment*, ed. Heywood and Watson, 11.

95. H. Mooney, J. Lubchenco, R. Dirzo, and O. Sala, "Biodiversity and Ecosystem Functioning: Basic Principles," section 5 in *Global Biodiversity Assessment*, ed. Heywood and Watson, 279.

Chapter 5
Interactions and Social Effects

1. See General Readings on Environmental Security at the end of this book.

2. The term "ecological marginalization" comes from Jeffrey Leonard, "Overview," in *Environment and the Poor: Development Strategies for a Common Agenda* (New Brunswick, N.J.: Transaction, 1989), 5–7.

3. For example, a person might own some land that can be leased for either farming or commercial use; the going lease rate for farming is $10/hectare per year, whereas the rate for commercial use is $100/hectare per year. If the landowner is economically rational, he will rent the land for commercial use. The "economic rent" in this case is the $90 difference between the two lease rates. If the commercial lease rate were to drop (perhaps because there was greater competition to lease land for commercial purposes), the landowner would not transfer his land from commercial to farming use until the commercial lease rate dropped to $10 per hectare or lower. (The value of the alternative use is sometimes called the "transfer earning.") Rent is therefore a return to the factor owner that is not needed to keep the factor in its current use, and large economic rents indicate significant economic inefficiency.

Note that neither the $10 nor the $100 rates have anything to do with the cost to the landowner of supplying the land. Nonetheless, many political economists have muddied the concept of "rent," broadening its use to encompass any differential between costs and returns. In this case, "economic rent" becomes synonymous with "profit." Government subsidies of irrigation water, for example, reduce costs and therefore increase profits. However, since some profit on production is regarded as reasonable, "rent"—by this broader usage—usually has a pejorative connotation of "surplus" profit that is not economically justified.

4. The figures in the following paragraphs are drawn from Miriam Lowi, *West Bank Water Resources and the Resolution of Conflict in the Middle East*, Occasional Paper No. 1, Project on Environmental Change and Acute Conflict (Cambridge, Mass.: American Academy of Arts and Sciences and the University of Toronto, 1992). For further information on this case, see Miriam Lowi, "Bridging the Divide: Transboundary Resource Disputes and the Case of West Bank Water," *International Security* 18, no. 1 (1993): 113–38; Miriam Lowi, *Water and Power: The Politics of a Scarce Resource in the Jordan River Basin* (Cambridge: Cambridge University Press, 1995); Stephen Lonergan and David Brooks, *Watershed: The Role of Fresh Water in the Israeli-Palestinian Conflict* (Ottawa: International Development Research Centre, 1994); and Natasha Beschorner, *Water and Instability in the Middle East*, Adelphi Paper 273, International Institute for Strategic Studies (London: Brassey's, 1992).

5. There appears to be an impending crisis from salinization of aquifers beneath the Gaza Strip, where the pressure on water resources is "rapidly becoming intolerable." See Beschorner, *Water and Instability*, 14–15. The Gaza aquifers are connected to the coastal aquifer that is vital to Israel. Salinization can cause irreversible physical changes in aquifers; even if replenished with freshwater, their capacity is reduced. See Fred Pearce, "Wells of Conflict on the West Bank," *New Scientist* 130, no. 1771 (1 June 1991): 37–38.

6. Alex Marshall, ed., *The State of World Population, 1996* (New York: United Nations Population Fund (UNFPA), 1996).

7. Lowi, "West Bank Water Resources," 34.

8. Beschorner, *Water and Instability*, 14, 78.

9. Global Assessment of Soil Degradation, *World Map on Status of Human-Induced Soil Degradation*, Sheet 2, Europe, Africa, and Western Asia (Nairobi, Kenya/Wageningen, The Netherlands: United Nations Environment Programme/International Soil Reference Centre, 1990).

10. Sadik, *The State of World Population 1991* (New York: United Nations Population Fund (UNFPA), 1991), p. 24; World Resources Institute (WRI), *World Resources 1992–93* (New York: Oxford University Press, 1992), 246, 262.

11. Despite popular perception and the past claims of the United Nations Environment Program, many experts now believe that the African Sahel (which includes southern Mauritania) is a robust ecosystem that does not exhibit extensive human-induced desertification. There is no clear southward march of the Sahara desert, and ecosystem recovery can be rapid if there is adequate rainfall and reduced grazing pressures. See "The Ebb and Flow of the Sahara," *New York Times*, 23 July 1991, p. B9, national edition. Overgrazing across the western Sahel, and the consequent migration of people from the region, appear to arise from the expansion of sedentary farming and population growth that together concentrate pastoralists on smaller areas of land (an example of ecological marginalization). In general, pastoralists are weak in face of modern African states; state development since decolonization has often changed property rights at their expense. See chapter 3 of Olivia Bennett, ed., *Greenwar: Environment and Conflict* (London: Panos, 1991), 33–53.

12. G. M. Higgins et al., *Potential Population Supporting Capacities of Lands in the Developing World*, Technical Report of Project INT/75/P13, "Land Resources for Populations of the Future," undertaken by The Food and Agriculture Organization of the United Nations in collaboration with The International Institute for Applied Systems Analysis and The United Nations Fund for Population Activities, Rome, 1982, p. 137, table 3.5.

13. Michael Horowitz, "Victims of Development," *Development Anthropology Network*, Bulletin of the Institute for Development Anthropology, 7, no. 2 (1989): 1–8; and Michael Horowitz, "Victims Upstream and Down," *Journal of Refugee Studies* 4, no. 2 (1991): 164–81. See also Runa Midtvåge, "Water, Resource Use and Conflict: The Case of the Senegal River" (master's thesis, Agricultural University of Norway, 1993).

14. Jacques Belotteau, "Senegal-Mauritanie: les graves événements du printemps 1989," *Afrique Contemporaine* 28, no. 152 (1989): 41–42.

15. The best cropland lies, for the most part, in the coastal plains of the archipelago's islands. Landowning and manufacturing elites are closely linked, and their relative economic power has actually grown since independence: the top 10 percent of the

country's families controlled 37 percent of the nation's total income in 1985, up from 27 percent in 1956. See Richard Kessler, *Rebellion and Repression in the Philippines* (New Haven, Conn.: Yale University Press, 1989), 18.

16. Using a standardized figure of 100 for 1972, average real wages dropped from 150 in the early 1950s to about 100 in 1980. Kessler, *Rebellion and Repression*, 26.

17. A full account can be found in Maria Concepcion Cruz et al., *Population Growth, Poverty, and Environmental Stress: Frontier Migration in the Philippines and Costa Rica* (Washington, D.C.: World Resources Institute, 1992).

18. World Bank, *Philippines: Environment and Natural Resource Management Study* (Washington, D.C.: World Bank, 1989).

19. Gareth Porter and Delfin Ganapin, Jr., *Resources, Population, and the Philippines' Future: A Case Study*, WRI Paper No. 4 (Washington, D.C.: World Resources Institute, 1988). Robin Broad with John Cavanagh, *Plundering Paradise: The Struggle for the Environment in the Philippines* (Berkeley: University of California Press, 1993).

20. Leonard, "Overview," 5. On the example of El Salvador, see Chapter 2 in William Durham, *Scarcity and Survival in Central America: The Ecological Origins of the Soccer War* (Stanford, Calif.: Stanford University Press, 1979), 21–62; on Honduras, see Susan Stonich, "The Dynamics of Social Processes and Environmental Destruction: A Central American Case Study," *Population and Development Review* 15, no. 2 (1989): 269–95.

21. For a complete account, see Philip Howard and Thomas Homer-Dixon, *Environmental Scarcity and Violent Conflict: The Case of Chiapas, Mexico*, Occasional Paper of the Project on Environment, Population, and Security (Washington, D.C.: American Association for the Advancement of Science and the University of Toronto, 1996). The material in this and the following paragraph is drawn from this publication. A version of this paper can be found in Thomas Homer-Dixon and Jessica Blitt, eds., *Ecoviolence: Links among Environment, Population, and Security* (Boulder, Colo.: Rowman & Littlefield: 1998).

22. Although these five effects deserve special attention, they are not precisely comparable. As Warrick and Riebsame point out, agricultural systems are best thought of as "intermediate" systems involving both physical and social variables; on the other hand, economic, institutional, and habitat systems are more purely social, and are therefore perhaps more flexible and resilient in the face of environmental shock. Richard Warrick and William Riebsame, "Societal Response to CO_2-Induced Climate Change: Opportunities for Research," *Climatic Change* 3, no. 4 (1981): 393–94.

23. The role of contextual and intervening variables is emphasized in Nazli Choucri, ed., *Multidisciplinary Perspectives on Population and Conflict* (Syracuse, N.Y.: Syracuse University Press, 1984).

24. Useful discussions of these systems include World Resources Institute (WRI), "Food and Agriculture," chap. 10 in *World Resources 1996–97* (New York: Oxford University Press, 1996), 225–46; World Resources Institute (WRI), "Food and Agriculture," chap. 6 in *World Resources 1994–95* (New York: Oxford University Press, 1994), 107–28; Pierre Crosson and Jock Anderson, *Resources and Global Food Prospects: Supply and Demand for Cereals to 2030*, World Bank Technical Paper Number 184 (Washington, D.C.: World Bank, 1992), especially chapters 3, 4, and 6; World Commission on Environment and Development (commonly known as the Brundtland Commission), "Food Security: Sustaining the Potential," chap. 5 in *Our Common*

Future (Oxford: Oxford University Press, 1987), 118–46; and Vaclav Smil, *Energy, Food, Environment: Realities, Myths, Options* (Oxford: Oxford University Press, 1987), especially chapters 3 and 5.

25. There is scientific debate about the likely magnitude, rate, and timing of global warming and its climatic, ecological, and social impacts. See the discussion in chapter 4 of this book. For assessments of climate change and agriculture, see M. L. Parry, T. R. Carter, and N. T. Konijn, eds., *The Impact of Climatic Variations on Agriculture*, vol. 1, *Assessments in Cool Temperate and Cold Regions,* vol. 2, *Assessments in Semi-Arid Regions* (Dordrecht, Netherlands: Kluwer, 1989); and John Reilly et al., "Agriculture in a Changing Climate: Impacts and Adaption," chap. 13 in *Climate Change 1995—Impacts, Adaptions and Mitigation of Climate Change: Scientific-Technical Analyses,* ed. Robert T. Watson, Marufu C. Zinyowera, and Richard H. Moss, contribution of Working Group II to the Second Assessment Report of the Intergovernmental Panel on Climate Change (IPCC) (Cambridge: Cambridge University Press, 1996), 427–67.

26. Smil, *Energy, Food, Environment,* 226–27.

27. See R. A. Warrick, R. M. Gifford, and M. L. Parry, "CO_2, Climatic Change and Agriculture: Assessing the Response of Food Crops to the Direct Effects of Increased CO_2 and Climatic Change," in *The Greenhouse Effect, Climatic Change, and Ecosystems,* SCOPE 29, ed. Bert Bolin et al. (New York: Wiley, 1986), 393–474.

28. T. M. L. Wigley, "Impact of Extreme Events," *Nature* 316, no. 6024 (11 July 1985): 106–7; Fakhri A. Bazzaz and Eric D. Fajer, "Plant Life in a CO_2-Rich World," *Scientific American* 266, no. 1 (January 1992): 68–74; Eric D. Fajer and F. A. Bazzaz, "Is Carbon Dioxide a 'Good' Greenhouse Gas?" *Global Environmental Change* (December 1992): 301–10; Harlod A. Mooney and George W. Koch, "The Impact of Rising CO_2 Concentrations on the Terrestrial Biosphere," *Ambio* 23, no. 1 (1994): 74–76; and T. W. Boutton, S. R. Archer and L. C. Nordt, "Climate, CO_2 and Plant Abundance," *Nature* 372, no. 6507 (15 December 1994): 625–26.

29. Cynthia Rosenzweig and Martin L. Parry, "Potential Impact of Climate Change on World Food Supply," *Nature* 367, no. 6459 (13 January 1994): 133–38; John Reilly, "Crops and Climate Change," *Nature* 367, no. 6459 (13 January 1994): 118; and G. Fischer, K. Frohberg, M. L. Parry and C. Rosenzweig, "Climate Change and World Food Supply, Demand and Trade: Who Benefits, Who Loses?" *Global Environmental Change* 4, no. 1 (1994): 7–23. A critique of this research team's results, and a more pessimistic assessment of the consequences of climate change for world agriculture, is provided by Barrie Pittock, in his review of "Climate Change and World Food Supply and special issues of *Global Environmental Change* and *Food Policy,*" *Environment* 37, no. 9 (1995): 25–30; see also letter by A. Barrie Pittock, Peter Whetton, and Yingping Wang, "Climate and Food Supply," *Nature* 371, no. 6492 (1 September 1994): 25.

30. Christopher Finney and Stanley Western, "An Economic Analysis of Environmental Protection and Management: An Example from the Philippines," *The Environmentalist* 6, no. 1 (1986): 56. For an additional account of the ecological impacts of deforestation, see Salah Eddine Zaimeche, "The Consequences of Rapid Deforestation: A North African Example," *Ambio* 23, no. 2 (1994): 136–40.

31. Even skeptics admit the importance of land degradation at the local level. For example, Pierre Crosson contends that degradation's effects on global agricultural pro-

duction are not substantial, but he acknowledges that its regional and local effects can be large. "While erosion and other degradation-induced problems do not as a whole represent a major threat to global agricultural capacity, for the people who must deal with them, they are very important." Pierre Crosson, "Will Erosion Threaten Agricultural Productivity?" *Environment* 39, no. 8 (1997): 4–9 and 29–31.

32. Indonesia was a particularly dramatic example. See Peter Timmer, "Indonesia: Transition from Food Importer to Exporter," in *Food Price Policy in Asia: A Comparative Study*, ed. Terry Sicular (Ithaca, N.Y.: Cornell University Press, 1989), 24–64.

33. Experts heatedly debate the social and economic consequences of the green revolution. The critical camp is well-represented by Frances Moore Lappe and Joseph Collins, *World Hunger: Twelve Myths* (New York: Grove Press, 1986); and Vandana Shiva, *The Violence of the Green Revolution* (Mapusa, Goa: The Other India Press, 1991). These authors suggest that green revolution technologies increased income differentials within and among farming communities. Although most experts agree that this was an initial effect, recent research shows that the technologies eventually narrowed income differentials. The longer-term result has generally been a decline in absolute poverty and an improvement of income distribution, because of technological diffusion and an increase in noncrop and off-farm job opportunities. (Nonetheless, there is still evidence that green revolution technologies have widened regional disparities by favoring regions with abundant water for irrigation.) See Peter Hazell and C. Ramasamy, *The Green Revolution Reconsidered: The Impact of High-Yielding Rice Varieties in South India* (Baltimore: Johns Hopkins University Press, 1991); and Rita Sharma and Thomas Poleman, *The New Economics of India's Green Revolution: Income and Employment Diffusion in Uttar Pradesh* (New Delhi: Vikas, 1994). Nathan Keyfitz provides an anecdotal yet insightful account of these effects in an Indonesian village in Nathan Keyfitz, "An East Javanese Village in 1953 and 1985: Observations on Development," *Population and Development Review* 11, no. 4 (1985): 695–719.

34. World Resources Institute, *World Resources 1988–89* (New York: Basic Books, 1988) 52.

35. Per Pinstrup-Andersen, *World Food Trends and Future Food Security*, Food Policy Report (Washington, D.C.: The International Food Policy Research Institute, 1994), 3.

36. Estimates of the maximum population that the earth could feed—if all arable land and the best current agricultural technologies were used—range from 10 to 40 billion. See Vaclav Smil, "How Many People Can the Earth Feed?" *Population and Development Review*, 20, no. 2 (1994): 255–92.

37. Pinstrup-Andersen, *World Food Trends*, 3.

38. Pinstrup-Anderson, *World Food Trends*, 1. This figure is down from forty-five countries at the end of the 1970s.

39. Celestine Bohlen, "Conference on Food Aid Starts in Rome," *New York Times*, 13 November 1996, p. A5, national edition.

40. Nikos Alexandratos, "The Outlook for World Food and Agriculture to Year 2010," chap. 3 in *Population and Food in the Early 21st Century: Meeting Future Food Demand of Increasing Population*, ed. Nural Islam (Washington, D.C.: The International Food Policy Research Institute (IFPRI), 1995), 25–48.

41. Pinstrup-Anderson, *World Food Trends*, 6.

42. For a discussion, see Rosamond Naylor, Walter Falcon, and Erika Zavaleta, "Variability and Growth in Grain Yields, 1950–94: Does the Record Point to Greater Instability?" *Population and Development Review* 23, no. 1 (1997): 41–58.

43. All yield statistics in this paragraph are taken from Pinstrup-Andersen, *World Food Trends*, 6.

44. For a thorough review, see Piers Blaikie and Harold Brookfield, *Land Degradation and Society* (London: Methuen, 1987).

45. Ester Boserup, *The Conditions of Agricultural Growth: The Economics of Agrarian Change Under Population Pressure* (Chicago: Aldine, 1965), 56.

46. See, for example, Yujiro Hayami, "Elements of Induced Innovation: A Historical Perspective for the Green Revolution," *Exploration in Economic History* 8, no. 4 (1971): 445–72. The green revolution involved both new technologies (such as short-stalked grains that would not "lodge"—or fall over—when carrying a heavy load of kernels) and resource substitution (the use of fertilizer in place of inadequate or degraded soil nutrients).

47. For an excellent treatment of the importance of institutions in boosting agricultural productivity, see Iftikhar Ahmed and Vernon Ruttan, *Generation and Diffusion of Agricultural Innovations: The Role of Institutional Factors* (Aldershot, U.K.: Gower, 1988).

48. See "Session No. 1: The Green Revolution As an Historical Phenomenon: What Has Happened, How and Why," in *Symposium on Science and Foreign Policy: The Green Revolution*, Proceedings before the Subcommittee on National Security Policy and Scientific Development of the Committee on Foreign Affairs, House of Representatives, 5 December 1969, 3–42.

49. John Kerry King, "Rice Politics," *Foreign Affairs* 31, no. 3 (1953): 453–60.

50. Anne Booth, "Indonesian Agricultural Development in Comparative Perspective," *World Development* 17, no. 8 (1989): 1249.

51. "Prospects for biotechnology to provide a significant breakthrough in yield in the next 10–15 years are limited; its major near-term contribution will be to provide greater resistance to pests and diseases as well as enhanced stability by reducing periodic decline in yields." Nural Islam, "Overview," chap. 1 in *Population and Food in the Early 21st Century: Meeting Future Food Demand of an Increasing Population*, ed. Nural Islam (Washington, D.C.: The International Food Policy Research Institute (IFPRI), 1995), 4. A similar skepticism is expressed by Alex McCalla, Chair of the Technical Advisory Committee of the Consultative Group on International Agricultural Research: "One must be somewhat cautious in assuming that future biological yield increases at past rates will be easy. Research by the International Rice Research Institute and the International Center for the Improvement of Maize and Wheat found significant slowing in the rate of yield increase of rice and wheat under experimental conditions." Alex McCalla, *Agriculture and Food Needs to 2025: Why We Should Be Concerned*, Sir John Crawford Memorial Lecture (Washington, D.C.: Consultative Group on International Agricultural Research, 1994), 21.

52. Crosson and Anderson, *Resources and Global Food Prospects*, 12.

53. Per Pinstrup-Andersen, "Prospects for Meeting Future Food Demands," *World Scientists' Warning Briefing Book*, ed. Union of Concerned Scientists (Cambridge, Mass.: Union of Concerned Scientists (UCS), 1993), 89–91. "It is extremely unlikely that the region will have the necessary foreign exchange to import such large amounts

of food. It is equally unlikely that the governments will be able to count on food aid in these amounts."

54. Smil, "How Many People Can the Earth Feed?"

55. Sara Scherr and Satya Yadav, *Land Degradation in the Developing World: Implications for Food, Agriculture, and the Environment to 2020*, IFPRI Food, Agriculture, and the Environment Discussion Paper 14 (Washington, D.C.: International Food Policy Research Institute, 1996).

56. WRI, *World Resources 1996–97*, 238.

57. Robert Repetto, "Population, Resources, Environment: An Uncertain Future," *Population Bulletin* 42, no. 2 (1987): 34.

58. Mark Rosegrant, Mercedita Agcaoili-Sombilla, and Nicostrato Perez, *Global Food Projections to 2020: Implications for Investment*, IFPRI Food, Agriculture, and the Environment Discussion Paper 5 (Washington, D.C.: International Food Policy Research Institute, 1995).

59. J. D. Longstreth et al., "Changes in Ultraviolet Radiation Reaching the Earth's Surface," *Ambio* 24, no. 3 (1995): 153–65; and Harry Slaper et al., "Estimates of Ozone Depletion and Skin Cancer Incidence to Examine the Vienna Convention Achievements," *Nature* 384, no. 6606 (21 November 1996): 256–58. Slaper and his colleagues estimate that ozone depletion would have produced a "runaway increase in skin cancer incidence" by the year 2100 in the absence of strict controls on the production of ozone-depleting chemicals.

60. Per Pinstrup-Andersen, "Global Perspectives for Food Production and Consumption," *Tidsskrift for Land Okonomi* 4, no. 179 (1992): 145–69.

61. Leonard, "Overview," 27.

62. This estimate does not include the economic costs of lost rooting depth and increased vulnerability to drought, which may be even larger. See Wilfrido Cruz, Herminia Francisco, and Zenaida Conway, "The On-Site and Downstream Costs of Soil Erosion in the Magat and Pantabangan Watersheds," *Journal of Philippine Development* 15, no. 1 (1988): 88.

63. Ed Barbier, "Environmental Degradation in the Third World," in *Blueprint 2: Greening the World Economy*, ed. David Pearce (London: Earthscan, 1991), 90, box 6.8.

64. Repetto carefully analyzed soil types, cropping practices, logging, and erosion rates in upland areas of Java. Applying a 10 percent discount rate to the future stream of lost income, Repetto calculated the total present economic cost of one year of erosion to be $481 million; this was "approximately 40 percent of the annual value of upland farm production." He continued: "Nearly 40 cents in future income is sacrificed to obtain each dollar for current consumption." He also estimated that off-site costs, including the higher expense of clearing waterways and irrigation channels of silt, came to $30 to $100 million a year. Robert Repetto, "Balance-Sheet Erosion—How to Account for the Loss of Natural Resources," *International Environmental Affairs* 1, no. 2 (1989): 103–37, especially 131.

65. Ibid., 129.

66. The following text and material on Gaza are drawn largely from Kimberley Kelly and Thomas Homer-Dixon, *Environmental Scarcity and Violent Conflict: The Case of Gaza*, Occasional Paper of the Project on Environment, Population, and Security (Washington, D.C.: American Association for the Advancement of Science and the

University of Toronto, 1996). A version of this paper can be found in Homer-Dixon and Blitt, eds., *Ecoviolence.*

67. Official Israeli sources tend to blame the state of Gaza's water supply on the Egyptian administration that preceded them. Overexploitation almost certainly occurred before the annexation of Gaza in 1967. Under the Egyptian authorities, water consumption was not regulated, and the massive influx of refugees after 1948 put tremendous strain on the area's resources. Nonetheless, although the Israeli authority introduced regulations that may have slowed down the rate of consumption, the resources continued to be overexploited. One commentator writes that "the water system in Gaza [was] managed by Israel for 27 years; it cannot wash its hands of the problem by blaming it . . . on the Egyptian administration." Sharif Elmusa, "The Israeli-Palestinian Water Dispute Can Be Resolved," *Palestine-Israel Journal* no. 3 (summer 1994): 26.

68. This figure represents the differential between estimates of safe renewable yield and actual consumption. Safe renewable yield is estimated at 60 to 65 mcm; consumption is estimated at 100 to 140 mcm. If we subtract a midpoint estimate of 120 to 125 mcm from the 60 to 65 mcm available, we are left with a deficit in the area of 60 mcm per year. Some sources, including the Israeli Defense Forces and the UN Conference on Trade and Development estimate this deficit to be much lower, approximately 30 mcm per year (still, however, a very large figure). But the balance of evidence from all sources appears to support the higher estimates cited here.

69. David Brooks and Stephen Lonergan, *Economic, Ecological and Geopolitical Dimensions of Water in Israel* (Victoria, British Columbia: Centre for Sustainable Regional Development, 1992), 77.

70. Hisham Zarour, Jad Isaac, and Violet Qumsieh, "Hydrochemical Indicators of the Severe Water Crisis in the Gaza Strip," in *Final Report on the Project Water Resources in the West Bank and Gaza Strip: Current Situation and Future Prospects* (Jerusalem: Applied Research Institute in Jerusalem, 1994), 9; Beschorner, *Water and Instability,* 15.

71. Anna Bellisari, "Public Health and the Water Crisis in the Occupied Palestinian Territories," *Journal of Palestinian Studies* 23, no. 2 (1994).

72. Zarour, Isaac, and Qumsieh, "Hydrochemical Indicators," 13.

73. Water sources in Gaza that fall below salinity levels of 600 ppm chloride are considered acceptable for irrigation; in Israel, levels between 200 and 300 ppm chloride are considered dangerous to citrus. Sara Roy, *The Gaza Strip: The Political Economy of De-Development* (Washington, D.C.: The Institute for Palestinian Studies, 1995), 163.

74. Beschorner, *Water and Instability,* 15.

75. Zaher Kuhail and Zaki Zaorob, *Potable Ground Water Crisis in the Gaza Strip, 1987–1994* (UNWRA and the Palestinian Health Authority, 1994), 40.

76. Bellisari, "Public Health and Water Crisis," 56.

77. World Bank, *Developing the Occupied Territories: An Investment in Peace,* vol. 6, *Human Resources and Social Policy* (Washington, D.C.: World Bank, 1993), 20–21.

78. The results of this team's work are available in Vaclav Smil and Mao Yushi, coordinators, *The Economic Cost of China's Environmental Degradation,* Occasional Paper of the Project on Environmental Scarcities, State Capacity, and Civil Violence

(Cambridge, Mass.: American Academy of Arts and Sciences and the University of Toronto, 1998). This Occasional Paper can be found at www.library.utoronto.ca/www/ pcs/state/china.htm, and contains: Mao Yushi, "The Economic Cost of China's Environmental Degradation: Summary;" Wang Hongchang, "Deforestation and Desiccation in China: A Preliminary Study;" Xia Guang, "An Estimate of the Economic Consequences of Environmental Pollution in China;" and Ning Datong, "An Assessment of the Economic Losses Resulting from Land Degradation in China," "An Assessment of the Economic Losses Resulting from Rangeland Degradation in China," "An Assessment of the Economic Costs of Wetland Disturbance and Destruction in China," and "An Assessment of the Economic Losses Resulting from Desertification." For an early estimate of the economic costs of environmental damage in China, see Vaclav Smil, *Environmental Change as a Source of Conflict and Economic Losses in China*, Occasional Paper No. 2, Project on Environmental Change and Acute Conflict (Cambridge, Mass.: American Academy of Arts and Science and the University of Toronto, 1992), republished and expanded as Vaclav Smil, *Environmental Problems in China: Estimates of Economic Costs* (Honolulu, Hawaii: East-West Center, 1996). Smil's estimate of a total economic cost of at least 15 percent of Chinese GDP corresponds closely with the total estimate of the above Chinese scholars.

79. Elizabeth Economy, *Reforms and Resources: The Implications for State Capacity in the People's Republic of China*, Occasional Paper of the Project on Environmental Scarcities, State Capacity, and Civil Violence (Cambridge, Mass.: American Academy of Arts and Sciences and the University of Toronto, 1997). This paper can be found at www.library.utoronto.ca/www/pcs/state/china.htm.

80. Robert Repetto, "Wasting Assets: The Need for National Resource Accounting," *Technology Review* 93, no. 1 (1990): 40.

81. Ibid., 42.

82. Repetto, "Balance-Sheet Erosion," 129–32.

83. For example, see Jodi Jacobson, *Environmental Refugees: A Yardstick of Habitability*, Worldwatch Paper 86 (Washington, D.C.: Worldwatch Institute, 1988); Arthur H. Westing, "Environmental Refugees: A Growing Category of Displaced Persons," *Environmental Conservation* 19, no. 3 (1992): 201–7; Norman Myers, *Ultimate Security: The Environmental Basis of Political Stability* (New York: W. W. Norton, 1993); Norman Myers, "Environmental Refugees in a Globally Warmed World," *Bio-Science* 43, no. 11 (1993): 752–61; and Norman Myers and J. Kent, *Environmental Exodus: An Emergent Crisis in the Global Arena* (Washington, D.C.: Climate Institute, 1995).

84. Astri Suhrke, *Pressure Points: Environmental Degradation, Migration, and Conflict*, Occasional Paper No. 3, Project on Environmental Change and Acute Conflict (Cambridge, Mass.: American Academy of Arts and Sciences and the University of Toronto, 1993); and Astri Suhrke, "Environmental Degradation and Population Flows," *Journal of International Affairs* 47, no. 2 (1994): 473–524.

85. Motivation to migrate will be influenced, of course, by numerous other factors, including the perceived costs of migration, the perceived probability of success in the new land, and the potential migrants' risk adversity, which is often influenced by their culture. Harris and Todaro proposed the best-known model of migration that emphasizes differences in perceived well-being (in this case, differences in expected earnings)

between sending and receiving regions. See John Harris and Michael Todaro, "Migration, Unemployment and Development: A Two-Sector Analysis," *American Economic Review* 60, no. 1 (1970): 126–42.

86. William Overholt, correspondence with author, 1995. See also William Overholt, *China: The Next Economic Superpower* (London: Weidenfeld & Nicolson, 1993).

87. Sanjoy Hazarika, *Bangladesh and Assam: Land Pressures, Migration, and Ethnic Conflict*, Occasional Paper No. 3, Project on Environmental Change and Acute Conflict, (Cambridge, Mass.: American Academy of Arts and Sciences and the University of Toronto, 1993), 52–54. The 1991 Indian Census showed that Assam's population growth rate had declined; the conflicts in Assam in the early 1980s appear to have encouraged many migrants from Bangladesh to go to West Bengal instead.

88. James Boyce, *Agrarian Impasse in Bengal: Institutional Constraints to Technological Change* (Oxford: Oxford University Press, 1987), 9. We will see in the next chapter, however, that Bangladesh's unequal distribution of wealth, power, and resources has played an important indirect role in maintaining high levels of resource scarcity. The combination of skewed distribution and rising absolute scarcities has stimulated local conflicts that impede the institutional reform necessary to deal with the underlying scarcity.

89. N. C. Dutta, *Census of India, 1991: Provisional Population Tables*, Series 4, Assam, Paper 1 of 1991 (Gauhati, India: Director of Census Operations, Assam, 1991), 1.

90. Boyce, *Agrarian Impasse*. The subdivision of land in Bangladesh through partible inheritance is discussed on pp. 44–45.

91. For further information on this case, see Shaukat Hassan, *Environmental Issues and Security in South Asia*, Adelphi Paper 262, International Institute for Strategic Studies (London: Brassey's, 1991), 42–43; P. C. Goswami, "Foreign Immigration into Assam," in *Northeast Region: Problems and Prospects of Development*, ed. B. L. Abbi (Chandigarh, India: Centre for Research in Rural and Industrial Development, 1984), 35–59; and Susanta Dass, *Spotlight on Assam* (Chanderpur, India: Premier Book Service, 1989).

92. I am indebted to Valerie Percival for her thought and writing on this issue. See, in particular, Valerie Percival and Thomas Homer-Dixon, *Environmental Scarcity and Violent Conflict: The Case of South Africa*, Occasional Paper of the Project on Environment, Population, and Security (Washington, D.C.: American Association for the Advancement of Science and the University of Toronto, 1995), 6–7. See also Valerie Percival and Thomas Homer-Dixon, "Environmental Scarcity and Violent Conflict: The Case of South Africa" *Journal of Peace Research* 35, no. 3 (May 1998): 279–98. A version of this paper can be found in Homer-Dixon and Blitt, eds., *Ecoviolence*.

93. Naomi Chazan, "Engaging the State: Associational Life in Sub-Saharan Africa," in *State Power and Social Forces*, ed. Joel Migdal, Atul Kohli, and Vivienne Shue (Cambridge: Cambridge University Press, 1994), 255–92. Chazan argues that under conditions of economic strain, both state and society become more insular.

94. For an excellent discussion of the utility and various uses of the concept of civil society, see Michael Foley and Bob Edwards, "The Paradox of Civil Society," *Journal of Democracy* 7, no. 3 (1996): 38–52.

95. On social capital, see Robert D. Putnam with Robert Leonardi and Raffaella Y. Nanetti, *Making Democracy Work: Civic Traditions in Modern Italy* (Princeton, N.J.:

Princeton University Press, 1993). The concept originates with James S. Coleman, "Social Capital," in *Foundations of Social Theory* (Cambridge, Mass.: The Belknap Press of Harvard University Press, 1990).

96. The following material is drawn largely from Percival and Homer-Dixon, *The Case of South Africa.*

97. Francis Wilson and Mamphela Ramphele, *Uprooting Poverty: The South African Challenge* (New York: Norton, 1989); George Quail et al., *Report of the Ciskei Commission* (Pretoria: Conference Associates, 1980), 73.

98. This estimate comes from the Urban Foundation. See Lesley Lawson, "The Ghetto and the Greenbelt," in *Going Green: People, Politics, and the Environment in South Africa,* ed. Jacklyn Cock and Eddie Koch (Cape Town: Oxford University Press, 1991), 47.

99. Anthony Minnaar, "Undisputed Kings: Warlordism in Natal," in *Patterns of Violence: Case Studies of Conflict in Natal,* ed. Anthony Minnaar (Pretoria: Human Science Research Council, 1992), 92.

100. Doug Hindson and Mike Morris, "Violence in Natal/KwaZulu: Dynamics, Causes, Trends," unpublished paper, March 1994, 6–7.

101. Doug Hindson, Mark Byerley, and Mike Morris, "From Violence to Reconstruction: The Making, Disintegration, and Remaking of an Apartheid City," *Antipode* 26, no. 4 (1994): 341.

102. A useful definition of institutions is provided by Douglass North. "Institutions are the rules of the game in a society or, more formally, are the humanly devised constraints that shape human interaction. In consequence they structure incentives in human exchange, whether political, social, or economic." Douglass North, *Institutions, Institutional Change and Economic Performance* (Cambridge: Cambridge University Press, 1990), 3.

103. Joel Migdal, *Strong Societies and Weak States: State-Society Relations and State Capabilities in the Third World* (Princeton, N.J.: Princeton University Press, 1988), 19. Migdal derives his definition from Max Weber, *The Theory of Social and Economic Organization,* ed. Talcott Parsons (New York: Free Press, 1964), 156.

104. Kal Raustiala, "States, NGOs, and International Environmental Institutions," *International Studies Quarterly* 41, no. 4 (1997): 719–740.

105. Peter Evans, *Embedded Autonomy: States and Industrial Transformation* (Princeton, N.J.: Princeton University Press, 1995); Migdal, *Strong Societies and Weak States*; Joel Migdal, Atul Kohli, and Vivienne Shue, eds., *State Power and Social Forces: Domination and Transformation in the Third World* (Cambridge: Cambridge University Press, 1994); Putnam with Leonardi and Nanetti, *Making Democracy Work*; and M. Mann, "The Autonomous Power of the State: Its Origins, Mechanisms, and Results," in *States in History,* ed. J. A. Hall (New York: Basil Blackwell, 1986).

106. Putnam with Leonardi and Nanetti, *Making Democracy Work,* especially 163–176; and Evans, *Embedded Autonomy,* p. 12.

107. I developed these indicators, in collaboration with Charles Barber, for the use within the Project on Environmental Scarcities, State Capacity, and Civil Violence.

108. The full set of reports of the Project on Environmental Scarcity, State Capacity, and Civil Violence is available from the American Academy of Arts and Sciences in Cambridge, Massachusetts. They can also be found at www.library.utoronto.ca/www/ pcs/state.htm.

109. Elizabeth Economy discusses the increased financial demands on the Chinese government arising from water scarcity. See Economy, *Reforms and Resources*.

110. Percival and Homer-Dixon, *The Case of South Africa*; and Peter Gizewski and Thomas Homer-Dixon, *Environmental Scarcity and Violent Conflict: The Case of Pakistan*, Occasional Paper of the Project on Environment, Population, and Security (Washington, D.C.: American Association for the Advancement of Science and the University of Toronto, 1996). Versions of these papers can be found in Homer-Dixon and Blitt, eds., *Ecoviolence*.

111. J. D. Kasarda and A. M. Parnell, eds., *Third World Cities: Problems, Policies and Prospects* (London: Sage, 1993), x.

112. The logging industry in the Philippines offers a good example of this elite behavior. See Broad and Cavanagh, *Plundering Paradise*.

113. Economy, *Reforms and Resources*.

114. Philip Shenon, "Gincun Journal: Good Earth is Squandered. Who'll Feed China?" *New York Times*, 21 September 1994, p. A10, national edition.

115. Charles Barber provides a detailed account of such processes in his account of elite rent-seeking behavior in the Indonesian forest sector. See Charles Barber, *Indonesia Case Study*, Occasional Paper of the Project on Environmental Scarcities, State Capacity, and Civil Violence (Cambridge, Mass.: American Academy of Arts and Sciences and the University of Toronto, 1997). This paper can be found at www.library.utoronto.ca/www/pcs/state/indon/indonsum.htm.

116. See C. S. Prasad, "The Resource Crunch in Bihar: Reconsideration of Current Land Revenue Policies," in *Land Reforms in India*, vol. 1, *Bihar—Institutional Constraints*, ed. B. N. Yugandhar and K. Gopal Iyer (New Delhi: Sage Publications, 1993), 70–83.

117. Barber, *Indonesia Case Study*.

Appendix to Chapter 5
The Causal Role of Environmental Scarcity

1. Although widely used by social scientists, the concept of causation is far more imprecise than usually acknowledged. For insightful discussion, see Paul Humphreys, *The Chances of Explanation: Causal Explanation in the Social, Medical, and Physical Sciences* (Princeton, N.J.: Princeton University Press, 1989); Wesley Salmon, *Scientific Explanation and the Causal Structure of the World* (Princeton, N.J.: Princeton University Press, 1984); Peter Van Inwagen, *Time and Cause: Essays Presented to Richard Taylor* (Dordrecht, Holland: Reidel Publishing, 1980); and Tom Beauchamp and Alexander Rosenberg, *Hume and the Problem of Causation* (New York: Oxford University Press, 1981). In addition, there are serious philosophical debates about whether and how causal claims in the social sciences differ from those in the natural sciences. These debates are particularly pertinent to environment-conflict research, because many causal claims in this field mix natural and social variables. For three decades, issues surrounding intentionality, causation, and generalization have been the subject of heated debate in philosophy of mind, language, and science. See Peter Winch, "The Idea of a Social Science," in *The Idea of a Social Science and Its Relation to Philosophy* (London: Routledge and Kegan Paul, 1958); Jerry Fodor, "Introduction: Two Kinds of Reductionism," in *The Language of Thought* (Cambridge: Har-

vard University Press, 1975), 1–26; Stephen Schiffer, "Ceteris Paribus Laws," *Mind* 100, no. 397 (1991): 1–17; and Alexander Rosenberg, "Obstacles to the Nomological Connection of Reasons and Actions," *Philosophy of Social Science* 10, no. 1 (1980): 79–91.

2. David Dessler introduces a different way of thinking about the causal role of environmental scarcity. He focuses on how environmental scarcity influences rational actors. See David Dessler, "How to Sort Causes in the Study of Environmental Change and Violent Conflict," in *Environment, Poverty, Conflict*, PRIO Report, ed. Nina Graeger and Dan Smith (Oslo: International Peace Research Institute (PRIO), 1994), 91–112.

3. See Benjamin Most and Harvey Starr, *Inquiry and International Politics* (Columbia: University of South Carolina Press, 1989), 47–67, for a discussion of necessity and sufficiency. The strength of a cause can be measured by the *probability* of the cause producing a given effect; if the probability is 1.0, then the cause is sufficient.

4. Goertz notes that causal proximity is influenced by theoretical and pragmatic concerns, because it is usually possible to specify the variables and links in the causal process with greater and greater detail, and thereby reduce proximity, especially by dropping down to lower levels of analysis. Gary Goertz, *Contexts of International Politics* (Cambridge: Cambridge University Press, 1994), 181–82.

5. When environmental degradation becomes irreversible, it takes on the character of a "barrier" cause—that is, a cause that constrains opportunities and precludes options. See chapter 6, "Barrier Models of Context," in Goertz, *Contexts*, 90–113.

6. In contrast, environmental determinists tend to assume that few factors operate and that the environmental ones are powerful.

7. Such a claim is like the assertion that the "3" in the product term "$2 \times 3 = 6$" contributes more to the "6" than the "2." The error of treating an interactive relationship among variables as an additive one is common in debates about the relative contribution of nature and nurture to human characteristics like height or intelligence; commentators will often claim that some proportion of measured height or intelligence—say, 60 percent—is a consequence of nature, while the remainder, additively, is a result of nurture. As Sober points out, such a claim is meaningless when applied at the "local" level— that is, at the level of the individual person. (It is not meaningful to say, for example, that 60 percent of Jim's height is a consequence of his genes and the remaining 40 percent of his environment.) At the level of the population of persons, however, the claim might be a meaningful interpretation of the results of an analysis of variance *if* it means that a certain proportion of the *variance* in the population can be explained by the factor in question. However, Lewontin argues that even this kind of claim is essentially tautological. See Elliott Sober, "Apportioning Causal Responsibility," *The Journal of Philosophy* 85, no. 6 (1988): 303–18; and Richard C. Lewontin, "The Analysis of Variance and the Analysis of Causes," in *The IQ Controversy: Critical Readings*, ed. N. J. Block and Gerald Dworkin (New York: Pantheon Books, 1976), 170–93. At the local level, the only time it is appropriate to weight the causal contribution of various factors differentially in an interactive relationship is when they have different rates of change over time. Holdren provides a mathematical method for estimating the relative causal importance of factors in such situations; John Holdren, "Population and the Energy Problem," *Population and Environment* 12, no. 3 (1991): 231–55, especially 243–44.

8. Such opportunistic exploitation of drought in Africa is discussed by Peter Wallensteen in "Food Crops as a Factor in Strategic Policy and Action," in *Global Resources and International Conflict: Environmental Factors in Strategic Policy and Action*, ed. Arthur Westing (New York: Oxford University Press, 1986), 154–55.

Chapter 6
Ingenuity and Adaptation

1. Indonesia is another excellent example of the use of both the above-mentioned strategies in response to critical cropland scarcity on the island of Java. See Anne Booth, "Indonesian Agricultural Development in Comparative Perspective," *World Development* 17, no. 8 (1989): 1235–54, especially 1242.

2. Drawing on the work of Burton and his colleagues, Warrick and Riebsame suggest that the societies most vulnerable to environmental stress are those transitional developing societies that have dismantled traditional coping mechanisms but have little of the technological prowess that comes with industrialization and that could aid adaptation. See Ian Burton et al., *The Environment as Hazard* (New York: Oxford University Press, 1978); and Richard Warrick and William Riebsame, "Societal Response to CO_2-Induced Climate Change: Opportunities for Research," *Climatic Change* 3, no. 4 (1981): 401.

3. See, for example, Paul Romer, "The Origins of Endogenous Growth," *Journal of Economic Perspectives* 8, no. 1 (1994): 3–22; and Elhanan Helpman, "Endogenous Macroeconomic Growth Theory," *European Economic Review* 36, no. 2/3 (1992): 237–67.

4. Paul Romer, "Two Strategies for Economic Development: Using Ideas and Producing Ideas," in *Proceedings of the World Bank Annual Conference on Development Economics, 1992*, by World Bank (Washington, D.C.: World Bank, 1993), 64.

5. Using a chemistry-set metaphor, Romer represents a given mixture of chemicals—his analogue to an "idea"—by a string of 0s and 1s. A position in the string is assigned to each substance in the chemistry set. The position shows 1 if the substance is included in the mixture and 0 if it is not. Romer, "Two Strategies," 68.

6. Pierre Crosson and Jock Anderson, "Trends in Global Agriculture" (paper presented at a NATO Advanced Research Workshop on Climate Change and World Food Security, University of Oxford, England, 11–15 July 1993), 17.

7. For similar arguments on how social institutions shape a society's capacity for technological development, see Alexander Gerschenkron, *Economic Backwardness in Historical Perspective* (Cambridge, Mass.: Belknap Press, 1962); Moses Abramovitz, "Catching Up, Forging Ahead, and Falling Behind," *Journal of Economic History* 46, no. 2 (1986): 386–406; and Björn Johnson, "Institutional Learning," in *National Systems of Innovation: Towards a Theory of Innovation and Interactive Learning*, ed. Bengt-Åke Lundvall (London: Pinter, 1992), 23–44. On the general relationship between institutions and economic growth, see Douglass North, *Institutions, Institutional Change and Economic Performance* (Cambridge: Cambridge University Press, 1990).

8. Surprisingly, people often are perplexed by the claim that something can be both an input and an output of the economic system. However, a moment's reflection shows this is the case for many goods. Physical and human capital, for example, are both

inputs and outputs: an economy needs factories to produce the components for further factories, and engineers to train engineers.

9. See, for example, Elinor Ostrom *Governing the Commons: The Evolution of Institutions for Collective Action* (Cambridge: Cambridge University Press, 1990).

10. I assume that there is a rough consensus within society on what constitutes social welfare, although the consensus may change across societies and over time. Economists acknowledge that it is difficult both to specify exactly what counts as individual welfare and to aggregate individual welfares to arrive at a measure for the whole society. See Amartya Sen, *Resources, Values and Development* (Oxford: Basil Blackwell, 1984), especially chapter 13 on "Rights and Capabilities," 307–24.

11. See Julian Simon, *The Ultimate Resource* (Princeton, N.J.: Princeton University Press, 1981); and Julian Simon, *The Ultimate Resource 2* (Princeton, N.J.: Princeton University Press, 1996).

12. Everett Rogers, *The Diffusion of Innovation*, 3d ed. (New York: Free Press, 1983) is the classic treatment of the second stage.

13. This general claim, while reasonable for heuristic purposes, needs several qualifications. First, some renewable resources—like agricultural soils, climate, and the stratospheric ozone layer—mainly provide economic services, not goods. In the case of agricultural land, the resource is not so much "consumed" as "used" (although there is some consumption of the nutrient stock in the soil); the ratio, in this case, is better stated as total cropland used to total potential cropland available. In the case of the ozone layer, the sink or absorptive capacity of the resource is degraded by human activity, and the appropriate ratio might be that of total emissions (of CFCs) to total absorptive capacity.

Second, it is notoriously hard to define, in any objective way, the total quantity of a resource available for consumption or use (the denominator of the ratio). Renewable resources are characterized by both a stock and a flow; resource availability, therefore, depends on whether one regards the underlying stock as available for consumption. In addition, the stated reserves of a resource tend to be affected by the resource's price, because the higher the price, the greater the incentive to obtain the resource. And, finally, technical ingenuity changes both the availability of resources (through more efficient extraction technologies, for instance) and the definition of what is, and what is not, a useful resource.

Third, while per capita resource consumption is rising rapidly in most developing countries, the 1970s saw a reversal of this trend in industrialized countries. Per capita consumption (and in some cases total consumption) of basic industrial materials—such as steel, cement, aluminum, and paper—began to decline, although the drop remains small compared to the growth that occurred in this century. In the United States, for example, steel consumption per capita increased from about 90 kilograms in 1890 to about 500 kilograms in 1972, and then declined to a modern low of 360 kilos by 1983. See Jose Goldemberg et al., *Energy for a Sustainable World* (Washington, D.C.: World Resources Institute, 1987), 38; and Eric Larson, Marc Ross, and Robert Williams, "Beyond the Era of Materials," *Scientific American* 254, no. 6 (June 1986): 34–41.

14. Many analysts use similar concepts. Daly and Cobb, for example, discuss the "optimal scale" of the global economy in relation to the planet's resource base. See Herman Daly and John Cobb, *For the Common Good: Redirecting the Economy Toward Community, the Environment, and a Sustainable Future* (Boston: Beacon Press,

1989), 143–47. See also David Pearce and Kerry Turner, *Economics of Natural Resources and the Environment* (Baltimore: John Hopkins University Press, 1990), 290–95; and Paul Raskin, Evan Hansen, and Robert Margolis, *Water and Sustainability: A Global Outlook* (Boston: Stockholm Environment Institute, 1994), 12–13.

15. Although demand-induced and supply-induced scarcities are worsening for many renewable resources, structural scarcities do not exhibit such a clear trend. Nonetheless, inequalities of resource access, wealth, and power are invariably severe in developing countries, and they tend to cause excessive and inefficient resource consumption (and higher supply-induced scarcity), particularly of forests and soils. Three mechanisms are key: first, without democracy and equity, the people who suffer from resource scarcity lack the power to block the activities of groups that benefit from scarcity; second, the low purchasing power of poor people means that the resources they depend on tend to be undervalued in the market; and third, inequality increases the discount rate of both poor and rich, which contributes to resource overexploitation. See James Boyce, "Towards a Political Economy of Sustainable Development" (paper presented at the Seminar on the Impact of Economic Policy on Sustainable Development in the Agricultural Sector, Inter-American Institute for Cooperation on Agriculture, Coronado, Costa Rica, 26 November 1992); James Boyce, "Inequality as a Cause of Environmental Degradation," *Ecological Economics* 11, no. 3 (1994): 169–78; and James Boyce, "Equity and the Environment," *Alternatives* 21, no. 1 (1995): 12–17.

16. On the cod fishery, see Leslie Harris, *Independent Review of the State of the Northern Cod Stock*, prepared by the Northern Cod Review Panel, submitted to the Honourable Thomas Siddon, Minister of Fisheries and Oceans (Ottawa, Canada: Department of Fisheries and Oceans, 1990); on Middle East water shortages, see House of Representatives, Committee on Foreign Affairs, Subcommittee on Europe and the Middle East, testimony on "The Middle East in the 1990s: Middle East Water Issues," 26 June 1990; and on Chinese cropland loss, see Vaclav Smil, *China's Environmental Crisis: An Inquiry into the Limits of National Development* (Armonk, N.Y.: M. E. Sharpe, 1993), 57.

17. On West African forests, see World Resources Institute (WRI), *World Resources 1992–93* (New York: Oxford University Press, 1992), 119; and on Antarctic fisheries, World Resources Institute (WRI), *World Resources 1990–91* (New York: Oxford University Press, 1990).

18. Gordon and his colleagues note, for example, that most successful substitutions among nonrenewables involve "the replacement of one scarce material by another that is more abundant but nevertheless geochemically scarce, as when molybdenum is used to replace tungsten as an alloying ingredient in steel." They argue that "modern technology has tended to make increased use of scarce and exotic metals." Robert Gordon et al., *Toward a New Iron Age? Quantitative Modelling of Resource Exhaustion* (Cambridge, Mass.: Harvard University Press, 1987), 154.

19. William K. Stevens, "Man Moves Down the Marine Food Chain, Creating Havoc," *New York Times*, 10 February 1998, p. B11.

20. See World Bank, *World Development Report 1992* (New York: Oxford University Press, 1992), 10, 69; and Robert Repetto, "Population, Resources, Environment: An Uncertain Future," *Population Bulletin* 42, no. 2 (1987): 6–7, 9.

21. Ironically, our technological ingenuity sometimes increases the risk of nonlinear effects in renewable-resource systems. For example, the cultural ecologist Roy Rappa-

port notes that our quest for higher crop yields has produced "some of the most delicate and unstable ecosystems ever to have appeared on the face of the earth." Roy Rappaport, "The Flow of Energy in an Agricultural Society," *Scientific American* 224, no. 3 (September 1971): 130.

22. Donald Ludwig, Ray Hilborn, and Carl Walters, "Uncertainty, Resource Exploitation, and Conservation: Lessons from History," *Science* 260, no. 5104 (2 April 1993): 17. See also Vaclav Smil, *Global Ecology: Environmental Change and Social Flexibility* (London: Routledge, 1993), especially chapter 5 on "Cascading Complications"; and Bo Wiman, "Implications of Environmental Complexity for Science and Policy," *Global Environmental Change* (June 1991): 235–47.

23. On the implications for system management of tight coupling and complex interactions among system elements, see Charles Perrow, "Complexity, Coupling, and Catastrophe," chap. 3 in *Normal Accidents: Living with High-Risk Technologies* (New York: Basic Books, 1984), 62–100.

24. Kenneth Watt and Paul Craig, "System Stability Principles," *Systems Research* 3, no. 4 (1986): 197.

25. Attempts to optimize system performance produce complexity, as do attempts to deal with the negative consequences of previous increases in complexity. See Brian Arthur, "Why Do Things Become More Complex?" *Scientific American* 268, no. 5 (May 1993): 144; and Brian Arthur, "On the Evolution of Complexity," in *Complexity: Metaphors, Models, and Reality*, ed. G. Cowan, D. Pines, and D. Meltzer, Proceedings of the Santa Fe Institute Studies in the Sciences of Complexity, vol. 19 (Reading, Mass.: Addison-Wesley, 1994), 65–81. Social systems that are dynamic, highly interactive, and tightly coupled are called "turbulent" or "hyperturbulent" by organizational theorists. A rich literature describes common sub-optimal organizational responses to such environments. See F. E. Emery and E. L. Trist, "The Causal Texture of Organizational Environments," *Human Relations* 18, no. 1 (1965): 21–32; Joseph McCann and John Selsky, "Hyperturbulence and the Emergence of Type 5 Environments," *Academy of Management Review* 9, no. 3 (1984): 460–70; and Todd La Porte, ed., *Organized Social Complexity: Challenge to Politics and Policy* (Princeton, N.J.: Princeton University Press, 1975).

26. The constraints influence the elasticity of substitution of ingenuity for a given resource; if the elasticity is low, then a large amount of ingenuity is needed to compensate for a small increase in the resource's scarcity. The second law of thermodynamics is a physical constraint that has received particular attention. As Dyke notes, the law "defines a space of possibilities for us, and does so rather tightly." See C. Dyke, "Cities as Dissipative Structures," in *Entropy, Information, and Evolution: New Perspectives on Physical and Biological Evolution*, ed. Bruce Weber, David Depew, and James Smith (Cambridge, Mass.: MIT Press, 1988), 355–68. The classic application of the second law to environmental degradation is Nicholas Georgescu-Roegen, "The Entropy Law and the Economic Problem," Distinguished Lecture Series, No. 1, Department of Economics, University of Alabama, 1971; and Nicholas Georgescu-Roegen, *The Entropy Law and the Economic Process* (Cambridge, Mass.: Harvard University Press, 1971). For a recent debate, see Jeffrey Young, "Is the Entropy Law Relevant to the Economics of Natural Resource Scarcity?" *Journal of Environmental Economics and Management* 21, no. 2 (1991): 169–79; and Herman Daly, "Comment: Is the Entropy Law Relevant to the Economics of Natural Resource Scarcity? Yes, of Course It Is!"

Journal of Environmental Economics and Management 23, no. 1 (1992): 91–95. Cultural constraints on social and economic development may also be intractable. See James Bradford De Long, "The 'Protestant Ethic' Revisited: A Twentieth Century Look," *The Fletcher Forum of World Affairs* 13, no. 2 (1989): 229–41; and Harry Eckstein, "A Culturalist Theory of Political Change," *American Political Science Review* 82, no. 3 (1988): 789–804.

27. Aaron Wildavsky, *Searching for Safety* (New Brunswick, N.J.: Transaction Books, 1988); Todd La Porte and Paula Consolini, "Working in Practice but Not in Theory: Theoretical Challenges of 'High Reliability Organizations,'" *Journal of Public Administration Research and Theory* 1, no. 1 (1991): 19–47; Dennis Avery, *Global Food Progress 1991* (Indianapolis, Ind.: Hudson Institute, 1991); Thomas Schelling, "Some Economics of Global Warming," *American Economic Review* 82, no. 1 (1992): 1–14; and Jesse Ausubel, "Does Climate Still Matter?" *Nature* 350, no. 6320 (25 April 1991): 649–52.

28. Simon, *The Ultimate Resource*, 345.

29. Schmookler suggests, for example, that "the S-shaped long-run growth curve for individual industries, in which output tends to grow at a declining percentage rate, usually reflects demand, not supply, conditions." The growth curve reflects the declining marginal utility of production, rather than its increasing marginal cost. In other words, Schmookler implies that there are no intrinsic limits, including no limits on the requisite human creativity or innovation, to indefinite expansion of individual industries. Jacob Schmookler, *Invention and Economic Growth* (Cambridge: Harvard University Press, 1996), 204.

30. Jan Fagerberg, "Technology and International Differences in Growth Rates," *Journal of Economic Literature* 32, no. 3 (1994): 1149.

31. Ester Boserup, *The Conditions of Agricultural Growth: The Economics of Agrarian Change under Population Pressure* (Chicago: Aldine, 1965); Ester Boserup, *Economic and Demographic Relationships in Development*, essays selected and introduced by T. Paul Schultz (Baltimore: Johns Hopkins University Press, 1990).

32. A recent close study of the semi-arid Machakos District in Kenya lends support to these various arguments. See Mary Tiffen, Michael Mortimore, and Francis Gichuki, *More People, Less Erosion: Environmental Recovery in Kenya* (Chichester, U.K.: John Wiley, 1994). Such arguments have a long history: see, for instance, Eugène Dupréel, *Population et Progrès* (1928), excerpted in *Population and Development Review* 8, no. 4 (1982): 821–28.

33. Simon, *The Ultimate Resource*. This argument, however, naively assumes that the marginal social benefit arising from the ideas of an additional person always exceeds the marginal cost that the additional person imposes on society.

34. The Coase theorem is "based upon the argument that externalities do not give rise to a misallocation of resources provided there are no transaction costs, and given property rights that are well-defined and enforceable." See David Pearce, ed., *The MIT Dictionary of Modern Economics*, 3d edition (Cambridge, Mass.: MIT Press, 1986), 66.

35. David Feeny, "The Demand for and Supply of Institutional Arrangements," in *Rethinking Institutional Analysis and Development: Issues, Alternatives, and Choices*, ed. Vincent Ostrom, David Feeny, and Hartmut Picht (San Francisco: International Center for Economic Growth, 1988), 159–209, especially 164–68. Feeny discusses a

host of factors that affect the supply of institutions, including the cost of institutional design, the stock of knowledge, the expected cost of implementation, the constitutional order, existing institutional arrangements, normative behavioral codes, and benefits to elite decision makers. Several of these factors are incorporated in the supply model discussed in this chapter.

36. For a technical discussion, see Partha Dasgupta and Karl-Göran Mäler, *Poverty, Institutions, and the Environmental Resource Base*, World Bank Environment Paper No. 9 (Washington, D.C.: World Bank, 1994), 22–30.

37. As Repetto notes, "prices can guide market adjustment processes only if resources can be bought and sold, which presupposes that they can be owned. Many important resources are not privately owned, usually because it is impossible to segregate one person's portion from another's and reserve it for exclusive use." Repetto, "Population, Resources, Environment," 6–7.

38. The World Bank notes that "clear property rights may induce private users to adopt the 'correct' pattern of timber extraction, taking into consideration the current and future benefits from logging, but give no incentive to take into account the costs of deforestation to those living outside the forests—for example, increased soil erosion or lost biodiversity." World Bank, *World Development Report 1992*, 70. Certain externalities of resource depletion or degradation—such as decreases in quality of life—are particularly hard to price within a market system. As Warrick and Riebsame note, "displacement of families, abandonment of livelihood, community disruption, and malnutrition are difficult effects to place on common yardsticks. Yet these are the appropriate descriptions of societal impact in most parts of the world." See Warrick and Riebsame, "Societal Response," 409.

39. Romer contends that "we must recognize that ideas are economic goods that are unlike conventional private goods, and that markets are inherently less successful at producing and transmitting them than they are with private goods." Paul Romer, "Two Strategies," 47.

40. Many analysts acknowledge the importance of state intervention if markets are to respond effectively to natural-resource scarcity. In a gentle but decisive critique of the Boserupian hypothesis, for example, Lele and Stone highlight the role of policy intervention in land and agricultural markets if cropland scarcity induced by population growth is to generate increased productivity without serious land degradation. They argue that "a policy-led approach to intensification is critical to maintaining and preserving resources otherwise degraded through more intensive use." A combination of higher population density and "the freeplay of market forces" is unlikely by itself to produce "the expected gains in per capita agricultural production and rural income." Uma Lele and Steven Stone, *Population Pressure, the Environment and Agricultural Intensification: Variations on the Boserup Hypothesis*, MADIA Discussion Paper 4 (Washington, D.C.: World Bank, 1989), 7. For similar arguments, see Olmstead and Rhode, "Induced Innovation in American Agriculture: A Reconsideration," *Journal of Political Economy* 101, no. 1 (1993): 110; Food and Agriculture Organization (FAO), *The State of Food and Agriculture 1990* (Rome: FAO, 1991), 96–97; and Elinor Ostrom, Larry Schroeder, and Susan Wynne, *Institutional Incentives and Sustainable Development: Infrastructure Policies in Perspective* (Boulder, Colo.: Westview, 1993), especially 220. The role of the state in establishing the conditions for markets has long been noted; of particular importance is Karl Polanyi, *The Great Transformation*

(Boston: Beacon Press, 1957), 139–140; for a contemporary policy-oriented treatment, see World Bank, *World Development Report, 1997: The State in a Changing World* (Oxford: Oxford University Press, 1997).

41. Peter Evans, "The State as Problem and Solution: Predation, Embedded Autonomy, and Structural Change," in *The Politics of Economic Adjustment: International Constraints, Distributive Conflicts, and the State*, ed. Stephan Haggard and Robert Kaufman (Princeton, N.J.: Princeton University Press, 1992), 141, 148.

42. Mancur Olson, *The Rise and Decline of Nations: Economic Growth, Stagflation, and Social Rigidities* (New Haven, Conn.: Yale University Press, 1982).

43. Bargaining costs are lower within small groups; group homogeneity tends to be higher, which reduces disputes over the nature of the collective good sought; the need for selective incentives is lower because collective benefits are shared by fewer members; and small groups can provide "social" selective incentives, such as ostracism and respect.

44. Olson, *Rise and Decline*, 165.

45. Ibid., 44.

46. Many analysts emphasize how narrow coalitions impede sustainable economic development and adaptation to resource scarcity. See David Reed's review of the World Bank's *World Development Report 1992* in *International Environmental Affairs* 4, no. 4 (1992): 367–71. See also Elinor Ostrom, Larry Schroeder, Susan Wynne, *Institutional Incentives and Sustainable Development*; Ludwig, Hilborn, and Walters, "Uncertainty, Resource Exploitation, and Conservation"; and Vernon Ruttan, "Institutional Innovation and Agricultural Development," *World Development* 17, no. 9 (1989): 1375–87, especially 1384–85.

47. Olson, *Rise and Decline*, 62.

48. Scarcity also causes a *diversion* of ingenuity to serve the interests of narrow coalitions; thus, even if society's total supply of ingenuity does not decrease, the supply of ingenuity for public institution-building can go down. As I will discuss in the conclusion of this chapter, to be fully complete my model of ingenuity's aggregate supply must be supplemented by models of its distribution and use.

49. Feeny, "The Demand for and Supply of Institutional Arrangements," 169–170. North and Thomas focus on property rights. A sharp divergence between the private and social rates of return may cause governments to establish property institutions that "hinder rather than promote growth." For example, rulers "may find short-run advantage in selling exclusive monopoly rights which may thwart innovation and factor mobility." Douglass North, and Robert Thomas, *The Rise of the Western World: A New Economic History* (Cambridge: Cambridge University Press, 1973), 6–8.

50. Vernon Ruttan and Yujiro Hayami, "Toward a Theory of Induced Institutional Innovation," *The Journal of Development Studies* 20, no. 4 (1984): 213. Feeny provides several important illustrations. In Thailand, for example, conflicting elite interests hindered the adoption of new irrigation institutions. Feeny, "The Demand for and Supply of Institutional Arrangements," 167.

51. James Boyce, *Agrarian Impasse in Bengal: Institutional Constraints to Technological Change* (Oxford: Oxford University Press, 1987).

52. Paul Wallich, "The Analytical Economist: The Wages of Haiti's Dictatorship," *Scientific American* 271, no. 6 (December 1994): 36.

53. The text in this paragraph is drawn from Peter Gizewski and Thomas Homer-

Dixon, *Environmental Scarcity and Violent Conflict: The Case of Pakistan*, Occasional Paper of the Project on Environment, Population, and Security (Washington, D.C.: American Association for the Advancement of Science and the University of Toronto, 1996), 18–19. A version of this paper can be found in Thomas Homer-Dixon and Jessica Blitt, eds., *Ecoviolence: Links among Environment, Population, and Security* (Boulder, Colo.: Rowman & Littlefield, 1998).

54. Pakistan Administrative Staff College, *Environmental Issues and Problems in Pakistan*, National Management Paper (Lahore: Pakistan Administrative Staff College, July 1994), 43.

55. Sungi Development Foundation, *Forests, Wealth and Politics: A Focus on Hazara* (Islamabad: Sungi Development Foundation, April 1995), 1–4.

56. Richard Kessler, *Rebellion and Repression in the Philippines* (New Haven, Conn.: Yale University Press, 1989), 18.

57. George Guthrie, ed., *Six Perspectives on the Philippines* (Manilla: Bookmark, 1968), 79.

58. See, for example, Amitai Etzioni, *The Moral Dimension: Towards a New Economics* (New York: Free Press, 1988); Albert Hirschman, "Against Parsimony: Three Easy Ways of Complicating Some Categories of Economic Discourse," chap. 6 in *Rival Views of Market Society, and Other Recent Essays* (Cambridge, Mass.: Harvard University Press, 1992), 153–57; Charles Sabel, "Studied Trust: Building New Forms of Cooperation in a Volatile Economy," in *Industrial Districts and Local Economic Regeneration*, ed. F. Pyke and W. Sengenberger (Geneva: International Institute for Labor Studies, 1992), 215–50; and Robert D. Putnam with Robert Leonardi and Raffaella Y. Nanetti, *Making Democracy Work: Civic Traditions in Modern Italy* (Princeton, N.J.: Princeton University Press, 1993).

59. Clifford Geertz, *Agricultural Involution: The Process of Ecological Change in Indonesia* (Berkeley: University of California Press, 1963), 96–100.

60. North and Thomas, *The Rise of the Western World*, 98–99.

61. Atul Kohli, "The Political Economy of Development Strategies: Comparative Perspectives on the Role of the State," *Comparative Politics* 19, no. 2 (1987): 242. Jackson argues that highly penetrated and ineffective states—what he calls "quasi-states"—are more common today than previously. Because of international norms of sovereignty and nonintervention, "ramshackle states today are not . . . allowed to disappear juridically—even if for all intents and purposes they have already fallen or been pulled down in fact." Robert Jackson, *Quasi-States: Sovereignty, International Relations, and the Third World* (Cambridge: Cambridge University Press, 1990), 23.

62. Olson, *Rise and Decline*, 73.

63. A move to authoritarianism might reduce the obstruction of state policy by narrow distributional coalitions, while allowing leaders to command more directly the system's resources in response to immediate social crises. It might therefore permit a temporary (and I emphasize temporary) narrowing of the ingenuity gap. In terms of organization theory, we can interpret such a move as a radical effort to simplify or "partition" the decision-making setting in order to preserve and allocate adaptive capacity. See McCann and Selsky, "Hyperturbulence," 464–65.

64. Putnam with Leonardi and Nanetti, *Making Democracy Work*, 176.

65. Albert Hirschman addresses this issue directly. He asks, "Is it possible to distinguish between two varieties of social conflict, those that leave behind a positive residue

of integration and those that tear society apart?" See Albert Hirschman, "Social Conflict as Pillars of Democratic Market Society," *Political Theory* 22, no. 2 (1994): 209.

66. Sheri Berman makes a related argument that draws on the classic work of Samuel Huntington: the activities of civil society, she argues, can sometimes be too vigorous for the capacity of society's political institutions. "Absent strong and responsive political institutions, an increasingly active civil society may serve to undermine, rather than strengthen, a political regime." Berman argues that high levels of "associationism" helped undermined the Weimar Republic and facilitated Hitler's rise to power. Sheri Berman, "Civil Society and the Collapse of the Weimar Republic," *World Politics* 49, no. 3 (1997): 401–29.

67. Peter Evans, "The State as Problem and Solution," 144.

68. Gene Grossman and Elhanan Helpman, *Innovation and Growth in the Global Economy* (Cambridge, Mass.: MIT Press, 1991).

69. See Mamman Aminu Ibrahim, *The Information Drain: Obstacles to Research in Africa,*" Gatekeeper Series, No. 32 (London: International Institute for Environment and Development, 1992).

70. Dr. Celso Roque, former Undersecretary for Environment and Research, Environment and Natural Resources, Philippines, interview by author, November 1991.

71. Repetto, "Population, Resources, Environment," 37.

72. United Nations Development Program, *Human Development Report, 1992* (New York: Oxford University Press, 1992), 57.

73. On the technical capacity of East African countries in the area of water management, see Charles Okidi, "Environmental Stress and Conflicts in Africa: Case Studies of African International Drainage Basins," paper prepared for the Project on Environmental Change and Acute Conflict, Peace and Conflict Studies Program, University of Toronto, May 1992.

74. "An Unwelcome Export Success," *Nature* 366, no. 6456 (16 December 1993): 618.

75. For a review, see Langdon Winner, "Complexity and the Limits of Human Understanding," in *Organized Social Complexity: Challenge to Politics and Policy*, ed. Todd LaPorte (Princeton, N.J.: Princeton University Press, 1975), 40–76.

76. Michael Manning and David Rejeski, "Sustainable Development and Risk: A Fit?" (paper presented at the conference on Comparative Risk and Priority Setting of Air Pollution Issues, Keystone, Colo., 7–11 June 1993). See also E. O. Wilson, "Is Humanity Suicidal?" *New York Times Magazine*, 30 May 1993, p. 29. Many natural/social systems are probably computationally "intractable," which means they cannot be accurately modeled using any realistic amount of computational power. See Joseph Traub and Henryk Wozniakowski, "Breaking Intractability," *Scientific American* 270, no. 1 (January 1994): 102–7. Scientists are additionally handicapped because they cannot conduct controlled experiments with large-scale natural and social systems; see Ludwig, Hilborn, and Walters, "Uncertainty, Resource Exploitation, and Conservation."

77. For an interesting argument to this effect, see Robert Ornstein and Paul Ehrlich, *New World, New Mind: Moving toward Conscious Evolution* (New York: Touchstone, 1989).

78. Perrow, *Normal Accidents*, 317.

79. Derek de Solla Price, *Little Science, Big Science . . . and Beyond* (New York: Columbia, 1986), 82.

80. Even if a discovery has a clear use, its diffusion in useable form throughout society often takes decades. For example, research shows a historically consistent interval of twenty to forty years for substitutions involving metals. Gordon et al., *Toward a New Iron Age?*, 65.

81. Watt and Craig, "System Stability Principles," 199.

82. Robert Wright, "The Experiment that Failed: Why Soviet Science Collapsed," *The New Republic* 205, no. 18 (28 October 1991): 20–25; and Sergei Kapitza, "Antiscience Trends in the USSR," *Scientific American* 265, no. 2 (August 1991): 32–38.

Appendix to Chapter 6
Can Poor Countries Attain Endogenous Growth?

1. R. E. Lucas, "On the Mechanics of Economic Development." *Journal of Monetary Economics* 22, no. 1 (1988): 3–42; S. Rebelo, "Long-Run Policy Analysis and Long-Run Growth," *Journal of Political Economy* 99, no. 3 (1991): 500–521; Paul Romer, "Increasing Returns and Long-Run Growth," *Journal of Political Economy* 94, no. 5 (1986): 1002–37; Romer, "Endogenous Technological Change."

2. R. J. Barro and X. Sala-I-Martin, *Economic Growth* (New York: McGraw-Hill, 1995).

3. Barro and Sala-I-Martin, *Economic Growth*; N. G. Mankiw, D. Romer, and D. N. Weil, "A Contribution to the Empirics of Economic Growth," *Quarterly Journal of Economics* 107, no. 2 (1992): 407–37; H. Pack, "Endogenous Growth Theory: Intellectual Appeal and Empirical Shortcomings," *Journal of Economic Perspectives* 8, no. 1 (1994): 55–72; Romer, "Origins of Endogenous Growth."

4. Romer, "Two Strategies for Economic Development," 63–91.

5. Pack, "Endogenous Growth Theory."

6. Edward Barbier, "Natural Capital and the Economics of Environment and Development," in *Investing in Natural Capital: The Ecological Economics Approach to Sustainability*, ed. A. M. Jansson et al. (Washington, D.C.: Island Press, 1994).

7. Recent efforts to extend endogenous growth models to incorporate environmental considerations have generally focused on the short- and long-run implications of pollution and its disutility. See A. Bovenberg and S. Smulders, "Environmental Quality and Pollution-Augmenting Technological Change in a Two-Sector Endogenous Growth Model," *Journal of Public Economics* 57, no. 3 (1995): 369–91; I. Musu, "Transitional Dynamics to Optimal Sustainable Growth" (paper presented at the 6th Annual European Association of Environmental and Resource Economics Conference, Umeå, Sweden, 24–26 June, 1995); I. Musu and M. Lines, "Endogenous Growth and Environmental Preservation," in *Environmental Economics: Proceedings of European Economic Associations at Oxford, 1993*, ed. G. Boero and A. Silberstein (London: St. Martins Press, 1995); and N. Vellinga, "Short Run Analysis of Endogenous Environmental Growth," (paper presented at the 6th Annual European Association of Environmental and Resource Economics Conference, Umeå, Sweden, 24–26 June, 1995).

8. P. S. Dasgupta and G. E. Heal, *The Economics of Exhaustible Resources* (Cambridge, U.K.: University Press, 1979); and J. E. Stiglitz, "Growth with Exhaustible

Natural Resources: Efficient and Optimal Growth Paths," *Review of Economic Studies*, Symposium on the Economics of Exhaustible Resources (1974), 123–38.

9. Stiglitz, "Growth with Exhaustible Natural Resources."

10. Ibid.

11. E. B. Barbier, *Endogenous Growth and Natural Resource Scarcity*, EEEM Discussion Paper 9601 (York, U.K.: Department of Environmental Economics and Environmental Management, University of York, 1996).

12. Stiglitz, "Growth with Exhaustible Natural Resources"; and Paul Romer, "Endogenous Technological Change," *Journal of Political Economy* 98, no. 5 (1990): S74–75.

13. Romer, "Endogenous Technological Change."

14. Barbier, "Endogenous Growth and Natural Resource Scarcity."

15. A third possible scenario of "negative" innovation is ruled out in the models developed by Barbier, because it is assumed that "decumulation" of the stock of ideas is not feasible; that is, resource scarcity may disrupt the social conditions and institutions necessary to generate new innovations, but once created, technical designs or other forms of technological knowledge do not simply disappear. Some may argue, however, that this is an unnecessarily restrictive condition and that the actual process of innovation in an economy is more complex. For example, Homer-Dixon distinguishes between the generation of ingenuity and its dissemination or implementation (see the main body of this chapter). If this distinction is valid then, although the generated ideas themselves may be hard to lose or "decumulate," their implementation may be affected to the point that the stock of ideas is no longer functional in the broader economic and social system. In this sense, the stock of ingenuity in society may for all intents and purposes appear to "decumulate."

Chapter 7
Violence

1. World Resources Institute (WRI), *World Resources, 1992–93* (New York: Oxford University Press, 1992), 286; Laurence Lewis and William Coffey, "The Continuing Deforestation of Haiti, *Ambio* 14, no. 3 (1985): 158–60.

2. Global Assessment of Soil Degradation, *World Map on Status of Human-Induced Soil Degradation*, Sheet 1, North and South America (Nairobi, Kenya/Wageningen, The Netherlands: United Nations Environment Programme/International Soil Reference Centre, 1990).

3. Jessica Tuchman Mathews, "Redefining Security," *Foreign Affairs* 68, no. 2 (1989): 168.

4. Thomas Weil et al., *Haiti: A Country Study* (Washington, D.C.: United States Government, Department of the Army, 1982), 28–33.

5. Anthony Catanese, *Haiti's Refugees: Political, Economic, Environmental*, Field Staff Reports, No. 17 (Sausalito, Calif.: Universities Field Staff International, Natural Heritage Institute, 1990–91), 5.

6. Elizabeth Abbott, "Where Waters Run Brown," *Equinox* 10, no. 59 (1991): 43.

7. Marko Ehrlich et al., *Haiti: Country Environmental Profile, A Field Study* (Washington, D.C.: USAID, 1986), 89–92.

8. United Nations Population Division, *World Population Prospects: The 1996 Re-

vision, Demographic Indicators 1950–2050, Diskettes 1–4 (New York: United Nations, 1996).

9. World Resources Institute (WRI), *World Resources, 1996–97* (New York: Oxford University Press, 1996), 239. Some of this decline was due, of course, to the country's chronic civil strife during this period.

10. All simple theories of conflict posit that the main cause of conflict is a property of either *individuals*, *groups*, or the *system* of interacting individuals or groups. Consequently, scholars often categorize theories of conflict according to such individual, group, or systemic "levels of analysis." They also often contend that conflicts explained by group-level or system-level theories exhibit "emergent" properties that cannot be predicted or explained even with a complete knowledge of the elements making up the prior or "lower" level of analysis. (In the natural world, the properties of wetness of water and of consciousness of mind are often used as examples of emergence, because, it is said, the property of wetness cannot be predicted from a complete knowledge of the characteristics of the hydrogen and oxygen that make up water, nor can the property of consciousness be predicted from a complete knowledge of the neurons that make up the human brain. In the vernacular, emergence is close to the common idea that "the whole is more than the sum of the parts.") Emergent properties of social phenomena—such as the feeling of collective identity shared by members of an ethnic group or the interstate anarchy that affects the behavior of states in the international system—are thus said to be entirely novel properties of the group or system in question.

11. John Dollard et al., *Frustration and Aggression* (New Haven, Conn.: Yale University Press, 1939); Leonard Berkowitz, *Aggression: A Social Psychological Analysis* (New York: McGraw-Hill, 1962). On relative deprivation, see James Davies, "Toward a Theory of Revolution," *American Sociological Review* 27, no. 1 (1962): 5–19; Ted Gurr, *Why Men Rebel* (Princeton, N.J.: Princeton University Press, 1970); and Ted Gurr and Raymond Duvall, "Civil Conflict in the 1960s: A Reciprocal Theoretical System with Parameter Estimates," *Comparative Political Studies* 6, no. 2 (1973): 135–69.

12. See M. Sherif, *Group Conflict and Cooperation: Their Social Psychology* (London: Routledge & Kegan Paul, 1966); Henri Tajfel, ed., *Differentiation between Social Groups* (London: Academic Press, 1978); Henri Tajfel, *Human Groups and Social Categories: Studies in Social Psychology* (Cambridge: Cambridge University Press, 1981); Edward Azar and John Burton, *International Conflict Resolution: Theory and Practice* (Sussex: Wheatsheaf, 1986); Lewis Coser, *The Functions of Social Conflict* (London: Free Press, 1956); Donald Horowitz, *Ethnic Groups in Conflict* (Berkeley: University of California Press, 1985).

13. As Wendt notes, the view of structure as constraint is only one of three possible positions on the issue. Structure can also be thought of as generating the actors rather than constraining them, or structure and actor can be seen as dialectically related—that is, generating but not reducible to each other (as Giddens suggests). See Alexander Wendt, "The Agent-Structure Problem," *International Organization* 41, no. 3 (1987): 335–70; and Anthony Giddens, *The Constitution of Society: Outline of the Theory of Structuration* (Berkeley: University of California Press, 1984).

14. Scholars who emphasize such constraints usually also acknowledge the causal importance of internal factors, such as the actor's particular interests and beliefs. By stressing power relations almost exclusively, perhaps Waltz comes closest to presenting a purely structural theory of international behavior and war. De Mesquita contends

that the geographic proximity of actors is an important structural determinant of international conflict, whereas Choucri and North emphasize differences in states' resource endowments. See Kenneth Waltz, *Theory of International Politics* (Reading, Mass.: Addison-Wesley, 1979); and Bruce Bueno de Mesquita, *The War Trap* (New Haven, Conn.: Yale University Press, 1981).

15. See in particular Doug McAdam, *Political Process and the Development of Black Insurgency, 1930–1970* (Chicago: University of Chicago Press, 1982); Charles Tilly, *From Mobilization to Revolution* (Reading, Mass.: Addison-Wesley, 1978); and Sidney Tarrow, *Power in Movement: Social Movements, Collective Action and Politics* (Cambridge: Cambridge University Press, 1994).

16. The adjective "simple" does not mean "unimportant." Rather, it distinguishes this type of conflict from others that involve psychological and social processes more complex than those posited by rational-choice theorists.

17. For a general and skeptical analysis of the role of scarcity of nonrenewable resources in interstate conflict, see Ronnie D. Lipschutz, *When Nations Clash* (Cambridge, Mass.: Ballinger Publishing, 1989).

18. Realism focuses on states as rational maximizers of power in an anarchic international system; state behavior—including conflictual behavior—is mainly a function of the structure of power relations *among* states in the system, not of events or pressures operating inside these states. Because environmental scarcity's most important social effects unfold inside countries, realism therefore encourages scholars to ignore or downplay the consequences of environmental problems for peace and conflict. If these scholars do consider environmental problems, they focus disproportionately on simple-scarcity conflicts among states over "strategic" environmental resources such as water. Classic modern realist texts include Waltz, *Theory of International Politics*; and Robert Gilpin, *War and Change in World Politics* (Cambridge: Cambridge University Press, 1981). For a discussion of views of political change in realist theory, see R. B. J. Walker, "Realism, Change, and International Political Theory," *International Studies Quarterly* 31, no. 1 (1987): 65–86.

19. Nazli Choucri and Robert North, *Nations in Conflict* (San Francisco: Freeman, 1975).

20. Arthur Westing, "Appendix 2. Wars and Skirmishes Involving Natural Resources: A Selection from the Twentieth Century," in *Global Resources and International Conflict: Environmental Factors in Strategic Policy and Action*, ed. Arthur Westing (New York: Oxford University Press, 1986), 204–10.

21. See William Durham, *Scarcity and Survival in Central America: The Ecological Origins of the Soccer War* (Stanford, Calif.: Stanford University Press, 1979).

22. Robert Albion, *Forests and Sea Power: The Timber Problem of the Royal Navy, 1652–1863* (Cambridge, Mass.: Harvard University Press, 1926).

23. Peter Gleick, *Water and Conflict*, Occasional Paper No. 1, Project on Environmental Change and Acute Conflict (Cambridge, Mass.: American Academy of Arts and Sciences and the University of Toronto, 1992); and Peter Gleick, "Water and Conflict: Fresh Water Resources and International Security," *International Security* 18, no. 1 (1993): 79–112.

24. Ismail Serageldin, "Earth Faces Water Crisis," Press Release, World Bank, Washington, D.C., 6 August 1995.

25. Quoted in Norman Myers, "Environment and Security," *Foreign Policy*, no. 74

(spring 1989): 32. See also Thomas Naff and Ruth Matson, eds., "The Nile River," chap. 6 in *Water in the Middle East: Conflict or Cooperation?* (Boulder, Colo.: Westview Press, 1984), 125–55.

26. "Pretoria Has Its Way in Lesotho," *Africa Report* 31, no. 2 (1986): 50–51; Patrick Laurence, "A 'New Lesotho'?" *Africa Report* 32, no. 1 (1987): 61–64; "Lesotho Water Project Gets Under Way," *Africa Report* 33, no. 3 (1988): 10. See also Charles Okidi, "Environmental Stress and Conflicts in Africa: Case Studies of African International Drainage Basins," paper prepared for the Project on Environmental Change and Acute Conflict, Peace and Conflict Studies Program, University of Toronto, May 1992.

27. The two countries have recently reached an agreement on sharing Ganges water. However, as India has violated Ganges water agreements in the past—agreements that decisively favored India—there is little assurance that this latest deal will hold. See "India and Bangladesh End Dispute on Ganges," *New York Times*, 13 December 1996, p. A6, national edition. See also Khurshida Begum, *Tension over the Farakka Barrage: A Techno-Political Tangle in South Asia* (Dhaka, Bangladesh: University Press, 1987); and Ben Crow with Alan Lindquist and David Wilson, *Sharing the Ganges: The Politics and Technology of River Development* (New Delhi: Sage Publications, 1995).

28. See Ashok Swain, "Environmental Destruction and Acute Social Conflict: A Case Study of the Ganges Water Dispute," Department of Peace and Conflict Research, Uppsala University, Uppsala, Sweden, November 1992; Ashok Swain, "Conflicts Over Water: The Ganges Water Dispute," *Security Dialogue* 24, no. 4 (1993): 429–39; and Ashok Swain, "Displacing the Conflict: Environmental Destruction in Bangladesh and Ethnic Conflict in India," *Journal of Peace Research* 33, no. 2 (1996): 189–204.

29. John Kolars and William Mitchell, *The Euphrates River and the Southeast Anatolia Development Project* (Carbondale: Southern Illinois University Press, 1991); Nurit Kliot, *Water Resources and Conflict in the Middle East* (London: Routledge, 1994), especially chapter 2. See also Alan Cowell, "Water Rights: Plenty of Mud to Sling," *New York Times*, 7 February 1990, p. A4, national edition. "Send for the Dowsers," *The Economist* 313, no. 7633 (16 December 1989): 42.

30. On January 13, 1990, Turkey began filling the giant reservoir behind the Ataturk dam, the first in this complex. Turkey announced that for one month it would hold back the main flow of the Euphrates River at the dam, and this cut the downstream flow within Syria to about a quarter of its normal rate.

31. Thomas Naff, an expert on Middle East water at the University of Pennsylvania, estimates that annual per capita water consumption is between 999 and 1,072 cubic meters. The country suffers serious water loss through leaks in pipes and irrigation systems—in some areas wastage is nearly 50 percent of total consumption. As a result, even though Syria has a small water surplus on aggregate, some parts of Syria face severe water scarcity. Personal communication with author, February 9, 1998.

32. Françoise Chipaux, "Syria and Iraq Unite against Turkish Dam," *Manchester Guardian Weekly* (translated from *Le Monde*), 17 February 1996.

33. Aaron Wolf, "International Water Conflicts and Conflict Resolution: 'Water Wars' and Water Reality," (paper presented at the 1997 Annual meeting of the American Association for the Advancement of Science, Seattle, Wash., 13–18 February 1997).

34. See Thayer Scudder, "River Basin Projects in Africa," *Environment* 31, no. 2 (1989): 4–32; and Thayer Scudder, "Victims of Development Revisited: The Political

Costs of River Basin Development," *Development Anthropology Network* 8, no. 1 (1990): 1–5.

35. Sanjoy Hazarika, *Bangladesh and Assam: Land Pressures, Migration and Ethnic Conflict*, Occasional Paper No. 3, Project on Environmental Change and Acute Conflict (Cambridge, Mass.: American Academy of Arts and Sciences and the University of Toronto, 1993), 60–61.

36. Myron Weiner, "The Political Demography of Assam's Anti-Immigrant Movement," *Population and Development Review* 9, no. 2 (1983): 279–92.

37. Chaitanya Kalbag, "A State Ravaged," *India Today* 8, no. 5 (15 March 1983): 16–21; Sumanta Sen, "Spillover Tension," *India Today* 8, no. 5 (15 March 1983): 22.

38. Astri Suhrke, *Pressure Points: Environmental Degradation, Migration, and Conflict*, Occasional Paper No. 3, Project on Environmental Change and Acute Conflict (Cambridge, Mass.: American Academy of Arts and Sciences and the University of Toronto, 1993); and Astri Suhrke, "Environmental Degradation and Population Flows," *Journal of International Affairs* 47, no. 2 (1994): 473–524.

39. Myron Weiner has provided some of the most useful analysis of the costs and benefits, and of the effects on international relations, of large interstate migrations. See Myron Weiner, *The Global Migration Crisis: Challenge to States and to Human Rights* (New York: HarperCollins College Publishers, 1995); Myron Weiner, "Security, Stability and International Migration," *International Security* 17, no. 3 (1992–93): 91–126; and Myron Weiner, "On International Migration and International Relations," *Population and Development Review* 11, no. 3 (1985): 441–55.

40. Data suggest that the gap between the North and the South is widening fast. In 1960, the share of the global income of the richest 20 percent of the world's population was thirty times that of the poorest 20 percent; today, it is over sixty times as great. United Nations Development Program (UNDP), *Human Development Report 1994* (New York: Oxford University Press, 1994), 35.

Evidence also suggests that this widening gap is driving South-to-North migration. Although Demetrios Papademetriou notes that migration rates to developed countries, especially to Western Europe, actually declined in the mid-1990s, this decline was probably anomalous, because the early 1990s witnessed a surge of migration to the West after the fall of communism in the Soviet bloc. The medium- and long-term migration trends from poor to richer countries seem unquestionably upward. In a representative sample of twelve OECD countries (included in a 1993 United Nations report), eight showed substantial increases in entries of permanent settlers between the early 1980s and 1990; Germany, Australia, and the United States more than doubled their entries. Eight of the countries also showed large increases in the number of registered refugees; six countries showed an increase of over 300 percent. See Demetrios Papademetriou, review of Myron Weiner, *The Global Migration Crisis: Challenge to States and to Human Rights* (New York: Harper Collins College Publishers, 1995), *Population and Development Review* 22, no. 3 (1996): 569–73; and Alex Marshall, ed., *The State of World Population 1993* (New York: United Nations Population Fund, 1993).

41. Kurt Schock, "A Conjunctural Model of Political Conflict," *Journal of Conflict Research* 40, no. 1 (1996): 98–133.

42. A wealth of literature exists on the theoretical and empirical relationship among economic hardship, inequality, and violence. Mark Lichbach provides a survey in "An

Evaluation of 'Does Economic Inequality Breed Political Conflict?' Studies," *World Politics* 41, no. 4 (1989): 431–70. Much research has focused on links between inequality and insurgency. See Edward Muller and Mitchell Seligson, "Inequality and Insurgency," *American Political Science Review* 81, no. 2 (1987): 425–451; and Raj Desai and Harry Eckstein, "Insurgency: The Transformation of Peasant Rebellion," *World Politics* 42, no. 4 (1990): 441–465. Also valuable are studies of the relationship between poverty and urban violence in the United States. See William Ford and John Moore, "Additional Evidence on the Social Characteristics of Riot Cities," *Social Science Quarterly* 51, no. 2 (1970): 339–48; and Robert Jiobu, "City Characteristics and Racial Violence," *Social Science Quarterly* 55, no. 1 (1974): 52–64.

43. Steven Finkel and James Rule, "Relative Deprivation and Related Theories of Civil Violence: A Critical Review," in *Research in Social Movements, Conflicts, and Change*, ed. Kurt Lang and Gladys Lang (Greenwich, Conn.: JAI, 1986), 47–69.

44. Edward Muller and Karl-Dieter Opp have tried to deal with the free-rider problem within rational choice models of rebellious collective action. They propose that people adopt a "collectivist" rationality that recognizes that public goods can only be achieved through joint action. See Edward Muller and Karl-Dieter Opp, "Rational Choice and Rebellious Collective Action," *American Political Science Review* 80, no. 2 (1986): 471–88; and George Klosko, Edward Muller, and Karl-Dieter Opp, "Controversy: Rebellious Collective Action Revisited," *American Political Science Review* 81, no. 2 (1987): 557–67.

45. See Seymour Martin Lipset, *Political Man: The Social Bases of Politics* (Garden City, N.Y.: Doubleday, 1959); and Mitchell Seligson and Edward Muller, "Democratic Stability and Economic Crisis: Costa Rica, 1978–83," *International Studies Quarterly* 31, no. 3 (1987): 301–26.

46. These beliefs are grounded in historical and economic experience. See, for example, James Scott, *The Moral Economy of the Peasant: Rebellion and Subsistence in Southeast Asia* (New Haven, Conn.: Yale University Press, 1976), 1–11.

47. See Farrokh Moshiri, "Revolutionary Conflict Theory in an Evolutionary Perspective," and Jack Goldstone, "An Analytical Framework," both in *Revolutions of the Late Twentieth Century*, ed. Jack Goldstone, Ted Gurr, and Farrokh Moshiri (Boulder, Colo.: Westview Press, 1991), 4–36 and 37–51.

48. McAdam, *Political Process*, 41. Colin Kahl makes the important point that state weakening can promote civil strife not only by opening opportunities for groups to directly challenge the state but also by creating a domestic "security dilemma." Some groups may come to believe that the state can no longer assure their security; as a result, these groups may feel compelled to launch preemptive attacks against other, potentially hostile groups in the society. Colin Kahl, "States, Scarcity, and Civil Strife in the Developing World," paper prepared for the Environment and Security Project, Institute of War and Peace Studies, Columbia University, September, 1997.

49. For a review of some of these factors, see Jack Goldstone, "Theories of Revolution: The Third Generation," *World Politics* 32, no. 3 (1980): 425–53.

50. Much of the text in the remainder of this section is drawn from Philip Howard and Thomas Homer-Dixon, *Environmental Scarcity and Violent Conflict: The Case of Chiapas, Mexico*, Occasional Paper of the Project on Environment, Population, and Security (Washington, D.C.: American Association for the Advancement of Science

and the University of Toronto, 1996), 24–25. A version of this paper can be found in Thomas Homer-Dixon and Jessica Blitt, eds., *Ecoviolence: Links among Environment, Population, and Security* (Boulder, Colo.: Rowman & Littlefield: 1998).

51. George Collier, "The New Politics of Exclusion: Antecedents to the Rebellion in Mexico," *Dialectical Anthropology* 19, no. 1 (1994): 1–44.

52. See Christian Anglade and Carlos Fortin, "Accumulation, Adjustment, and the Autonomy of the State in Latin America," in *State and Capital Accumulation*, ed. Christian Anglade and Carlos Fortin (Pittsburgh: Pittsburgh University Press, 1985), 211–341.

53. For a rational choice analysis of the role of leadership in civil violence, see Douglas Van Belle, "Leadership and Collective Action: The Case of Revolution," *International Studies Quarterly* 40, no. 1 (1996): 107–32.

54. McAdam, *Political Process*, 48–51.

55. Leaders of challenger groups are not the only ones to manipulate grievances and blame systems this way. Leaders of states often do the same as part of a divide-and-rule strategy, or to mobilize attacks against opposition groups. Kenya provides one of the best contemporary examples: President Daniel arap Moi has exploited his followers' deep grievances—grievances arising in part from critical land scarcity and land competition among Kenya's diverse ethnic groups—to motivate his followers to launch violent attacks against opposition ethnic groups. See Colin Kahl "Chaos and Calm in East Africa: Population Growth, Land, and State-sponsored Violence in Kenya, 1991–1993," paper prepared for the Environment and Security Project, Institute of War and Peace Studies, Columbia University, October, 1997.

56. Neil Harvey, "Playing with Fire: The Implications of Ejido Reform," *Akwe:kon—Journal of Indigenous Issues* 11, no. 2 (1994): 23.

57. On the radicalization of peasants in eastern Chiapas, see George Collier, "The Building of Social Movements," in *Basta! Land and the Zapatista Rebellion in Chiapas* (Oakland, Calif.: Institute for Food and Development Policy, 1994); and Neil Harvey, "Rural Reforms, Campesino Radicalism and the Limits to Salinismo," in *Transformation of Rural Mexico*, Number 5 (La Jolla, Calif.: Ejido Reform Research Project, Center for U.S.–Mexican Studies, University of California at San Diego, 1994), 1–49. On the growth of social movements for rural reform, see Jonathan Fox, *The Politics of Food in Mexico* (Ithaca, N.Y.: Cornell University Press, 1993).

58. See George Collier, *Fields of the Tzotzil: The Ecological Bases of Tradition in Highland Chiapas* (Austin: University of Texas Press, 1975); James Nations, "The Ecology of the Zapatista Revolt," *Cultural Survival Quarterly* (spring 1994): 31–33; and Victor M. Toledo, "The Ecology of Indian Campesinos," *Akwe:kon—Journal of Indigenous Issues* 11, no. 2 (1994): 41–46.

59. This conclusion is supported by the research of Edward Muller and Mitchell Seligson in "Inequality and Insurgency," *American Political Science Review* 81, no. 2 (1987): 425–52. They find that "semi-repressive" regimes are more vulnerable to insurgency induced by income inequality than either highly repressive or democratic regimes. In semi-repressive societies, dissident groups can develop "relatively strong organizations," but "opportunities to engage in nonviolent forms of collective action that effectively exert influence on the political process are limited."

60. Peter Wallensteen, "Food Crops As a Factor in Strategic Policy and Action," in *Global Resources and International Conflict: Environmental Factors in Strategic*

Policy and Action, ed. Arthur Westing (New York: Oxford University Press, 1986), 154–55.

61. I am grateful to Monica Toft for pointing out the distinctiveness of this kind of enviromentally related violence. On the Ogoni conflict, see John Vidal, "Black Gold Claims a High Price," *Guardian Weekly*, 15 January 1995, p. 7; Howard French, "Rights Group Accuses Nigeria of a Civil War," *New York Times*, 28 March 1995, p. A5, national edition; Joshua Hammer, "Nigeria Crude," *Harper's Magazine* (June 1996): 58–70. On Bougainville, see Victor Böge, "Bougainville: A 'Classical' Environmental Conflict?" Occasional Paper No. 3, Environment and Conflicts Project (Zurich: Center for Security Studies and Conflict Research, Swiss Federal Institute of Technology, 1992).

62. The material in this and the following paragraph is drawn from Peter Gizewski and Thomas Homer-Dixon, *Environmental Scarcity and Violent Conflict: The Case of Pakistan*, Occasional Paper of the Project on Environment, Population and Security (Washington, D.C.: American Association for the Advancement of Science and the University of Toronto, 1996), 26. A version of this paper can be found in Homer-Dixon and Blitt, eds., *Ecoviolence*.

63. With the notable exception of the dacoits, rural violence in Pakistan has tended to be confined to familial conflicts and isolated disputes over land. See Pervaiz Naeem Tariq and Naeem Durrani, *Socio-Psychological Aspects of Crime in Pakistan*, Psychological Research Monograph 1 (Islamabad: National Institute of Psychology, 1983), 103–6.

64. Christina Lamb, *Waiting for Allah: Pakistan's Struggle for Democracy* (New Delhi: Penguin Books, 1991), 121.

65. Angus MacKay, "Climate and Popular Unrest in Late Medieval Castile," in *Climate and History: Studies in Past Climates and Their Impact on Man*, ed. T. M. Wigley, M. J. Ingram, and G. Farmer (Cambridge: Cambridge University Press, 1981), 356–76. MacKay pieced together quantitative data on local grain production from the records of tithe income kept in numerous Spanish cathedrals. Although this quantitative information indicates whether the harvest for a particular year was good or bad, it does not say why the harvest changed from year to year (whether, for example, a bad harvest resulted from drought or locusts). For this, MacKay used documentation on prayer processions, which were often illustrated in miniature. Other valuable sources of qualitative evidence were municipal records on the regulation of local food supply and trade with other regions.

66. Ibid., 369.

67. Durham, *Scarcity and Survival*.

68. For instance, see Paul Ehrlich, Anne Ehrlich, and John Holdren, *Ecoscience: Population, Resources and Environment* (San Francisco: Freeman, 1977), 908; and Shirley Hart, *Population Quantity Versus Quality: A Sociological Examination of the Causes and Consequences of the Population Explosion* (Englewood Cliffs, N.J.: Prentice-Hall, 1972).

69. The most recent United Nations statistics on El Salvador give a growth rate of about 2.0 percent (doubling time of about thirty-five years) and a density of three hundred persons per square kilometer. United Nations Population Division, *World Population Prospects*.

70. Durham, *Scarcity and Survival*, 31.

71. Ibid., 54.

72. Cynthia McClintock, "Why Peasants Rebel: The Case of Peru's Sendero Luminoso," *World Politics* 37, no. 1 (1984): 48–84; and Cynthia McClintock, "Peru's Sendero Luminoso Rebellion: Origins and Trajectory," in *Power and Popular Protest: Latin American Social Movements*, ed. Susan Eckstein (Berkeley: University of California Press, 1989), 61–101.

73. McClintock, "Why Peasants Rebel," 61, 63.

74. Ibid., 63.

75. Ibid., 82.

76. Daniel Lascon, interview by author, November 1991.

77. The Huk rebellion in the late 1940s and early 1950s provides some of the best evidence for the link between economic conditions (especially unequal land distribution) and Filipino civil strife. See Benedict Kerkvliet, *The Huk Rebellion: A Study of Peasant Revolt in the Philippines* (Quezon City, Philippines: New Day Publishers, 1979); and E. J. Mitchell, "Some Econometrics of the Huk Rebellion," *American Political Science Review* 63, no. 4 (1969), 1159–71.

78. Celso Roque and Maria Garcia, "Economic Inequality, Environmental Degradation and Civil Strife in the Philippines," paper prepared for the Project on Environmental Change and Acute Conflict, Peace and Conflict Studies Program, University of Toronto, 1993. See also Gareth Porter and Delfin Ganapin, Jr., *Resources, Population, and the Philippines' Future: A Case Study*, WRI Paper No. 4 (Washington, D.C.: World Resources Institute, 1988); Gregg Jones, *Red Revolution: Inside the Philippine Guerrilla Movement* (Boulder, Colo.: Westview Press, 1989); and Norman Myers, *Not Far Afield: U.S. Interests and the Global Environment* (Washington, D.C.: World Resources Institute, 1987).

79. Maria Concepcion Cruz and Robert Repetto, *The Environmental Effects of Stabilization and Structural Adjustment Programs: The Philippines Case* (Washington, D.C.: World Resources Institute, 1992). See also Francisco Lara, Jr., *Structural Adjustments and Trade Liberalization: Eating Away Our Food Security*, PPI Research Papers (Quezon City, Philippines: Philippine Peasant Institute, 1991); and Robin Broad, *Unequal Alliance, 1979–1986: The World Bank, the International Monetary Fund, and the Philippines* (Quezon City, Philippines, Ateneo de Manila University Press, 1988).

80. Gary Hawes, "Theories of Peasant Revolution: A Critique and Contribution from the Philippines, *World Politics* 42, no. 2 (1990): 261–98, quotation from 297–98.

81. Hawes, "Theories of Peasant Revolution," 282.

82. Richard Kessler, *Rebellion and Repression in the Philippines* (New Haven, Conn.: Yale University Press, 1989), 24–25.

83. Ibid., 16–19. See also Reynaldo Clemena Ileto, *Pasyon and Revolution: Popular Movements in the Philippines, 1840–1910* (Manila: Ateneo de Manila University Press, 1979).

84. Peter Gizewski was the primary author of much of the material in the following pages. See Peter Gizewski and Thomas Homer-Dixon, *Urban Growth and Violence: Will the Future Resemble the Past?* Occasional Paper of the Project on Environment, Population, and Security (Washington, D.C.: American Association for the Advancement of Science and the University of Toronto, 1995).

85. The statistics in this and the following paragraph are from John Kasarda and Allan Parnell, "Introduction: Third World Urban Development Issues," in *Third World*

Cities: Problems, Policies, and Prospects, ed. John Kasarda and Allan Parnell (New York: Sage, 1993), ix–x.

86. Philip Morgan, "Third World Urbanization, Migration, and Family Adaptation," in *Third World Cities,* ed. Kasarda and Parnell, 247.

87. A. S. Oberai, *Population Growth, Employment and Poverty in Third World Mega-Cities* (New York: St. Martin's Press, 1993), 26.

88. Ibid.

89. Ibid.

90. Ibid., 26–27.

91. See Alan Gilbert and Josef Guglar, *Cities Poverty and Development: Urbanization in the Third World* (Oxford: Oxford University Press, 1992), 187–200.

92. James B. Rule, *Theories of Civil Violence* (Berkeley: University of California Press, 1988), 119–21, 154–56.

93. Between 1976 and 1992, over 146 separate incidents of strikes, riots, and demonstrations took place, principally in Latin America. See John Walton and David Seddon, *Free Markets and Food Riots: The Politics of Global Adjustment* (Cambridge: Blackwell Publishers, 1994), 39–40.

94. P. R. Rajgopal, *Communal Violence in India* (New Delhi: Uppal Publishing House, 1987), 16–17.

95. Ibid., 20.

96. Anthony Minnaar et al., *An Overview of Political Violence and Conflict Trends in South Africa with Specific Reference to the Period January–June 1994* (Pretoria: Human Sciences Research Council, Center for Socio-Political Analysis, July 1994), 3–4.

97. Alba Zaluar, "Urban Violence, Citizenship and Public Policies," *Journal of Regional and Urban Affairs* 17, no. 1 (1993): 57.

98. Jose Carvalho de Noronha, "Drug Markets and Urban Violence in Rio de Janeiro: A Call for Action," *Urban Age* 1, no. 4 (1993): 9.

99. Wayne A. Cornelius, Jr., "Urbanization as an Agent in Latin American Political Instability: The Case of Mexico," *American Political Science Review* 63, no. 3 (1969): 833–57.

100. See for instance, Ted Robert Gurr and Don R. Bowen, "Deprivation, Mobility, and Orientation Toward Protest of the Urban Poor," *American Behavioral Scientist* 11 (March–April 1968): 20–24; R. H. Fitzgibbon, "Political Implications of Population Growth in Latin America," *The Sociological Review* 11 (February 1967): 41; Gláucio A. D. Soares, "The Politics of Uneven Development: The Case of Brazil," in *Party Systems and Voter Alignments: Cross-National Perspectives,* ed. Seymour M. Lipset and Stein Rokkan (New York: Free Press, 1967), 488–89.

101. Cornelius, "Urbanization," 835.

102. Kenneth F. Johnson, "Causal Factors in Latin American Political Instability," *Western Political Quarterly* 17, no. 3 (1964): 442; Dankwart Rustow, *A World of Nations: Problems of Political Modernization* (Washington, D.C.: Brookings Institution, 1967), 245.

103. For an excellent overview of the various arguments advanced see, Joan M. Nelson, *Migrants, Urban Poverty and Instability in Developing Nations,* Occasional Papers in International Affairs, No. 22 (Cambridge: Center for International Affairs, Harvard University, 1969), especially chapters 1 and 2.

104. Abdul Qaiyum Lodhi and Charles Tilly, "Urbanization, Crime and Collective Violence in 19th Century France," *American Journal of Sociology* 79, no. 2 (1973): 296–318; Cornelius, "Urbanization."

105. Lodhi and Tilly, 308.

106. Joan Nelson, *Access to Power: Politics and the Urban Poor in Developing Countries* (Cambridge, Mass.: Harvard Center for International Affairs, 1979).

107. William R. Kellie and Omar R. Galle, "Sociological Perspectives and Evidence on the Links Between Population and Conflict," in *Multidisciplinary Perspectives on Population and Conflict*, ed. Nazli Choucri (New York: Syracuse University Press, 1984), 107.

108. See, for instance, Cornelius, "Urbanization," 842.

109. Nelson, *Migrants, Urban Poverty and Instability*, 18–19.

110. See, for instance, Cornelius, "Urbanization," 855; Henry Bienen, "Urbanization and Third World Stability," *World Development* 12, no. 7 (1984): 666; and Barbara Ward, *The Home of Man* (New York: W. W. Norton, 1976).

111. Susan Eckstein, "Urbanization Revisited: Inner-City Slum of Hope and Squatter Settlement of Despair." *World Development* 18, no. 2 (1990): 168–69.

112. Ibid., 174–76.

113. John Walton and David Seddon, *Free Markets and Food Riots: The Politics of Global Adjustment* (Cambridge: Blackwell Publishers, 1994), especially chapter 1.

114. Ibid. See also John Walton and Charles Ragin, "Global and National Sources of Political Protest: Third World Responses to the Debt Crisis," *American Sociological Review* 55, no. 6 (1990): 876–90; and John Walton, "Debt, Protest and the State in Latin America," in *Power and Popular Protest*, ed. Susan Eckstein, 299–328.

115. Walton and Seddon, *Free Markets and Food Riots*, 336–37.

116. Arif Hasan, "Karachi and the Global Nature of Urban Violence," *Urban Age* 1, no. 4 (1993): 4.

117. Ibid.

118. Farida Shaheed, "The Pathan-Muhajir Conflicts, 1985–6: A National Perspective," in *Mirrors of Violence: Communities, Riots and Survivors in South Asia*, ed. Veena Das (New York: Oxford University Press, 1990), 205.

119. Hasan, "Karachi and the Global Nature of Urban Violence," 4.

120. Nafisa Shah, "Karachi Breakdown," *Newsline* (July 1994): 35, 37.

121. Ahmed Rashid, "Mean Streets: Chaos and Violence Rule in Karachi," *Far Eastern Economic Review* 157, no. 43 (27 October 1994): 19.

122. Hasan, "Karachi and the Global Nature of Urban Violence," 4.

123. See, for instance, Akmal Hussain, "The Karachi Riots of December 1986: Crisis of State and Civil Society in Pakistan," in *Mirrors of Violence: Communities, Riots and Survivors in South Asia*, ed. Veenas Das (New York: Oxford University Press, 1990), 188–89.

124. Hasan, "Karachi and the Global Nature of Urban Violence," 5.

125. Ibid.

126. Urban Management Programme, Regional Office for Latin America and the Caribbean, "Tackling Urban Violence: An Update," *Urban Age* 2, no. 2 (1994): 9.

127. "Praetorian" is a label used by Huntington for societies in which the level of political participation exceeds the capacity of political institutions to channel, moderate, and reconcile competing claims to economic and political resources. "In a praeto-

rian system, social forces confront each other nakedly; no political institutions, no corps of professional political leaders are recognized or accepted as the legitimate intermediaries to moderate group conflict." Samuel Huntington, *Political Order in Changing Societies* (New Haven, Conn.: Yale University Press, 1968), 196.

128. Ophuls notes that environmental scarcity "seems to engender overwhelming pressures toward political systems that are frankly authoritarian by current standards." William Ophuls, *Ecology and the Politics of Scarcity: A Prologue to a Political Theory of the Steady State* (San Francisco: Freeman, 1977), 163.

129. Jonathan Wilkenfeld, "Domestic and Foreign Conflict Behavior of Nations," *Journal of Peace Research* 5 (1968): 56–69.

130. See Theda Skocpol, "Social Revolutions and Mass Military Mobilization," *World Politics* 40, no. 2 (1988): 147–68. Stephen Walt suggests, in addition, that revolutions are a potent cause of instability and war, "because they alter the 'balance of threats' between the revolutionary state and the other members of the system." Stephen M. Walt, "Revolution and War," *World Politics* 44, no. 3 (1992): 321–68.

131. In both Indonesia and Nigeria, in fact, there is already evidence that internal ecological stresses are encouraging further hardening of these countries' authoritarian regimes.

Appendix to Chapter 7
Hypothesis Testing and Case Selection

1. For many years, political scientists generally thought that testing hinged on falsification: if data clearly contradicted a hypothesis, the theory from which the hypothesis had been deduced was "falsified" and, therefore, rejected. Knowledge cumulation progressed not by proof but by disproof. Although falsificationism is based on Karl Popper's interpretation of natural science, most methodological experts now acknowledge that this approach seriously misinterprets how natural science actually works. Years ago, for example, Quine showed decisively that theories are tested as a whole and that the discovery of evidence that contradicts a particular hypothesis deduced from a theory hardly every results in the wholesale rejection of the theory. See Willard van Orman Quine, "Two Dogmas of Empiricism," in *From a Logical Point of View: Nine Logico-Philosophical Essays*, 2d ed. (Cambridge, Mass.: Harvard University Press, 1953). For a general critique of falsificationism and a defense of an alternative understanding of hypothesis testing, see Paul Diesing, *How Does Social Science Work? Reflections on Practice* (Pittsburgh, Pa.: University of Pittsburgh Press, 1991), especially 248–54.

2. Barbara Geddes, "How the Cases You Choose Affect the Answers You Get: Selection Bias in Comparative Politics," in *Political Analysis: An Annual Publication of the Methodology Section of the American Political Science Association*, ed. James Stimson (Ann Arbor: University of Michigan Press, 1990), 2: 131–50; Gary King, Robert Keohane, and Sidney Verba, *Designing Social Inquiry: Scientific Inference in Qualitative Research* (Princeton, N.J.: Princeton University Press, 1994), 128–35; and David Collier and James Mahoney, "Insights and Pitfalls: Selection Bias in Qualitative Research," *World Politics* 49, no. 1 (1996): 56–91.

3. Douglas Dion, "Evidence and Inference in the Comparative Case Study," working paper, Department of Political Science, University of Michigan, Ann Arbor, 24 July

1994; see also, Benjamin Most and Harvey Starr, *Inquiry and International Politics* (Columbia: University of South Carolina Press, 1989), 52–54.

4. A statement of the form "If X, then Y" implies that the antecedent "X" is a sufficient cause or condition for the consequent "Y." When "X" is hypothesized to be a necessary cause, then the statement should be of the form "Only if X, then Y." When "X" is proposed as a necessary *and* sufficient cause, then the statement should be "If and only if X, then Y."

5. In research on environment and conflict, scope conditions are related to the contextual factors discussed in chapter 5. Both are sets of factors that must be present in addition to environmental scarcity for violent conflict to occur. However, while scope conditions operate at the level of a causal generalization or hypothesis (which purports to describe a causal process applying across numerous cases), contextual factors operate only at the level of the specific case. If certain contextual factors are found to operate in most cases examined, then they can be included as scope conditions within causal generalizations or hypotheses on environmental scarcity and conflict.

6. Alexander George and Timothy McKeown, "Case Studies and Theories of Organizational Decision Making," in *Advances in Information Processing in Organizations*, ed. Robert Coulam and Richard Smith (London: JAI Press, 1985), 2: 21–58, especially 2: 24.

7. Of course, as often noted, correlation does not prove causation.

8. Another common case-study approach is *crucial-case* analysis, in which a single case is selected that, should it disconfirm the hypothesis, cannot simply be dismissed as deviant, and that, should it confirm the hypothesis, cannot be equally well explained by a competing hypothesis. See Harry Eckstein, "Case Study and Theory in Political Science," in *Handbook of Political Science*, ed. Fred Greenstein and Nelson Polsby, vol. 1, *Political Science: Scope and Theory* (Reading, Mass.: Addison-Wesley, 1975), 118.

9. For a thorough discussion of counterfactual analysis, see Philip Tetlock and Aaron Belkin, eds., *Counterfactual Thought Experiments in World Politics: Logical, Methodological, and Psychological Perspectives* (Princeton, N.J.: Princeton University Press, 1996); see also James Fearon, "Counterfactuals and Hypothesis Testing in Political Science," *World Politics* 43, no. 2 (1991): 169–95.

10. Controlled case comparison and process tracing are both discussed in George and McKeown, "Case Studies and Theories of Organizational Decision Making," 24–43.

11. To the extent that these causal linkages are specified by the researcher's hypotheses, process tracing increases the number of empirical observations that can be used to test the hypotheses. This is one way of dealing with the problem of an inadequate number of observations for the number of causal variables hypothesized—the "small-N problem"—that many analysts believe bedevils comparative case-study methodology. See King, Keohane, and Verba, *Designing Social Inquiry*, 226–27.

12. George and McKeown, "Case Studies and Theories of Organizational Decision Making," 31–32. Process tracing provides a particular type of explanation of the dependent variable, which Abraham Kaplan calls the "pattern" model of explanation. Kaplan writes: "According to the pattern model . . . something is explained when it is so related to a set of other elements that together they constitute a unified system. We understand something by identifying it as a specific part in an organized whole." Kaplan notes that

the pattern model of explanation is distinct from the "deductive" model: "Very roughly, we know the reason for something either when we can fit it into a known pattern, or else when we can deduce it from other known truths." See Abraham Kaplan, *The Conduct of Inquiry* (San Francisco: Chandler, 1964), 332–35. Kaplan's deductive model corresponds to Hempel's "deductive-nomological" or "covering-law" model of explanation, whereby a phenomenon is said to be explained if its occurrence can be shown to be logically expected given certain general laws. However, Hempel similarly distinguishes between covering-law explanations and what he calls "genetic" explanations, which, he argues, are generally a better form of explanation for social events. A genetic explanation "presents the phenomenon under study as the final stage of a developmental sequence, and accordingly accounts for the phenomenon by describing the successive stages of that sequence." See Carl Hempel, *Aspects of Scientific Explanation* (New York: Free Press, 1965), 447. Thagard makes an analogous distinction among deductive, schematic and causal modes of explanation; Paul Thagard, *Conceptual Revolutions* (Princeton, N.J.: Princeton University Press, 1992), 118–126.

13. The conjunction in this statement could also be "or." Thus, an exhaustive statement of the conditions would be of the form "X causes Y, when conditions A and/or B and/or C . . . and/or N are true." The relationship between X and these conditions is interactive. Charles Ragin discusses the methodological implications of such "multiple conjunctural" causation in which multiple causes interact in different combinations to produce effects of interest to researchers. See Charles Ragin, *The Comparative Method: Moving Beyond Qualitative and Quantitative Strategies* (Berkeley: University of California Press, 1987), 23–30.

14. The problems of control in case-study research are highlighted in George and McKeown, "Case Studies and Theories of Organizational Decision Making," 27. See also, Fearon, "Counterfactuals," 174, n. 11.

15. Marc Levy advocates this strategy in Marc Levy, "Is the Environment a National Security Issue?" *International Security* 20, no. 2 (1995): 35–62.

Chapter 8
Conclusions

1. For an example of this kind of argument, see Ronnie Lipschutz, "Environmental Conflict and Environmental Determinism: The Relative Importance of Social and Natural Factors," in *Conflict and the Environment*, ed. Nils Petter Gleditsch (Dordrecht, The Netherlands: Kluwer, 1997), 35–50; see also Wenche Hauge and Tanja Ellingsen, Beyond Environmental Scarcity: "The Causal Pathways to Conflict:" *Journal of Peace Research* 35, no. 3 (1998): 299–317.

2. See, for example, Jack Goldstone, "Environmental Scarcity and Violent Conflict: A Debate," *Environmental Change and Security Project Report*, Issue 2 (Washington, D.C.: Woodrow Wilson Center, 1996): 68.

3. See chapters 3 and 6 for a detailed discussion of these positions.

4. For an optimistic assessment of democracy's effects, see Nils Petter Gleditsch, "Environmental Conflict and the Democratic Peace," in *Conflict and the Environment*, ed. Nils Petter Gleditsch (Dordrecht, The Netherlands: Kluwer, 1997), 91–106; see also, Rodger Payne, "Freedom and the Environment," *Journal of Democracy* 6, no. 3 (1995): 41–55.

General Readings on Environmental Security _____

THE FOLLOWING LIST presents some of the key articles and books in the emerging field of research on the environmental causes of violence.

Bennett, Olivia. *Greenwar: Environment and Conflict*. Washington, D.C.: Panos Institute, 1991.

Brown, Janet Welsh, ed. *In the U.S. Interest: Resources, Growth, and Security in the Developing World*. Boulder, Colo.: Westview Press, 1990.

Brown, Neville. "Climate, Ecology and International Security." *Survival* 31, no. 6 (1989): 519–32.

Byers, Bruce. "Ecoregions, State Sovereignty, and Conflict." *Bulletin of Peace Proposals* 22, no. 1 (1991): 65–76.

Choucri, Nazli, ed. *Multidisciplinary Perspectives on Population and Conflict*. Syracuse, N.Y.: Syracuse University Press, 1984.

Dabelko, Geoffrey, and P. J. Simmons. "Environment and Security: Core Ideas and U.S. Government Initiatives." *SAIS Review* 17, no. 1 (1997): 127–46.

Dalby, Simon. "Ecopolitical Discourse: 'Environmental Security' and Political Geography." *Progress in Human Geography* 16, no. 4 (1992): 503–22.

———. "Security, Modernity, Ecology: the Dilemmas of Post Cold War Security Discourse." *Alternatives* 17, no. 1 (1992): 95–134.

Deudney, Daniel. "Environment and Security: Muddled Thinking." *Bulletin of Atomic Scientists* (April 1991): 23–28.

———. "The Case Against Linking Environmental Degradation and National Security." *Millennium* 19, no. 3 (1990): 461–76.

———. "The Mirage of Eco-War: The Weak Relationship Among Global Environmental Change, National Security and Interstate Violence." In *Global Environmental Change and International Relations*, edited by Ian Rowlands and Malory Green, 169–91. Basingstoke: Macmillan, 1992.

Environmental Change and Security Project Report. Published annually since 1995. Washington, D.C.: Woodrow Wilson Center.

Gleditsch, Nils Petter, ed. *Conflict and The Environment*. Proceedings of the NATO Advanced Research Workshop on Conflict and the Environment, Bolkesjø, Norway, 11–16 June, 1996. Dordrecht, Netherlands: Kluwer, 1997.

Gleick, Peter. "Climate Change and International Politics: Problems Facing Developing Countries." *Ambio* 18, no. 6 (1989): 333–39.

———. "Environment and Security: the Clear Connections." *Bulletin of Atomic Scientists* (April 1991): 17–21.

———. "Global Climatic Changes and Geopolitics: Pressures on Developed and Developing Countries." In *Climate and Geo-Sciences*, edited by A. Berger et al., 603–21. Boston: Kluwer Academic Publishers, 1989.

———. "The Implications of Global Climatic Changes for International Security." *Climatic Change* 15, no. 1/2 (1989): 309–25.

Gurr, Ted. "On the Political Consequences of Scarcity and Economic Decline." *International Studies Quarterly* 29, no. 1 (1985): 51–75.

Homer-Dixon, Thomas. "On The Threshold: Environmental Changes as Causes of Acute Conflict." *International Security* 16, no. 2 (1991): 76–116.

———. "Environmental Scarcities and Violent Conflict: Evidence from Cases," *International Security* 19, no. 1 (1994): 5–40.

———. "The Ingenuity Gap: Can Poor Countries Adapt to Resource Scarcity?" *Population and Development Review* 21, no. 3 (1995): 587–612.

———. "Strategies for Studying Causation in Complex Ecological-Political Systems." *Journal of Environment & Development* 5, no. 2 (June 1996): 132–48.

Homer-Dixon, Thomas, J. H. Boutwell, and G.W. Rathjens. "Environmental Change and Violent Conflict." *Scientific American* 268, no. 2 (February 1993): 38–45.

Homer-Dixon, Thomas, and Marc Levy. "Environmental Scarcity and Violent Conflict: a Debate." In *Environmental Change and Security Project Report*, issue 2. Washington, D.C.: Woodrow Wilson Center, 1996.

Kakonen, Jyrki, ed. *Perspectives on Environmental Conflict and International Politics.* New York: Pinter, 1992.

Kaplan, Robert. "The Coming Anarchy." *Atlantic Monthly* 272, no. 2 (1994): 44–76.

Lipschutz, Ronnie. *When Nations Clash: Raw Materials, Ideology and Foreign Policy.* New York: Ballinger, 1989.

Lipschutz, Ronnie, and John Holdren. "Crossing Borders: Resource Flows, the Global Environment, and International Security." *Bulletin of Peace Proposals* 21, no. 2 (1990): 121–33.

Mathews, Jessica Tuchman. "Redefining Security." *Foreign Affairs* 68, no. 2 (1989): 162–77.

McNicoll, Geoffrey. Review of Robert Kaplan. *The Ends of the Earth: A Journey at the Dawn of the 21st Century.* New York: Random House, 1996. In *Population and Development Review* 22, no. 3 (1996): 575–77.

Myers, Norman. *Not Far Afield: U.S. Interests and the Global Environment.* Washington, D.C.: World Resources Institute, 1987.

———. "Environment and Security." *Foreign Policy*, no. 74 (spring 1989): 23–41.

———. "The Environmental Dimension to Security Issues." *Environmentalist* 6, no. 4 (1986): 251–57.

———. *Ultimate Security: the Environmental Basis of Political Stability.* New York: W. W. Norton, 1993.

Porter, Gareth. "Post-Cold War Global Environment and Security." *Fletcher Forum of World Affairs* 14, no. 2 (1990): 332–44.

Renner, Michael. *Fighting for Survival: Environmental Decline, Social Conflict, and the New Age of Insecurity.* New York: W. W. Norton, 1996.

———. *National Security: The Economic and Environmental Dimensions.* Worldwatch Paper 89. Washington, D.C.: Worldwatch Institute, 1989.

Romm, Joseph J. *Defining National Security: The Nonmilitary Aspects.* New York: Council on Foreign Relations Press, 1993.

Rowlands, Ian. "The Security Challenges of Global Environmental Change." *Washington Quarterly* 14, no. 1 (1991): 99–114.

Shabecoff, Philip. *A New Name for Peace.* Hanover, N.H.: University Press of New England, 1996.

Simon, Julian. "Paradoxically, Population Growth May Eventually End Wars." *Journal of Conflict Resolution* 33, no. 1 (1989): 164–180.

Stern, Erik. "Bringing the Environment In: The Case for Comprehensive Security." *Cooperation and Conflict* 30, no. 3 (1995): 211–37.

Stoett, Peter. "Global Environmental Security, Energy Resources and Planning: A Framework and Application." *Futures* 26, no. 7 (1994): 741–58.

Trolldalen, Jon Martin. *World Foundation for Environment and Development.* Oslo: World Foundation for Environment and Development, 1992.

Ullman, Richard. "Redefining Security." *International Security* 8, no. 1 (1983): 129–53.

Westing, Arthur, ed. *Global Resources and International Conflict: Environmental Factors in Strategic Policy and Action.* New York: Oxford University Press, 1986.

Winnefeld, James A., and Mary E. Morris. *Where Environmental Concerns and Security Strategies Meet: Green Conflict in Asia and the Middle East.* Santa Monica, Calif.: Rand, 1994.

ENCOP Materials

The following list includes papers, reports, and books produced by the Project on Environment and Conflict (ENCOP) of the Swiss Peace Foundation and the Centre for Security Studies and Conflict Research. For further information, please contact Kurt Spillman, Centre for Security Studies and Conflict Research, Swiss Federal Institute of Technology, ETH Zentrum, 8092 Zurich, Switzerland.

ENCOP's theoretical publications include the following Occasional Papers, all published jointly in Berne and Zurich by the Swiss Peace Foundation and Centre for Security Studies and Conflict Research:

Bächler, Günther. *Conflict and Cooperation in the Light of Global Human-Ecological Transformation.* No. 9. 1993.

———. *Desertification and Conflict: The Marginalization of Poverty and of Environmental Conflicts.* No. 10. 1994.

Böge, Volker. *Proposal for an Analytical Framework to Grasp 'Environmental Conflict.'* No. 1. 1992.

Klötzli, Stephan. *Sustainable Development: A Disputed Concept.* No. 2. 1992.

Libiszewski, Stephen. *What is an Environmental Conflict?* No. 1. 1992.

Most of ENCOP's regional studies have recently been published in a three volume set:

Bächler, Günther et al. *Kriegsursache Umweltzerstörung.* Band I. *Ökologische Konflikte in der Dritten Welt und Wege ihrer friedlichen Bearbeitung.* Chur/Zürich: Verlag Rüegger, 1996.

Bächler, Günther and Kurt R. Spillman, eds. *Kriegsursache Umweltzerstörung/Environmental Degradation as a Cause of War.* Vol. II. *Regional-und Länderstudien von Projektmirtarbeitern/Regional and Country Studies of Research Fellows.* Chur/Zürich: Verlag Rüegger, 1996. This volume contains: M. Abdul Hafiz and Nahid Islam, "Environmental Degradation and Intra/Interstate Conflicts in Bangladesh"; Mohamed Suliman, "Civil War in Sudan: The Impact of Ecological Degradation"; Mohamed Suliman, "War in Darfur or the Desert versus the Oasis

Syndrome"; Peter B. Okoh, "Environmental Degradation, Conflicts and Peaceful Resolution in Nigeria and between Nigeria and Neighboring States"; Stephan Klotzli, "The Water and Soil Crisis in Central Asia: A Source for Future Conflicts?"; Stephen Libiszewski, "Water Disputes in the Jordan Basin Region and Their Role in the Resolution of the Arab-Israeli Conflict"; Günther Bächler, "Rwanda: The Roots of Tragedy, Battle for Elimination on an Ethno-Political and Ecological Basis"; and Volker Böge, "Bergbau—Umweltzerstörung—Krieg im Südpazifik."

Bächler, Günther and Kurt R. Spillman, eds. *Kriegsursache Umweltzerstörung/Environmental Degredation as a Cause of War*. Vol. III. *Länderstudien von externen Experten/Country Studies of External Experts*. Chur/Zürich: Verlag Rüegger, 1996.

Other ENCOP Occasional Papers, also published jointly in Berne and Zurich by the Swiss Peace Foundation and Centre for Security Studies and Conflict Research include:

Böge, Volker. *Bougainville: A 'Classical' Environmental Conflict?* No. 3. 1992.

———. *Sardar Sarovar Project at Narmada River in India: Subject of Environmental Conflict*. No. 8. 1993.

Klötzli, Stephan. *The Slovak-Hungarian Conflict on the Hydropower Station of Gabcikovo and on the Diversion of the Danube River*. No. 7. 1993.

Lang, Christopher I. *Environmental Degradation in Kenya as a Cause of Political Conflict, Social Stress, and Ethnic Tensions*. No. 12. 1995.

Spillman, Kurt R., and Günther Bächler, eds., *Environmental Crisis: Regional Conflicts and Ways of Cooperation*. No. 14. 1995.

Other papers produced by ENCOP include:

Klotzli, Stephan. "The 'Aral Sea Syndrome' and Regional Cooperation in Central Asia: Opportunity or Obstacle." Paper prepared for presentation at the NATO Advanced Research Workshop, "Conflict and the Environment," Bolkesjø, Norway, 12–16 June 1996.

Okoh, Peter B. "Environmental Conflicts in the Niger-Delta Region of Nigeria." Draft for ENCOP Project. 1994.

Suliman, Mohamed. *Environmental Degradation and Migration in Africa: The Predicament of Displaced People Inside the Sudan*. ENCOP/IFAA Sudan Paper II. London: Institute for African Alternatives (IFAA), 1992.

PRIO Materials

The following list includes papers, reports, and books produced by the International Peace Research Institute (PRIO) in Oslo, Norway. For further information, please contact International Peace Research Institute (PRIO), Fuglehauggata 11, 0260, Oslo, Norway.

Gleditsch, Nils P. "The Environment, Politics and Armed Conflict: A Critique and Research Proposal." Paper prepared for presentation at the NATO Advanced Research Workshop, "Conflict and the Environment," Bolkesjø, Norway, 12–16 June 1996.

Gleditsch, Nils P. and Bjorn O. Sverdrup. *Democracy and the Environment*. Oslo: International Peace Research Institute (PRIO), 1996.

Graeger, Nina and Dan Smith, eds. *Environment, Poverty, Conflict*. PRIO Report. Oslo: International Peace Research Institute (PRIO), 1994.

Hauge, Wenche, and Tanja Ellingsen. "Environmental Change and Civil War: A Multivariate Approach." Paper prepared for presentation at the NATO Advanced Research Workshop, "Conflict and the Environment," Bolkesjø, Norway, 12–16 June 1996.

Lodgaard, Sverre, and Anders H. af Ornas, eds. *The Environment and International Security*. PRIO Report. Oslo: International Peace Research Institute (PRIO), 1992.

Materials on the World Wide Web

Much of the research and data cited in this book can be referenced through the World Wide Web. Key papers can be found at www.library.utoronto.ca/www/pcs/catalog.htm. An environmental security database of some thirty thousand items is available at www.library.utoronto.ca/www/pcs/database/libintro.htm.

Index